LNWR WAGONS

This delightful photograph shows eight D14 24ft timber wagons and two low loader wagons loaded up and ready to depart, hauled by a '19in Goods' 4–6–0. The load of steam wagons built by Fodens of Sandbach were, we believe, bound for the Army in 1915-17. There appear to be at least three different models in the load, as can be seen from the two types of engine covering and two lengths of side sheet. The picture shows several of the D14 wagons labelled 'STEAM WAGON TRUCK'. The first appears to have been No. 77797, which was one of six built in 1914. It had a tare rating of 6-6-2 and the lettering at the right-hand end reads 'TO BE RETURNED TO SANDBACH'. The next wagon was No. 77762 whilst the brake van was No. 784B of the four-wheeled design to Diagram 16. The two low-loaders with a steel-plate frame immediately behind the engine are thought not to have been LNW stock. NATIONAL RAILWAY MUSEUM (88/97)

LNWR WAGONS

VOLUME ONE

by THE LONDON & NORTH WESTERN RAILWAY SOCIETY

EDITED BY CHRIS NORTHEDGE

Authors: Mike Williams, Peter Ellis,
John Shelley, Peter Davis, Tim Hughes
and Bob Williams

An LNWR G2 0–8–0 trundling a typical lengthy heavy goods, including many private owner wagons, over Castlethorpe troughs on the LNWR main line. HMRS (V1668)

WILD SWAN PUBLICATIONS

ISBN 1 874103 65 8

An interesting load carried on a Diagram 103 open wagon. The wagon had all the final LNWR features, including bulbous axleboxes and 2-rib buffers. The number painted on the side (426) probably indicates a date close to 1923 and the tare weight appears to read 6-0-2. This could be another photograph taken to record insecure fastening of a load, since, although there is no apparent damage, the ropes were clearly too slack to properly restrain the cylinders.

COLLECTION R. J. ESSERY

Designed by Paul Karau
Printed by Amadeus Press Ltd., Cleckheaton

Published by
WILD SWAN PUBLICATIONS LTD.
1-3 Hagbourne Road, Didcot, Oxon, OX11 8DP

CONTENTS

An official Earlestown photograph of wagons fitted with the Williams automatic sheet support. This device was used only experimentally by the LNWR. The wagon nearest the camera was Diagram 84 No. 10170 with a tare of 6–15–1 and displaying a paint date of 4/09. It exhibits all the standard features of that period and looks to have been new. The tarpaulin cleats are shown up well in this picture, fixed beneath the curb rail. The smaller wagons appear to have been elderly Diagram 2 wagons with wooden brake blocks and grease axleboxes. The first three bear numbers 52936, 36877 and 45347. Note the altered positions of the wagon number on the ends — moved due to the sheet support, no doubt. The bottom four rivets on the end of the corner plate on D2 No. 52936 had been replaced by bolts and square-headed nuts.
NATIONAL RAILWAY MUSEUM (ETN 46)

PREFACE AND ACKNOWLEDGMENTS

The locomotives and carriages of the London and North Western Railway have been the subjects of publications by other authors, locomotives most recently by Ted Talbot and carriages by David Jenkinson, Phillip A. Millard and Richard M. Casserley. Lineside items have been covered by Richard Foster (signals) and by inclusion in regional histories by various others.

There has long been a gap in the published material in that LNWR wagons have received very little attention. This publication attempts to rectify that by studying LNWR wagons from the earliest railways until the 1923 grouping. No attempt has been made to cover either North London Railway or Dundalk, Newry and Greenore Railway wagons, but those from other absorbed lines have been included in the relevant chapters where information is available.

No attempt has been made to cover post-1923 liveries, renumbering or scrapping dates although LMS and later photographs are included, and some later constructional changes are mentioned to aid reference back to the LNWR design.

The chapters in this volume were written and illustrated by Peter Davis, Peter Ellis, John Shelley, Bob Williams and Mike Williams; additional drawings were done by Tim Hughes. The late Jim Richards' knowledge of pre-group days from first-hand observation complemented official sources. Many of his photographs and drawings have been gratefully used as reference material. Assistance was also received from Richard Foster, Gordon Reid, Don Rowland, the late Dudley Whitworth, Philip Millard, the late Geoff Williams, Newton Reference Library and the St. Helens Reference Library. Bob Essery made his photograph and drawing collection available to the authors. Finally, Chris Northedge acted as Editor to draw together and publish the material, and added sections on liveries and slate wagons.

Official reference material is available for inspection from: the Public Records Office, Kew – building records; the National Railway Museum, York – photographs, both official and from their collections; and the Historical Model Railway Society – copies of official drawings.

The LNWR Society was instrumental both in bringing the authors together and in providing collections of drawings and photographs which proved invaluable. Further material is published regularly in the Journal and The Newsletter. The availability of this large pool of knowledge has been of considerable help to the authors, just as it will be to any person interested in the LNWR. The membership has grown over the years to a current total of about 500.

Membership details are available from: Bob Williams, 3 Chieveley Court, Emerson Valley, Milton Keynes, Bucks, MK4 2DD.

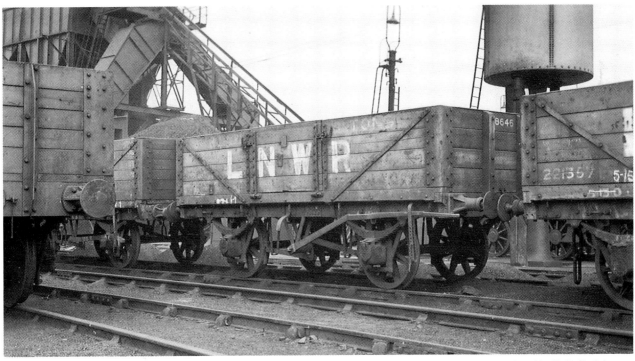

The mainstay of the LNWR's wagon fleet was the Diagram 84 open, at least in later years. Introduced in 1904 by Mr. H. D. Earl, it was designed with increased width and to the new standard length of 18ft. Other features such as axleboxes, brakes and buffers were consistent with the LNW standard of the time, and – a sign of the quality of workmanship at the LNW's Earlestown workshops – all the square nuts had been carefully lined up.

The goods yard at Builth Road on the LNW Central Wales line, looking towards Shrewsbury c.1909/10. LNW goods yard scenes are curiously rare. Here at the left can be seen a loco coal wagon; Diagram 88 van No. 76838; a Diagram 2 loaded with barrels and '6 TONS LNWR' visible; a Diagram 16 4-wheel brake van; four unidentified open wagons; another Diagram 16 brake van with another LNW open wagon across to the right.

G. M. PERKINS

INTRODUCTION

THE authors of this volume are all largely inexperienced in writing and publishing, but came together simply because of their love of the subject. Each author drafted a chapter on his allocated topic and others commented and added to this where possible. The draft was then returned to the author for re-writing. The process worked and we were all surprised at just how much material we had available to us which, without being encouraged to examine, we never knew we had.

One of the first things we had to do was to decide which wagons would appear in which volume. Notes on Earlestown appear first to set the scene. The LNWR benefited from great continuity throughout its life, and wagons followed the same pattern. Once established in the 1850s, Earlestown Works built almost all the wagons the LNWR had until the end of its separate existence. The few exceptions were certain steel wagons built at Crewe, wagons that came from absorbed companies, and a short period just before and during World War I when, like Crewe, armament work at Earlestown forced the company to use contractors for small batches of wagons built to standard LNWR design. The handful of other wagons built outside Earlestown will be discussed in the appropriate chapter.

We then cover construction and mechanical details which were highly standardised and have enabled us to avoid repeating this information for each wagon. When we came to research this chapter it was fascinating to realise why certain features developed the way they did. Wagons, after all, were built to perform a particular job and were often neglected, particularly in later years. They had to be simple and cheap to construct, but they also had to be strong enough to withstand the odd rough shunt and exposure to the British weather which was no better then than it is now! The very best materials were used, of course, but, even so, wood rots in the end and iron rusts, so Earlestown went to great trouble to protect each component as best it could.

The LNWR were realistic enough to accept that everything will wear out in the end and it even kept annual records to show the average age of each type of wagon. Unlike today's philosophy though, they were not designed to have a finite life span, but were simply built to last as long as possible. Should the traffic needs change, a wagon would rarely be scrapped, but converted or rebuilt for another use, an attitude very different from today's throw-away society.

The remainder of this volume is about individual wagon types. We start, as the LNWR did, with open goods wagons. Again like the LNWR, we have made a distinction between goods or general merchandise and coal/coke. The latter were quite different, usually having bottom doors and were sometimes hoppered. They were reserved for that traffic and were lettered accordingly. Having said that, there were, of course, cases when coal wagons were used for general merchandise and vice-versa but the principle holds good. Coal and coke wagons will be covered in a later volume.

Cattle wagons were probably the next type of vehicle to develop and are covered in chapter 4. The LMS could not make up its mind whether the special cattle wagons should be classified as goods or passenger vehicles but the LNWR always classed them as wagons, so they are included in this publication. Similarly, we do not intend to cover horseboxes, carriage trucks or ventilated fruit and milk vans built at Wolverton simply because the LNWR classed them as passenger vehicles. The same argument has been used for the otherwise apparently random decision to include tram car trolleys in a later volume but not cover omnibus trucks at all! We have followed the official designation exactly, and the LNWR classified omnibus trucks as passenger vehicles.

Finally, by way of contrast and perhaps light relief from the previous fairly meaty chapters, we have compiled a little group of special vehicles which, although quite different, nevertheless do exhibit similarities which enable them to be grouped together here.

MAIN REFERENCES

The primary sources of data on the quantities and types of LNWR goods wagons either built or in existence in any particular year, such as the original wagon shop registers, do not appear to have survived. Important official reference documents which have survived are as follows:

Wagon Stock Diagram Book 1903

H.D. Earl was appointed to the post of Wagon Superintendent at Earlestown in 1903 and soon had the Diagram Book produced. Each type of wagon then in use was allocated a numbered page in the Diagram Book (see example on p. 66).

It showed an outline (not to scale) of each type of wagon and included information relevant to the traffic department such as description, maximum pay load, tare weight and a few basic dimensions. In special cases it also showed route restrictions and even running numbers for some of the more limited types.

One page was used for each type and the original 1903 Diagram Book totalled 83 pages. Each new type of wagon developed after that date was usually issued with the next available page number. However, sometimes an updated or longer version was included on the same page as an original type, e.g. Diagram 5 was used for 18ft drop-sided wagons as well as the initial 16ft versions. Sometimes a later version was shown on the original type, e.g. 16ft gunpowder van on Diagram 43 with the original 13ft 6ins version, but subsequently allocated its own Diagram number, D43A. In such cases there was usually a cross reference from the original type to the later version.

The 1903 Diagram Book continued as the basic reference book through into LMS days and by 1923 had reached Diagram 110 with many pages having A, B, C or even D suffixes. Numerous copies of the Diagram Book were maintained over the LNWR system, each modification requiring

1

Number and Age of Wagons Stock.
— 30th November 1902. —

	No. record when built	No. of Vehicles	Total Years	Average Age
Brought forward	6	60253	829,278	10.41
Furniture Wagons		158	16444	13.00
Loco. valves Iron		2	36	18.00
Glass Wagons Stone Stanchions	1	145	1081	7.46
Gunpowder Vans	14	16	121	7.56
Hopper Wagons		1456	18,840	12.93
Meat		80	1166	14.57
Vans		819	5591	6.83
Refrigerator		558	2720	4.87
Covered Goods, fitted up for Meat Traffic		100	577	5.77
Slaughter Wagons		1	18	18.00
Rail sockets		83	1744	21.27
Standing Wagons		2	10	5.00
Tool Vans (LocKing)	3	13	168	12.93
Sleeper Road Wagons 2 tons		68425	977,20	14.19
20		1		0.00
Transhipe Vans		348	4517	12.98
Sundries		74	1054	14.24
Chemical Vans		6	72	12.00
Ballast	51	1555	14944	9.61
Road Wagons Carriage Department		69	723	10.46
Coke		19	210	11.05
Loco. 20 tons	2	3018	25,189	8.35
Coke		62		0.00
Locker		445	680	15.11
Tool Standard		1440	1225	9.46
Breakdown Wagon		20	200	10.00
Local		122	630	19.69
Coke		27	421	15.59
Slate		300	4250	14.17
	77	76245	1014,268	13.30
No record when built		77		
Total Stock		76322		

Number and Age of Wagons Stock.
— 30th November 1902. —

	No. record when built	No. of Vehicles	Total Years	Average Age
Open Goods Wagons " 9 tons. 7 tons	5	12960	306530	23.65
20 " 7 "		13126	276656	20.01
20 " 7 " End Doors		4441	58905	13.37
36 " 7 " Side		14903	45,116	3.03
20 " 10 " Augustine		12	125	10.42
30 " 10 " Vent		6	130	21.67
20 " 10 " State traffic		50	850	17.00
22 " 10 " N.B. District		85	2011	23.66
36 " 10 " Side Doors		262		0.00
36 " 10 " A.H. & Co.		319	2085	6.64
42 " 10 " Side Doors Stone traffic		100	579	5.79
20 "		50	2	0.04
Timber Ordinary. 7		447	14486	31.63
Timber Trucks 10		1625	16143	9.93
Tin. 10		1436	7115	4.95
Meat Vans 24 feet 10		661	8122	12.29
Stock Primary 10	1	1447	24451	16.49
20		335	31167	21.54
Cattle 20		335	642	2.73
Sutton Small		75	200	2.67
Cattle Medium		281	6117	21.77
Large		1152	13244	11.50
Special		891	130444	14.64
States		25	350	14.00
Nth. compartment for mares		2	38	19.00
worked by Mechanical Dept, S&C District		16	18	1.12
N.B.		100	838	8.38
Coal		53	694	13.09
Cattle		131	2031	15.50
Locke Northampton		8	39	4.87
Covered Goods Vans Doors each side 7 tons		3402	68300	20.08
	1	5381	15261	2.84
Carried forward	10	1		0.00

Wagons in the interchange sidings at Blaenau Ffestiniog, overshadowed by the imposing rock of Clogwyn Bwlch Y Gwynt. This view shows (from the left) on the nearer line a D7 slate transporter wagon, two open wagons to D4, a D2, another D4 and a D7 loaded with empty slate trucks. Behind the D7 we can just make out two slate trucks in front of two vans. To the left is a D32, with its side door away from the photographer, the other being a D33, with doors both sides. The roof doors are clearly apparent. In front of the two-storey building to the right of centre with prominent windows is a Festiniog Railway gunpowder van. The building itself was owned by the railway and for many years was rented out to the Oakeley Quarries to use as offices, accompanying their slate quay. The date is not known but must be between 1894 and 1908.

an update to all copies. For this reason, historians need to take great care since some updates marked on pages of the Diagram Book surviving today may date from the LMS period. For example, it is possible that Diagram 84A, the 18ft open goods wagon, was an LMS addition.

It must also be remembered what the Diagram Book was for, since several inaccuracies are included which may have been irrelevant to the users, the traffic department. Nevertheless, it is a very useful basic source of reference and forms the basis of the descriptions and format of this book.

There was also an LNWR publication describing the Government pool wagons of World War I allocated to the LNWR. Many of these were subsequently taken into LNWR stock. Although there are several copies in private hands today, copies can be inspected at the Public Record Office (Ref. Rail 410/1434) and the NRM, York.

Annual Stock Valuation Lists
These annual lists survive for the period 1861 to 1899 at the Public Record Office [Ref. Rail 410/1437 (1861–1876), Rail 410/1357 (1877–1893), Rail 410/1358 (1894–1899)]. They appear to have formed an extension of the annual accounts and hence covered mainly the financial aspects of locomotives, carriages, wagons, cranes and station equipment, etc. The wagon section gave total stock quantity and valuation by classes of use. The classes were neither consistent year on year nor compatible with the 1903 Wagon Stock Diagram Book when this was introduced.

The annual stock valuation lists are the only reference we have for earlier wagon types and helps establish introduction dates for several other types.

Wagon Stock Age Books
The Wagon Stock Age Book was a ledger used to calculate the average age of each type of wagon. It worked by using the totals of all the wagons of each type for each year multiplied by the years in service, thereby calculating the average age.

The first book is thought to have been produced in 1902 and may well have been in readiness for the succession of H.D. Earl in 1903. Again, the type descriptions were not fully consistent with the Wagon Stock Diagram Book but were closer than the Annual Stock Valuation Lists.

This hand-written ledger may be found at the Public Record Office (Ref. Rail 410/1449). It is interesting to note how different classes of wagons have very different life expectancies, depending on the loads and conditions of service they encountered. The contrast can be seen in figures from the 1902 Wagon Stock Age Book: Whilst 7-ton Diagram 12 timber wagons were calculated as lasting 31.6 years, 9in sided Diagram 1 open wagons 23.6 years, and covered vans 20.1 years, medium cattle wagons only lasted 11.5 years.

From 1909 the Wagon Stock Age Book was produced annually and they all survive at the Public Record Office [Ref. Rail 410/1450 (1909–1917), Rail 410/1451

London and North Western Railway.

WAGON DEPARTMENT, EARLESTOWN.

NUMBER AND AGE OF WAGON STOCK, 30th NOVEMBER, 1902.

Class of Vehicle *Junction Wagons*

When Built	Age in Years	4 tons No.	4 tons Total Years	10 tons No.	10 tons Total Years	twin No.	twin Total Years	24 ft No.	24 ft Total Years	TOTAL No.	TOTAL Years
1902	0			64	–	188	–	5	–	257	–
1901	1			68	68	265	265			323	333
1900	2			94	188	138	276	45	90	277	554
1899	3			129	387	107	321	45	135	381	843
1898	4			153	612	205	820			388	1432
1897	5			180	900	160	800			340	1700
1896	6			152	912	108	648			360	1560
1895	7			187	1309	124	868			311	2177
1894	8			161	1288	34	272	34	272	249	1832
1893	9							66	594	106	954
1892	10			12	120					12	120
1891	11			5	55			190	2090	195	2145
1890	12			1	12			99	1188	100	1200
1889	13							31	403	31	403
1888	14										
1887	15										
1886	16										
1885	17										
1884	18										
1883	19							50	950	50	950
1882	20			2	40					46	
1881	21			137	3014					137	2014
1880	22										
1879	23			3	69					3	69
1878	24										
1877	25			31	775			96	2400	177	3175
1876	26			4	104	44	1144			48	1248
1875	27			19	513	63	1707			87	2311
1874	28			31	868					31	868
1873	29	3	87	48	1392					51	1479
1872	30		30	74	2220					75	2250
1871	31	7	217	24	744					31	961
1870	32	26	1152	6	192					47	1344
1869	33										
1868	34										
1867	35										
Average Age		47	1486	162.5	16,142	143.6	7416	661	8177	3769	32,865
		31.61 years		9.93 years		4.76 years		12.29 years		8.72 years	

London and North Western Railway.

WAGON DEPARTMENT, EARLESTOWN.

Return of Working Stock, 30th November 1902.

Compiled from the Wagon Shop Register.

		Side Doors
Open Goods Wagons, 9' sides, 7 tons	Side Doors	12,965
" " 20' " 7 "		13,826
" " 20' " 7 "	Fall Doors	441
" " 36' " 7 "	Side Doors (including furniture wagons)	14,903
" " 20' " 10 "		12
" " 20' " 10 "	Vitriol	6
" " 22' " 10 "	W.C. District	85
" " 36' " 10 "		262
" " 24 feet 10 "	Slate Traffic	50
Timber Wagons, Ordinary, 7 tons		47
" " 10 "		1,625
" Twin 10 "		1,436
" 24 feet 10 "		661
Beer Vans		270
Break Vans — Birkenhead	144 & Ordinary	1,683
Shunting Wagons		2
Cattle 287 small	891 Large	2,324
(Fowler's) 2' Special 25'	1152 Medium	43
Coal Wagons in use by Merchandise Dept. S. & C. District		100
" "	W.C.	53
Coke "	W.C.	131
Covered Goods Wagons Ordinary		3,402
" " Doors each side		5,381
Furniture Wagons		158
Engine Trollies Iron		2
Glass Wagons, Iron Stanchions (No wells)		118
Iron Stanchions (with wells)		28
Gunpowder Vans		30
Hopper Wagons		1,455
Meat Wagons, Fall Doors, 7 tons		80
Vans		819
Refrigerator		558
Propeller Wagon		82
Rail Trucks		13
Tool Vans (Pooley's)		
Traffic Coal Wagons		6,845
Tranship Vans		348
Trollies		77
Chemical Pan		6
Ballast Wagons		1,606
Coal Wagons, Carriage Dept.		69
Coke "		19
Coke " Loco		3,082
Coal "		45
Coal " Steamboat		140
Cinder " Wagon		20
Coal "		32
Coke "		27
Slate		300
Narrow Gauge		319
Open Goods, 36 lids, 10 tons (including Ballast Wagons)		75
Butter Vans	Northampton	8
Cattle Wagons		
Covered Goods Fitted for Meat Traffic		100
Open Goods, 36 Lids, Stone Traffic		100
	Total	76,330

Average Age 13.30

(1918–1924)]. These last documents are particularly valuable because they show the quantities of each class of wagon built and scrapped each year. It is also sometimes possible to deduce when wagons of one type were rebuilt into another, by looking for corresponding increases and decreases in the numbers of wagon types built each year.

Earlestown Accounts Book

This book records the quantity of each type of wagon built on both the Capital and Renewal Accounts for each half year. It also records the average cost of each wagon; since it is an accounts book with the expenditure recorded to one old penny, we may be sure that its building data is highly accurate. The descriptions of each vehicle type generally match those in the 1903 Wagon Stock Diagram Book, so identifying which is which is generally fairly clear, except, of course, that the descriptions of some diagrams were very similar.

1919 Table from The Diagram Book

This table was an overall summary of the entire wagon fleet of the LNWR as at 30th November 1919. It was printed on one very large page (see pages 6/7) and was marked 'Private and Confidential'. It principally summarised capacities and dimensions, such as carrying capacity; number owned; tare; inside measurements; wheelbase; axlebox; 'break'; buffer and coupling type; door arrangements. Very usefully it includes intentions and comments about renewals etc., such as '6000 is number of 9-in. sided wagons to be permanently retained' and 'These wagons are fitted with end door only'. A section underneath the main table lists the duplicate wagon stock by location. An adjacent table details the numbers of wagons built, purchased and renewed together with the total stock each year from 1868 through to 1919.

Examples of other information which is contained in the table include that at this date 56,658 wagons had been fitted with brake levers on both sides, leaving 22,584 with levers on one side only. However, those with dumb buffers had been reduced to just three crane wagons. The 12,417 wagons remaining with small 6in x 3in journals were specifically listed with the plans to upgrade or replace them. Only one LNWR Refrigerator van was fully fitted with Westinghouse brakes, although 144 had through pipes.

Official General Arrangement Drawings

These survive for most wagons included in the 1903 Diagram Book but for very few wagons that were scrapped before then. Sometimes several drawings exist for one type of wagon, each showing different constructional details such as axleboxes, couplings and smaller details as these were changed. Although well-drawn, dimensioned, and to a large scale (usually 1in–1ft), smaller details are still not clear. Later drawings often included a table of these details with a list of detail drawing numbers. Unfortunately, very few detail drawings appear to have survived.

There are many inaccuracies in official drawings. The Diagram 53 Coal Wagon is correctly drawn as 15ft over headstocks. Although later vehicles were 15ft 6in long, the drawing office simply altered the dimension on the drawing to 15ft 6in, even though it obviously still scaled 15ft. One drawing of a Diagram 42A has the height of the sides dimensioned as 9in in one place but 9¼in in another, both on the same drawing! Another example is a five-plank coal wagon with side hinged cupboard type doors. No record can be found of this vehicle and it is generally thought that it was never built. The fact that a drawing was produced is no guarantee that anything was ever built to it. In this respect, photographs are much more reliable. While prints were occasionally marked-up or altered, this can usually be detected, so with that proviso, if a photograph exists, the wagon was built.

Generally, drawings of the more unusual wagons seem to have survived in better condition, perhaps because they were rarely used. Many drawings of common wagons are now rather dirty and dog-eared. In this volume we have reprinted some of the original drawings, rather than re-drawing, because they are of intrinsic value in themselves.

Earlestown drawings were all numbered in a straight sequence and it is encouraging that very few GAs seem to be missing from our collections.

Photographs

Photographs are perhaps the most attractive archive of all. Earlestown probably took official photographs of each new type of wagon built, sometimes from both ends or a three-quarter and broadside view. They also photographed an example of many of the older types as they received the new LNWR livery from 1908. These official photographs are of excellent quality and can be dated fairly accurately from the paint date or overhaul date which appears at the left-hand end of the solebar.

As with most historical documents, they should be treated with caution, as although the camera cannot lie, the print can be retouched and lettering in particular can be changed. Once again, it is the unusual which appears to have survived. There are, for instance, several photographs of Diagram 103 with what appears to be experimental brake gear but very few with the standard product. Official photographs are probably the best record we have of livery carried, surpassed perhaps only by amateur photographs which, although more typical, are usually of inferior quality and show vehicles in working condition, i.e. filthy! Livery varied: some views show everything below the solebar as black, whilst others show varying amounts of grey in that area. It is possible that some of the earlier wagons were painted in shop grey for the photograph. White-painted brake gear is often apparent in official photographs and was for the benefit of the camera and not an indication of standard livery.

No register of Earlestown photographs has yet been found, so although hundreds still exist at the NRM and elsewhere, we do not know how many more may have been taken and subsequently lost or destroyed.

In this book we have attempted to show wagons as they were, in their everyday working environment. We could

London & North Western Railway.   WAGON STOCK.   30th November,

Type of Stock.	Carrying Capacity.	Stock	Tare (averaged).	Measurements (inside). Length.	Breadth.	Wheel Base.	Axle Boxes. Oil.	Grease.	Couplings. Screw.	Link.	Lever. One side.	Both sides.	Breaks. Screw	Vacuum Pipes and Blocks. Single Hose.	Duplicate Hose.	Vacuum Pipes only. Single Hose.	Duplicate Hose.	Westinghouse. Complete.	Pipes only.	Small Journals 6 in. × 3 in.	Cubical Capacity	Doors. Roof.	One side.	Both sides.
	Tons.	No.	Tons cwt. qrs.	Ft. in.	Ft. in.	Ft. in.	No.	No.	No.	No.	No.	No.	No.	No.	No.	No.	No.	No.	No.	No.	No.			

OPEN WAGONS:—

Type of Stock.	Carrying Cap.	Stock													
Goods, 9 in. sides	6 & 7	32						32		8		24		81	
"	10	5,968					5,968			5,968		5,968			1,899
" 20 in.	6 & 7	1,899					1,899			1,899	1,799	100			92
" " fall doors	6 & 7	92						92		92	80	12			
"	10	40					23	26		40	10	30			
" " slate traffic	10	8						8		8	8				
" 36 in.	6 & 7	4,587						4,587		4,587	3,265	1,322		4,587	4,587
" "	10	17,931					9,196	8,735		17,931	1,458	16,473			17,931
" (Garston, Widnes, and St. Helens)	10	432					115	317		432	180	252			432
" (express traffic)	10	126					126		126		124	42	84		126
" (18 ft.)	10	12,516					12,448	68		12,516		12,516			12,516
" 40 ft.	20	150					150			150	80	70			150

COVERED WAGONS:—

Beer	10	249				52	197		249	107	142	83
Goods, Ordinary	6 & 7	83					83		83	83		
" D. E. S.	6 & 7	4,219					4,219	24	4,195	3,047	1,172	4,219
" 10 ft.	10	1,454				1,454	15	6	1,454	15	1,454	
" 16 ft. special	10	15					1		1			
" 18 ft.	10	5,003				5,003		137	4,866	1	5,003	
" 20 ft. special	10	1				1			1	1		
" 21 ft. 8 in. special	10	1				1			1	1		
" 27 ft.	18	1										
" express traffic	10	1,600				1,606		1,305	391	1	1,695	
" banana	6, 7, & 10	13				4	9	1	12		13	
" fruit	10	25				25		25		25		
Fruit-banana traffic, steam heated	10	525				525		525		525		
Gunpowder	5 & 7	35				10	25		35	20	15	
Meat	6	768				741	27	768		541	227	768
" refrigerators	6	741				741		741		377	364	741
Tranship	6 & 7	40					40	13	27	31	9	

MINERAL WAGONS:—

Coal, Carriage Department	6, 7, & 10	69				10	59		69	20	49	69
" Steamboat	10	140				21	119		110	120	20	140
" S. & C. District	10	100				14	86		103	58	42	
" Wagon Department	6, 7, & 10	63				19	44		63	36	27	
" W. C. District	10	138				83	55		138	20	118	138
Coke, Carriage Department	10	20				10	34		44	8	36	20
" Loco.	10	8					21		25	7	18	44
" Wagon Department	10	25				43	88		131	72	59	
" W. C. District (hoppered)	10	131					3		3	2	1	
" Widnes	10	3				174	1,269		1,443	1,164	279	
Hopper, Ordinary	10	1,443				60			60		60	
" Steel	20	80					3,366		3,366	3,385	1	3,366
Traffic Coal	8	3,366				2,504	960		3,464	817	2,647	3,464
"	10	3,464										
"	15	20				20			20	2	18	

SPECIAL WAGONS:—

Furniture	6 & 10	158				18	140		158	7	151	1
Glass	6, 7, & 10	145				15	130		145	108	37	118
Trollies—Agricultural engine						2	1		3	1	2	
" Boiler		39				21	18		39		27	
" Chemical pan		6				3	3		6		5	
" Glass		2				2			2		2	
" Gun	50 & 150	3				1	2	1				
" Platform		62				62			62		1	61
" Propeller		1				1			1			
" Tramcar		35				5	30		35	1	4	29
" Wire rope		1										

CATTLE TRUCKS:—

Medium	6, 7, & 10	1,433				601	832	1,433		654	779	1,433
Large	10	891				771	120	891		117	774	891
Special (late Fowler's)	6	24					24	24		24		24
"	6	1					1			1		1
With compartment for man	10	18				18		18		10	8	18

RAIL AND TIMBER TRUCKS:—

Timber, Ordinary	10	1,583				80	1,503		1,583	1,024	539	
" Twin	20	710				25	685		710		710	
" 24 ft.	10	768				185	583		768	60	708	

BREAK VANS:—

10 tons	...	604					602	604		604	2	
15 "	...	32				32		32		32	31	
20 "	...	1,169					1,169		1,169		1,169	

MISCELLANEOUS:—

Shunting Wagons	...	101					101	101		33	68	99
Slate—Narrow Gauge	...	300					300	300				

RAILWAY SERVICE VEHICLES:—

Locomotive Department (Coal)—

10 tons	...	3,062				266	2,786	1	3,051	2,519	532	
15 "	...	568				568			568		568	
20 "	...	63				63			63		63	63
Ballast Stock:— Break Vans	...	96				21	75	96			96	
Cranes	...	18					18		18			
Rail Trucks	...	47				3	44		47		33	
Wagons, &c.	...	2,009				261	1,748		2,009	1,177	832	

MISCELLANEOUS:—

Cinder—Wagon Department	6	20					20		20			
Tool Vans (Pooley's)	6 & 10	16				4	12	16		9	7	

| **TOTAL** | ... | 81,642 | | | | 45,338 | 36,284 | 7,957 | 73,685 | 23,584 | 66,688 | 2,031 | 2,855 | 229 | 1,854 | 72 | 1 | 144 | 92,441 | 3 | 6,907 | 83 | 60,18... |

DUPLICATE WAGONS:—

Birkenhead	...	4
Broadheath	...	26
Crewe	...	20
Earlestown	...	20
Garston	...	600
Holyhead	...	5

CHIEF GOODS MANAGER'S OFFICE, EUSTON STATION.

March, 1920.

2/3/20

Remarks.

6 and 7-ton wagons are those with small journals. They will be replaced in renewal by 10-ton vehicles, and a number of them converted into 10-ton wagons. 6,000 is number of 9-in. sided wagons to be permanently retained.]

Will be replaced in renewal by 36-in. sided 10-ton vehicles.]

Will be replaced in renewal by 36-in. sided 10-ton vehicles.
Will be replaced in renewal by 36-in. sided 10-ton vehicles. Some will be converted into 10-ton wagons.

Will be replaced by 10-ton vehicles.
Small journals vehicles. They will be replaced in renewal by 10-ton wagons. Some will be converted into 10-ton wagons

Will be replaced in renewal by 10-ton vehicles.

Will be replaced in renewal by 7-ton vehicles.

Will in renewal be replaced and merged in stock of covered 10-ton vans.

Will be replaced in renewal by 10-ton vehicles.

These wagons are fitted with end door only
Will be replaced in renewal by 10-ton vehicles.

Will be replaced in renewal by 10-ton vehicles.

Will be replaced in renewal by 10-ton vehicles.

Will be replaced in renewal by 10-ton vehicles.

20-ton is now standard break van.

Steel bodies and frames.

Will be replaced in renewal by 10-ton vehicles.
Will be replaced in renewal by 10-ton vehicles.

WAGONS BUILT, PURCHASED, RENEWED, AND THE TOTAL STOCK, EACH YEAR FROM 1868.

Year.	Built on Capital Account.	Built at Cost of Revenue.	Purchased or taken over.	Total added to Stock.	Number Renewed.	Total Stock.
1868	91	...	123	214	1,130	28,304
1869	545	30	...	575	1,095	28,879
1870	1,218	...	75	1,293	1,133	30,172
1871	2,010	123	13	2,146	1,184	32,316
1872	2,894	29	498	3,421	1,211	35,730
1873	3,324	...	2	3,326	1,257	39,065
1874	2,027	...	80	2,107	1,302	41,172
1875	1,026	...	10	1,036	1,402	42,208
1876	320	...	39	359	1,608	42,567
1877	1,014	...	1	1,015	1,755	43,582
1878	27	...	872	899	1,918	44,481
1879	38	...	106	144	1,899	44,925
1880	1,882	2	80	1,964	2,017	46,589
1881	1,550	...	...	1,550	2,072	48,139
1882	1,118	25	...	1,143	2,076	49,292
1883	2,279	...	...	2,279	2,059	51,561
1884	1,343	...	...	1,343	1,031	52,904
1885	220	...	...	220	709	53,124
1886	204	...	...	204	383	53,382
1887	107	20	...	127	451	53,518
1888	435	36	...	471	274	53,986
1889	1,297	24	...	1,321	470	55,307
1890	1,993	48	20	2,061	664	57,368
1891	1,974	48	...	2,099	660	59,988
1892	1,715	...	...	1,710	448	61,098
1893	1,096	...	...	1,096	657	62,194
1894	1,065	...	2	1,067	905	63,261
1895	1,618	...	4	1,622	1,387	64,283
1896	1,123	...	...	1,123	1,361	65,406
1897	1,382	...	...	1,382	1,931	66,788
1898	1,827	...	...	1,827	2,128	68,615
1899	1,420	2	...	1,422	2,372	70,037
1900	2,938	...	24	2,962	2,026	72,999
1901	1,894	...	4	1,898	2,430	73,997
1902	2,325	...	...	2,325	2,476	76,322
1903	380	...	...	380	2,363	76,367
1904	3	...	...	3	2,162	76,370
1905	60	...	4	64	2,203	76,434
1906	715	...	15	730	2,243	77,164
1907	490	...	...	490	2,321	77,654
1908	361	...	2	363	2,181	78,017
1909	...	...	50	50	2,328	78,067
1910	...	...	...	...	2,234	78,067
1911	...	...	11	11	2,786	78,078
1912	1	...	1,576	1,577	3,461	79,655
1913	280	...	1,190	1,470	2,786	80,426
1914	273	...	1	274	2,991	80,700
1915	86	...	4	90	2,319	80,790
1916	46	...	1	47	1,984	80,837
1917	14	...	...	14	1,582	80,851
1918	243	...	...	243	1,172	81,094
1919	542	...	6	548	1,214	81,642

CONVERSION OF 6 AND 7 TON WAGONS WITH SMALL JOURNAL.

Number of 6 or 7-ton goods wagons converted since 31st May, 1911, and now 10-ton wagons :—

To 30th November, 1919 10,551

7-ton wagons with small journals reduced in carrying capacity to 6 tons :—

To 30th November, 1919 ... 30,748, of which 19,261 have since been renewed by or converted into 10-ton wagons.

1919 Table from Diagram Book.

Three generations of open wagons on the quayside at Garston Docks, Liverpool: (from the left) an unidentified D9, D84 No. 24014 (tare 6.15.1), D84 No. 30642, D4 No. 70527 and another D4 with a number starting 3088X. The date was between 1909 and 1910. There is little evidence of actual paint inside the wagons. The knees had gone rusty and the loads had made scuff marks on the insides. Note the period dock cranes with their wooden control cabins.
NATIONAL RAILWAY MUSEUM (CR MC431)

An atmospheric scene of timber being loaded on the quayside: Nos. 40300 (on the right-hand road) and what we think was 39257 to D12 loaded with timber at Garston Docks in 1913. Twin timber trucks to D13 often ran with a D12 single-bolster timber truck at either end, so some of these wagons could have been D13s. This view shows numerous sailing barges but only two steamships can be seen.

NATIONAL RAILWAY MUSEUM (LMS 3030)

have restricted plates to rather sterile side and end views, but we think you will agree the goods yards, sheds, docks, etc, shown are all of great interest and will be fascinating to modellers, historians and enthusiasts alike. Photographs of adequate quality of LNWR goods yards are not common, and so in deciding what to include and what must be omitted, the decision was made to include a wide variety of working environment scenes, including yards of other companies but they must include at least one LNWR wagon. In some cases it may play a very minor part in the scene.

Other sources

In addition to the above, there are numerous non-official sources of information ranging from personal recollection to amateur sketches, drawings and photographs. These are invaluable because they were taken from wagons actually in service and corroborate the official records. Sometimes, of course, the official records even disagree with themselves and that has caused us to be very careful before going into print. If the Wagon Stock Age Book shows that 6,589 of a certain wagon were built, it probably does not matter very much

This October 1938 view of Thomas W. Ward's Albion Works yard in Sheffield shows ex-LNWR D84 open No. 78914 in LMS livery amid the highly industrialised environment that such wagons necessarily had occasion to visit. The tare was evidently 6.5.2, and we can see four-bolt two-rib buffers, bulbous axleboxes and a great deal of dirt.   CTY. T. W. WARD

that the Annual Stock Valuation Lists show 6,586, but we have had to be very careful as to which figure we use. Another example is where the 1902 Wagon Stock Age Book shows twelve glass wagons built in 1895 and eight in 1894 whereas from 1909 editions of this book all twenty are shown as having been built in the latter year.

WAGON NUMBERING

The now familiar LNWR method of wagon numbering with a unique number carried on a cast-iron plate fixed to the centre of each solebar originated in 1861/62 rather than at the birth of the company in 1846. Evidence for this is to be found in the minutes of the General Stores and Locomotive Expenditure Committee for May 1861 when the committee agreed to a new system of numbering in which all the company's wagons were to be renumbered consecutively with the exception of ballast wagons and brake vans. Prior to that time the Northern and Southern Divisions had numbered their wagons independently. This situation must have been causing concern for some time because in 1858 there was a report on duplicate numbers to the above committee.

After considering the report, the committee resolved that the Southern Division wagons should be renumbered beginning at 10,001.

Whether this decision was implemented is uncertain, for a year later the committee was discussing the marking and numbering of the wagon stock again. This time they resolved that all wagons be lettered only L&NW, with a white diamond, and that each class be numbered from 1 upwards. The wording of the minute makes it clear that brake vans, ballast wagons, sheep and cattle wagons, box wagons and open wagons each constituted a separate class. We do not know if this decision was carried out, but we do know that a year later, in May 1861, the General Manager attended the committee's meeting to ensure that they agreed to his request to rescind their previous decision and instead agree to renumber the whole of the wagons consecutively with the exception of the ballast wagons and brake vans.

We do know that this decision was implemented, for in November 1861 it was reported to the committee that 8,984 wagons had already been renumbered and that it was hoped to complete the renumbering of the whole stock and verify them by the end of May 1862. By the end of 1862 the total wagon stock excluding ballast wagons and brake vans was 17,644. It is believed that any wagons built after that date on capital account (i.e. additions) would have taken the next unused number and any wagons built on revenue account (i.e. replacements) would then have taken the number of the wagon being replaced.

There are references to 'register numbers' on some LNWR documents but for simplicity here we shall simply refer to wagon 'numbers'.

Brake vans had their own number series starting at 1 and their plates were suffixed with a small letter 'B'. Ballast wagons each carried two different numbers. The solebar plate carried the wagon department number for repair and renewal purposes and was in a sequence also starting at 1 and suf-

fixed 'BALLAST'. The other plate, positioned on one end of each wagon, gave its number in the appropriate engineering department division.

Whilst it was normal to replace a wagon by one of a similar but more modern type, this was not always the case, e.g. many open wagons were replaced by vans as traffic requirements changed. So, although the original 1862 numbering is thought to have allocated a block of numbers to each type of wagon, this neat pattern was gradually destroyed so that by 1923 numbering appeared to be almost random. It seems certain that no renumbering occurred after 1862 or before 1923, but older wagons relegated to departmental use were sometimes prefixed 'o'.

The LMS renumbered most LNWR wagons by the addition of 200,000 to the running number. However brake vans and narrow gauge slate and coal wagons had 280,000 added, whilst ballast wagons also bore numbers in the 280,000 series.

Photographs exist of LNWR wagon designs carrying LMS numbers in the 100,000 series. These are mostly cattle wagons and 'Crystal Palace' brake vans (Diagram 17B). They are believed to relate to the LNWR/L&Y merger of 1922, where the stock may have been counted with the L&Y.

LIVERIES

We shall give here a basic overview of the standard LNWR livery and outline common type-specific variations which were applied to the wagons covered in this volume. Wagons in later volumes will have their variations outlined in that volume. There will be enough information to meet the needs of most modellers, but for a more complete coverage in depth the reader is referred to the excellent HMRS publication *LNWR Liveries*. A note on early liveries follows at the end of this section.

It is important to remember that wagons came in for re-painting on a cycle of several years; accordingly any changes in livery took several years to implement on the existing stock. Repainting was not always complete – there is plenty of photographic evidence of patch-painting and repairs. Wagons bearing the LNWR livery could commonly be seen up until about 1930, and a few could be noted up until the Second World War.

THE STANDARD LIVERY

From the 1850s onwards the bodies of goods wagons and vans were painted a medium lead grey colour. It has sometimes been termed 'invisible grey', a 'lead colour' or even 'light grey' in some references. The grey was mixed from equal parts of black and white pigments, and was slightly darker than LMS grey.

This colour was applied to the body, solebars and buffer stocks of the wagon. All the running gear below the solebars was painted black including buffer heads and couplings. Goods vans had white roofs when new, but from 1908 onwards the roofs of ordinary covered vans began to be painted grey. Refrigerator, banana, fruit and other 'special' vans continued with white roofs after this date.

The wagon number and ownership were shown on a cast-iron rectangular plate 13in x 6½in affixed to the middle of the solebar. It carried the initials 'L.N.W.' with the number beneath it in 2in characters. It was painted black with the raised lettering and border painted white. Up until 1878 it was fitted to only one side but was on both sides thereafter.

Up to 1908 the only markings of ownership, apart from the cast-iron number plate on each solebar, were the two white diamonds, 11in x 5½in, on each side of the body. The exact position varied according to the position of the framing, strapping and other markings. It is best to refer to photographs to check positions. After 1910 the diamonds were omitted when vehicles were repainted, but were still commonly to be seen after the Grouping in 1923. The diamonds have been referred to as 'illiterate symbols' but were much more likely to have been company logos, since railwaymen were not uneducated. The North Staffordshire similarly used a knot, the Cambrian the Prince-of-Wales feathers, the Lancashire & Yorkshire a solid triangle within a circle, and the North British both a quatrefoil and an inverted crescent for the paint date.

In February 1908 the Goods Conference minuted that the legend 'LNWR' should be added in large prominent letters to the two white diamonds on each side of the body. This was initially overruled by the higher Loco & Engineering Committee who decided a month later that an ampersand should be inserted between the 'L' and the 'N'. However, the 'LNWR' form prevailed and the only photographic evidence of the intervention is on some hired coal wagons where the 'L & NWR' can be seen on the top plank. The letters were 16in. high where practicable.

The wagon number was painted in white 4in letters centrally on the top plank of each end from 1882 onwards, except on brake vans which never had numbers on the end, and cattle wagons from which they were omitted after 1896. Some photographs exist of wagons from 1921 onwards where the number has been moved onto the sides (Ref: No. 68410, page 69).

The tare weight was painted in white 3in figures adjacent to the left-hand axlebox on each side. Until 1912 it appeared on the solebar, but after that date it was moved up onto the curb rail or bottom plank of the body side. The style could be 6.9.0 or 6·9·0, but variations 6_9_0 and 6—9—0 have been noted.

The painting date was shown in numbers 1¼in high in month/year format, eg. '6/06', normally positioned between the lower two leftmost bolt heads on the solebars.

This standard colour scheme continued right up to the grouping with just a few variations. Where these apply to particular types of wagon, the variations will be detailed in the exceptions below.

Old wagons no longer fit for mainline service were sometimes transferred to service stock, in which case some evidence suggests they were painted red and their running number prefixed by zero.

OPEN WAGONS
Open wagons were usually given the standard livery but there could be variations in the lettering. On wagons with 36in sides it was usual to paint the maximum permitted load, for example, '7 TONS', in 6in characters on each side on the top plank. A Minute of 1896 ordered this after complaints of damage by overloading, which was presumably much easier to accomplish in higher-sided vehicles.

The earliest style placed the weight, eg. '7', to the left of the door and the word 'TONS' to the right, above the diamond symbols. When the 'LNWR' legend was added, the rating, eg. '10 TONS', was placed near the left-hand end on the top plank. From 1921 on, the 'LNWR' was moved higher up the sides and the rating moved to or repeated on the bottom plank at the right-hand end.

Wagons used in the West Cumberland district had the legend 'WEST CUMBERLAND DIST.' painted centrally on the sides on the top plank but one.

When wagons were fitted with the Williams automatic sheet support, there was no space for the number on the end. On D84 wagons it was moved to a central position on the bottommost end plank, and on D2 wagons it was moved to the right-hand side on the top plank (see page IV).

On narrow gauge slate and coal wagons, the numberplate could only be 5in long x 3½in high due to the restricted space available (Appendix 5 refers).

VANS
The wagon numbers of vans were being painted on the insides of the doors by 1914, and this practice is believed to have continued until the Grouping. Having the number clearly displayed above platform level during loading and unloading would have been of great use to the staff.

CATTLE WAGONS
The livery worn by the majority of cattle wagons followed the standard colour scheme, but for many years a white lime wash was used to disinfect the bodywork between each journey. Photographs show that characteristically this dribbled down the outside of the lower planks. Although in no way part of the official livery, this whitening is essential to an accurate portrayal of a 19th century cattle wagon in service. Use of lime wash was prohibited as being injurious to the animals sometime after the early 'twenties.

After 1896 the wagon register number was transferred to the top plank on the right-hand side panel in white 2in numbers (see page 125) to make it more easily accessible to the cattle inspectors. Note also that the wagon label holder was raised to the second plank from the solebar so as to keep it out of the mire! Up to 1908 the two white diamonds were placed on each side of the body centrally on the next to the top plank of the outer side panels.

SPECIAL CATTLE WAGONS
The 'Prize Cattle' wagons to Diagrams 23–26 were painted in the brown/lake 'quick brown' colour worn by horseboxes and other non-passenger coaching stock. The raised framing was lined in yellow in a simplified style. All lettering was in white.

They were sometimes lettered 'CATTLE BOX' and from 1908 the tonnage appeared on the bottom plank at the left-hand end at each side.

TIMBER WAGONS

The letters 'LNWR' adopted in 1908 could only be 6in high due to the limited space on the single side plank or curb rail. Similarly the wagon number painted on the ends was only 3in high, and the diamonds were only 8in x 4in. The tare weight lettering was also reduced in size, to 2½in. The bolsters themselves were numbered separately and painted with the vehicle number and a diamond. Subsequently the 'LNWR' was added in the centre above the number, both being in 2in letters.

GLASS WAGONS

On glass wagons, for similar space reasons, the 'LNWR' legend added from 1908 could only be 9in high. Glass wagons were normally lettered 'FOR GLASS TRAFFIC' and almost invariably, 'EMPTY TO S.T HELENS'.

FURNITURE VAN WAGONS

The letters 'LNWR' adopted in 1908 could only be 6in high due to the limited space on the single side plank or curb rail.

Similarly the wagon number painted on the ends was only 3in high, and the diamonds were only 8in x 4in. The tare weight lettering was also reduced in size to 2½in.

EARLY LIVERIES

It is uncertain how long before 1860 the standard grey livery was being applied, but cattle and merchandise wagons were known to be usually blue in 1849. At this time wagons for sheep were green.

It is now known that the Grand Junction Railway were using the diamond mark as early as 1838.

It is also believed that the Prince of Wales feathers appearing on Chester and Holyhead Railway wagons had its origins on the C&HR even before absorption into the LNWR in 1853. Due to the difficulties there would be in obtaining suitable wagons for the coal and slate traffic in the Chester and Holyhead area, Mr. J.O. Binger, the genial Superintendent of the C&HR, requested that the feathers be retained. They were needed to distinguish the Division as well as the number, since at that time each Division numbered its wagons in a separate sequence starting at one. They were retained until September 1860 when the LNWR Locomotive Committee ordered their discontinuance.

It may have been posed but this shot is charged with atmosphere and interest. It shows an 'Overland' lorry being offloaded from a Motor Car Van with the aid of a D14 24ft timber wagon in use as a 'motor runner wagon'. D14 was probably being used in lieu of an end-loading dock, and the prominent side lettering 'HOLYHEAD. NOT TO WORK ON THE MAIN LINE' suggests maybe this was not the first time it had been used in this way. Note the rings on the solebars and worn condition of the floor planking.
NATIONAL RAILWAY MUSEUM (LMS 4503)

RLESTOWN

348

Earlestown
345·899

Wood

270 G.
9·005

269
12·203

314
8·570

Engineering Works

310
1·378

315
2·556

317·580

316·916

Vitriol
Square

313
1·025

312
·789

311
5·571

319
7·528

310
7·176

309
1·199

Larkfield

308
5·112

307
3·236

303
2·490

304
2·401

302
1·199

289
·845

Viaduct Works
(Wagon)

321
13·389

320
13·423

Recreation Ground

Griffin Hotel

L I V E R P O O L   &   M A N C H E S T E R   L I N E

HAYDOCK COLLIERY RAILWAY

WELLINGTON STREET

VIADUCT STREET

SANKEY STREET

BANK STREET

Sankey Hill

Sankey Viaduct

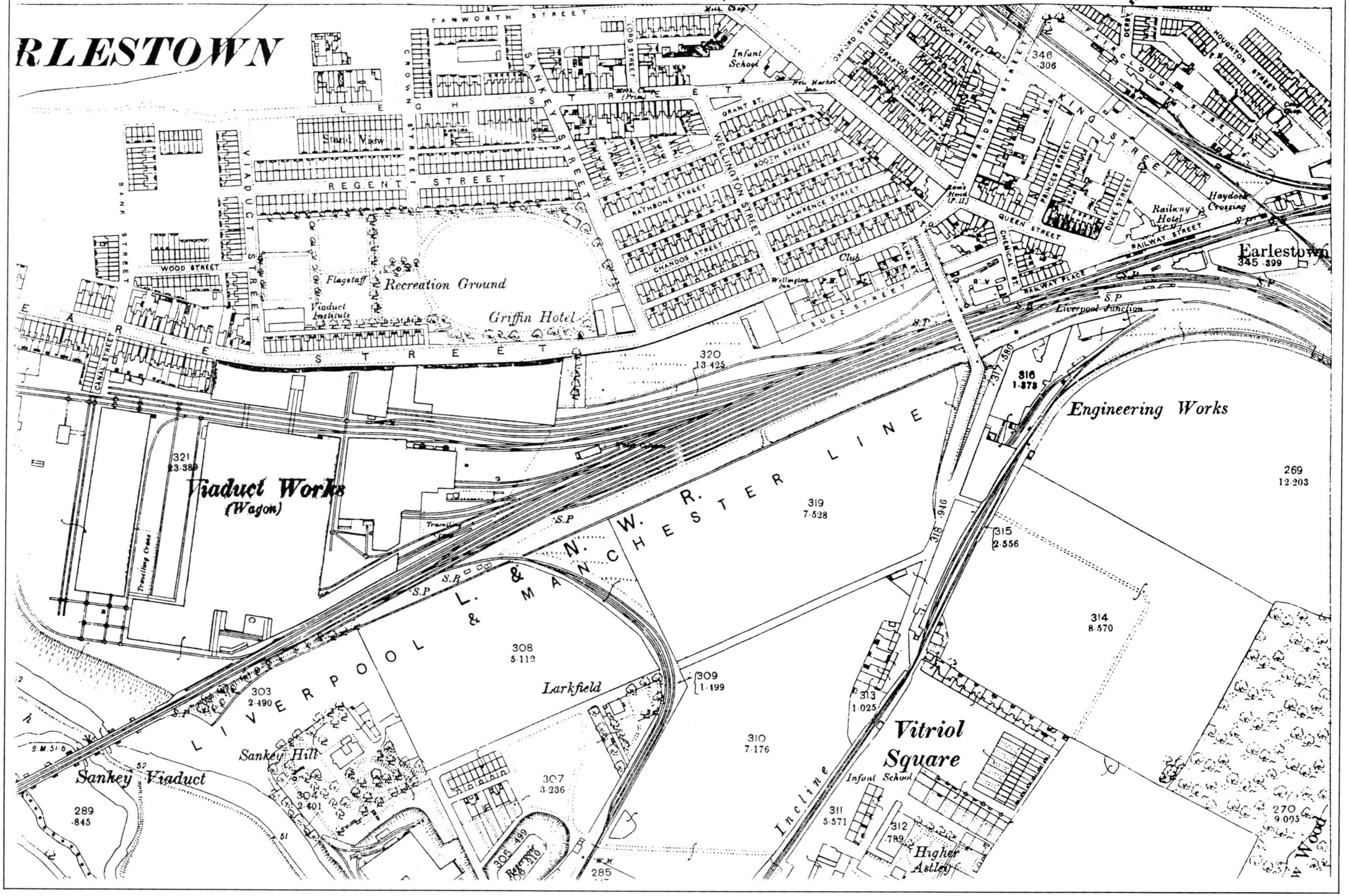

Earlestown Wagon Works in LNWR days, before construction of the 'White Shop' in 1913.

CHAPTER ONE

EARLESTOWN WAGON WORKS

A '19in Goods' 4–6–0 speeding past Earlestown Wagon Works with an eastbound train in LMS days. Note the large quantity of lime on the two cattle wagons standing outside the Works.
HMRS (AAJ200)

EARLESTOWN came to be the primary wagon manufacturing and repair works for the LNWR. The origin of the Works can be traced back to before the formation of the company. The Grand Junction Railway (GJR) was opened in 1837 from Birmingham to Newton Junction and connected with the Liverpool and Manchester Railway (L&MR). The GJR rented premises from the L&MR which they used as a locomotive repair shop. This was situated at Edge Hill, Liverpool, which surprisingly was 15 miles from the nearest GJR line at Newton Junction.

When the GJR took over the Chester and Crewe Railway (C&CR) in 1840 they found that they had acquired powers to purchase land around the junction of the C&C at Crewe. Joseph Locke, the engineer-in-chief, quickly realised that a new and larger works would be needed to build and service locomotives for the planned expansion. On 12th August 1840 the GJR board approved the building of Crewe Works for the construction and repairs of GJR locomotives, wagons and carriages. It opened in 1843.

With the formation of the LNWR in July 1846 the demand for more locomotives stretched the resources of Crewe Works, and in February 1847 it was decided to transfer the wagon construction to Edge Hill, Liverpool, and to transfer the small locomotive repair shop back to Crewe

Works. With the transfer to Edge Hill, Owen Owens, who was the wagon foreman at Crewe Works, was put in charge. The small wagon works at Ordsall Lane, Manchester was also placed under his control. The demands for locomotive work at Crewe were still increasing and not all the repairs could be transferred from Edge Hill. Very soon the locomotive work undertaken at Edge Hill increased again and this restricted the space available for wagon building, so as soon as 1852 the LNWR again began a search for a new works to centralise wagon building.

Success came on 1st March 1853 when the LNWR took a lease on the Viaduct Foundry from Messrs Jones and Potts. This was a small works of eight acres situated at the eastern end of the famous viaduct over the Sankey Brook and St. Helens canal, built by George Stephenson for the Liverpool & Manchester Railway, and just west of Newton-le-Willows. The LNWR were offered a lease at £650 per annum for two years or £600 per annum for seven years. The latter option was taken up, and after seven years the property was purchased outright for £15,000. The works, when first let, was said to include 'one 24 horse engine, an 18 horse engine, 40 smiths' fires, one large hooping furnace, one foundry, three cupolas, one brass foundry, gas apparatus, one office and drawing room, warehouse, dining room for

200 men and stables for eight horses.' It had capacity for building 1,000 wagons and 50 engines per year. Included in the lease were thirty-three workers' cottages in Owen Street and Norris Street.

The Viaduct Foundry had been a small engineering works begun by Messrs Jones Turner & Evans in 1833. It is known to have built at least one locomotive, *Black Diamond*, for the nearby Haydock Collieries of which Richard, Evans and Turner were owners. Among other things produced were pumping machines for local mines. It had a rail connection at the eastern end of the viaduct, and claims are made that *Rocket* was serviced at the works. There is no proof of this but excavations under the floor of the 'Square Smithy' on the spot where the watering is said to have taken place, revealed a line of stone blocks with cast-iron rail chairs with chair bolts set in lead, matching the early L&MR permanent way.

From 1853 rapid development began and the area covered by the works increased from the eight acres purchased to 36 acres in the 1900s. The first order received was for 300 wagons and, to accommodate the work, a new wagon shed was authorised in early 1854 on land recently purchased adjacent to the 'Long Smithy'.

By the year 1864 wagon production was in full swing and Mr Owens reported that the production for the first half of that year was:

Capital Account
640	Open Goods
6	Break Vans
2	Parcels Vans (4 wheeled)
2	Lorries (4 wheeled)
1	Cart (2 wheeled)
1	Float (2 wheeled)
———	
652	vehicles

Renewal Account
136	Open wagons
11	Covered wagons
16	Cattle wagons
4	Coal wagons
3	Break Vans
9	Ballast wagons
1	Lorry
———	
180	vehicles

and for the second half of the year:

Capital Account
508	Open Goods
2	Glass wagons
15	Break Vans
3	Lorries
1	Parcel Cart
———	
529	vehicles

Renewal Account
142	Open Goods
17	Covered goods
19	Cattle Vans

Sir Hardman Earle, director of the LNWR and former GJR.

2	Break Vans
8	Coal wagons
14	Ballast wagons
———	
202	vehicles

This totalled 1,552 rail vehicles and 11 road vehicles.

The full extent of the activities at Earlestown and district is clearly indicated in the first half-yearly report for 1865, which was as follows:

New wagon output	1,099
Vehicle frames renewed	48
Heavy repairs	774
Ordinary repairs	33,260
(outstations included)	

The country lane giving access to the works was called Pepper Alley Lane but this was later renamed Earle Street as a compliment to Sir Hardman Earle, a director of the LNWR and former GJR. With the transfer of the men from Ordsall Lane Works, more housing was needed, and when built these became known as Earle's Town, which later became corrupted to Earlestown, the name it bears today. The streets within Earlestown were named Rathbone, Booth, Lawrence and Chandos after LNWR directors and officials. Haydock Place, Newton and Sankey Terraces were built to continue the expansion of housing accommodation and at a later date Regent Street is thought to have been added. In 1854 a house was built on Earle Street at the western end of the works and was named Earle Cottage. This became the residence of Mr Owen Owens and subsequent Works Superintendents.

The Works Superintendents from 1853–1964 were:

Mr Owen Owens	1853–1867
Mr J.W. Emmett	1867–1903
Mr H.D. Earl	1903–1910
Mr A.R. Trevithick	1910–1916
Mr W.W.H. Warneford	1916–1924
Mr E. Lemon	1924–1931
Mr Anthony	1931–1946
Mr A.E. Bates	1946–1964 (?)

In 1867 Mr Owens retired and J.W. Emmett was appointed his successor.

J. Watson Emmett had served his apprenticeship under first his father and then his uncle who were Wagon Superintendents of the Lancashire and Yorkshire Railway, working on the bench for a further five years before being promoted to foreman and then daughterman. With the death of his uncle in 1865, he succeeded him as Wagon Superintendent of the L&Y. He was appointed to move to the LNWR and take charge of Earlestown in 1867. He was immediately faced with a wholesale reduction in the building programme, resulting in 124 of the staff being discharged. Fortunately, this was a short phase and Emmett quickly began to develop the Works. In December 1867 the roof of the original smithy was found to be unsafe and it was decided to pull it down, giving more yard space. At the same time an additional bay was added to the Foundry to become the new smithy.

The development of the works is shown by the following extracts from the Northern Section of the Locomotive and Engineering Committee Minutes:

February 1868: LNWR chairman visited the works and agreed Mr Emmett's proposals to build a new shed for the tyre press at £460, the existing Iron and Brass Foundries to be enlarged by taking in one bay of the old smithy £300.

New Wagon and Machine Shop. The existing outside wall of the Wagon Shop to be replaced by pillars and girders at £500.

October 1868: New Spring Shop and furnace ordered.

February 1869: Shop heating by hot water and steam ordered in Fitting, Carpentering and Wood Machine Shops. Other shops heated by stoves.

January 1870: Wheel-making plant authorised.

April 1870: Plans for new stores authorised.

September 1870: New Paint Shop approved owing to wagon production encroaching on existing Paint Shop.

July 1871: Timber Shed approved £7,800.

June 1872: Plan for new Wagon Shop approved £8,500.

November 1872: Authority given to re-site stables to make way for new offices.

Mr. J. Watson Emmett, Superintendent of the Works 1867-1903.

February 1873: Additional bay to forge and appropriate equipment authorised. Cost £2,135.

With the increase of workers at the works, a further fifty houses were authorised to be built in 1873. With the enlarged community, the need for a meeting place for recreation and education was recognised by the company, and they built the Viaduct Institute in 1877. Workers paid 1d. per week to be members for those earning over 10/- per week, and a halfpenny for those earning less. The Institute was sited on land to the north side of Earle Street across the road from the Works. It was a two-storey building which had a dining room for 400 on the ground floor, and on the first floor there was a library of 5,000 books, a reading room and class rooms. On five nights a week classes were run in subjects such as book-keeping, shorthand, arithmetic and geometry. There were also classes for female members of the workers' families, in millinery, dressmaking, cooking and other activities. Scholarships were offered annually by Lancashire County Council and there was a company scheme founded by Sir Richard Moon, who was Chairman of the LNWR for many years.

The importance of Earlestown as the principal wagon works of the LNWR was recognised in 1895 when the Works was visited by the International Railway Congress on 28th June.

A remarkable achievement and highlight of Mr Emmett's long tenure as Superintendent was the building of a low-sided Diagram 2 open wagon with single-sided wood handbrake in 1 hr. 41 mins. on 8th March 1878.

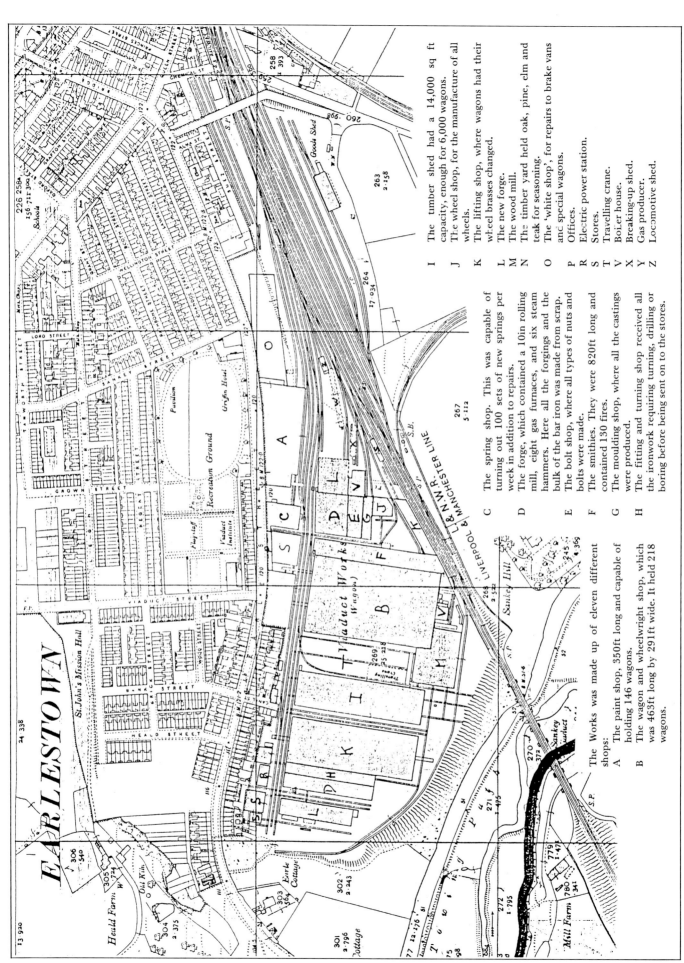

The Works was made up of eleven different shops:

A   The paint shop, 350ft long and capable of holding 146 wagons.

B   The wagon and wheelwright shop, which was 463ft long by 291ft wide. It held 218 wagons.

C   The spring shop. This was capable of turning out 100 sets of new springs per week in addition to repairs.

D   The forge, which contained a 10in rolling mill, eight gas furnaces, and six steam hammers. Here all the forgings and the bulk of the bar iron was made from scrap.

E   The bolt shop, where all types of nuts and bolts were made.

F   The smithies. They were 820ft long and contained 130 fires.

G   The moulding shop, where all the castings were produced.

H   The fitting and turning shop received all the ironwork requiring turning, drilling or boring before being sent on to the stores.

I   The timber shed had a 14,000 sq ft capacity, enough for 6,000 wagons.

J   The wheel shop, for the manufacture of all wheels.

K   The lifting shop, where wagons had their wheel brasses changed.

L   The new forge.

M   The wood mill.

N   The timber yard held oak, pine, elm and teak for seasoning.

O   The 'white shop', for repairs to brake vans and special wagons.

P   Offices.

R   Electric power station.

S   Stores.

T   Travelling crane.

V   Boiler house.

X   Breaking-up shed.

Y   Gas producer.

Z   Locomotive shed.

Map of Earlestown Works in LNWR days with the different shops indicated, after the 'White Shop' was built in 1913.

By the 1900s the works employed approximately 2,000 men plus 750 at various outlying repair shops and examining stations. It was reported to be able to produce 4,000 new wagons, perform 13,000 heavy repairs and produce 300 new horse-drawn vehicles per year.

The works was able to turn out eighteen finished wagons during a 9-hour day, a rate of one every half hour.

There were about 500 various machines employed in the works including 43 boring and drilling machines, 17 for making nuts and bolts, 63 lathes, 22 steam hammers, 52 wood-working machines and many others. The power for the machines was supplied by steam, hydraulic power and in later years by electricity. The electric power unit consisted of two Willan's Triple Expansion high-speed engines of 175 and 75 IHP which drove two Crewe dynamos. The plant was self-sufficient and manufactured everything it required.

Once built, a wagon would only return to Earlestown for major repairs. Minor repairs could be handled by the repair shops around the system. Nevertheless, the volume of work was such that Earlestown often received several trains of crippled wagons per week to be repaired.

Besides minor repair work, a most important duty performed by the 'outside staff' of 300 men was the examination and greasing of wagons in transit. These men were deployed singly or in groups at every important station or junction throughout the system. They had to satisfy themselves that every wagon starting from or stopping at their station was in proper running order. They tested the wheels and axles and examined the springs, buffers, drawgear, brakes and all working parts of the wagon. If a wagon was found to be defective, it was shunted out of the train and a label attached indicating that it was not to travel until the defect was remedied. They also checked that the axleboxes were well supplied with grease. The LNWR used nearly a thousand tons of grease per year.

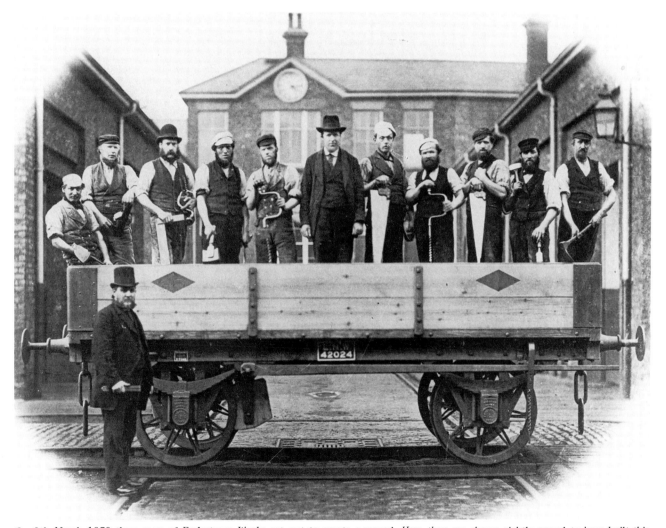

On 8th March 1878 these men of Earlestown Works set out to create a record. Here they are shown rightly proud to have built this Diagram 2 low-sided open wagon in just 1 hour 41 minutes. The men have recently been identified by Ian Fisher of Newton-le-Willows as: standing by the wagon, F. Harwood (Chief Foreman); in the wagon, G. Mottram, G. Profit, Crampton, L. Sydes, J. Hatton, J. Massey (Foreman), Wills, M. Watkins, Jones, D. Owen, C. James.   LNWR SOCIETY (9576)

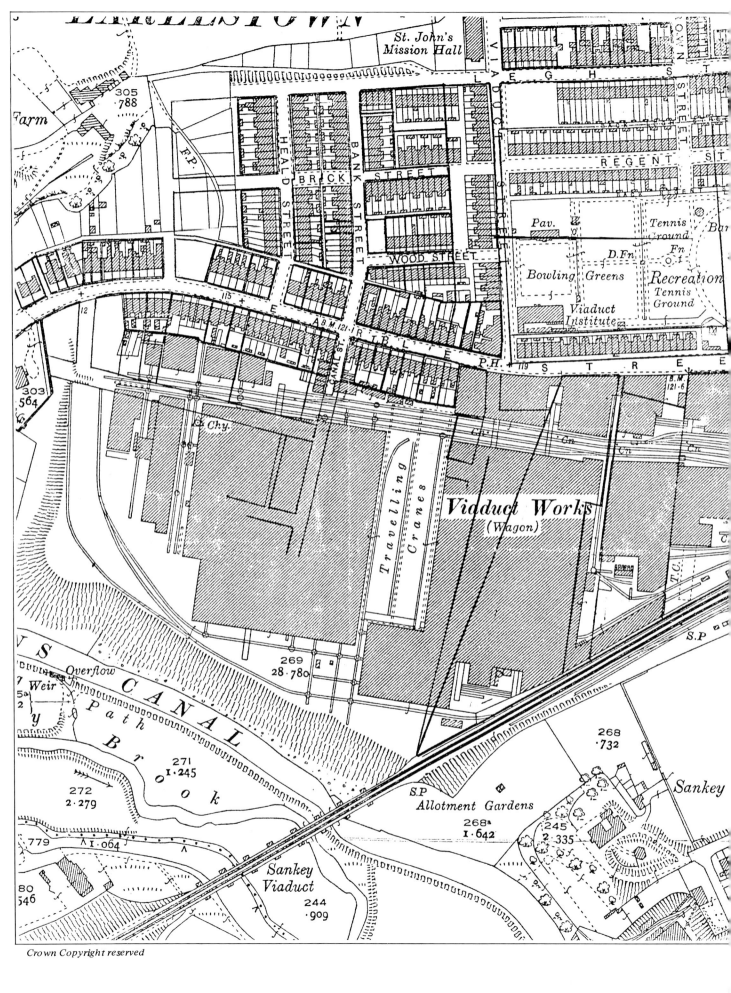

St. John's
Mission Hall

Farm

305
·788

F.P.

HEALD STREET

BRICK STREET

BANK STREET

WOOD STREET

VIADUCT

OWN ST

LEIGH ST

REGENT STREET

REGENT ST

Pav.

Tennis
Ground

D.Fn

Bowling Greens

Recreation

Fn

Viaduct
Institute

Tennis
Ground

303
·564

12

115

B.M.121.1

CANAL ST

TRIBLE

P.H.

119

STREET

B.M.
121·6

Chy.

Ch

Cn

Cn

Cn

Cn

Travelling Cranes

Viaduct Works
(Wagon)

S.P

T.C.

Overflow

Weir

269
28·780

CANAL

Path

Brook

268
·732

271
1·245

Sankey

272
2·279

S.P
Allotment Gardens

779
1·064

268a
1·642

245
2·335

80
·546

Sankey
Viaduct

244
·909

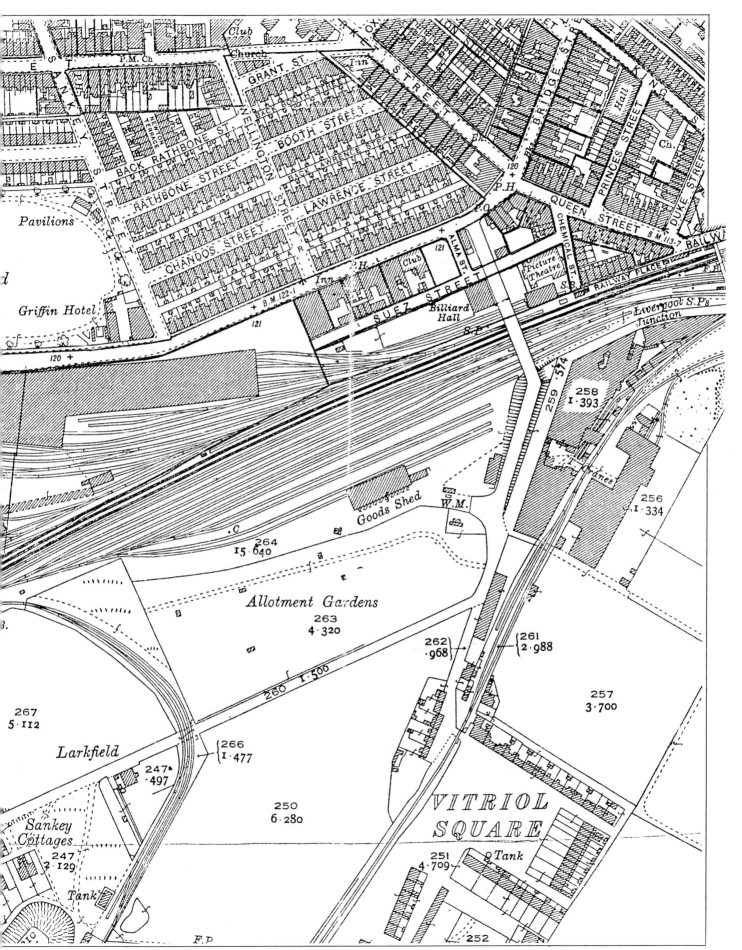

Map of Earlestown Works in LNWR days.

J.W. Emmett retired in 1903 after running Earlestown for 36 years and his place was taken by H.D. Earl. Henry Douglas Earl began his career as an apprentice at Crewe in March 1869 and later served in the drawing office from June 1874. In June 1875 he was appointed Assistant Works Manager under T.W. Worsdell and was responsible for the steel works and also for new works building construction. In 1888 he succeeded C. Dick as Locomotive Works Manager. In July 1903 he was appointed to Earlestown. In May 1910 he left Earlestown to become Carriage Superintendent at Wolverton, from where he retired in May 1916. His place at Earlestown was taken by A.R. Trevithick.

Arthur Reginald Trevithick was born at Crewe, the son of Francis Trevithick. He became a Crewe premium apprentice in 1877 and, on completion of his time, he went into the running side, becoming foreman at Preston in 1880 and District Locomotive Superintendent at Carlisle in 1889. In 1899 he returned to Crewe as Assistant Works Manager under Earl and succeeded him in 1903. He followed Earl to Earlestown in 1910 and later to Wolverton.

During the period of management by Earl and Trevithick, there were no dramatic changes, just a slow process of absorbing the best of current technology, including a gradual changeover to electricity as the main power source. In

Staff in the Stores at Earlestown. Apart from the canteen, this must have been one of the few departments largely staffed by women.

A group of Works staff arranged proudly in front of a D26 Special Cattle wagon. The width of some of the caps indicates the fashion of the Twenties, although sartorial elegance may not have been top of the workers' minds. Notice how the track in the foreground was paved with wagon solebars, presumably in a 'well-used' condition. The staff were: Jim Bowen looking through the window; Tim Forber immediately to his right. L. Mullins stood fourth from left in the fourth row back. Seated in second row back at extreme right was William Carman.
CTY. IAN FISHER

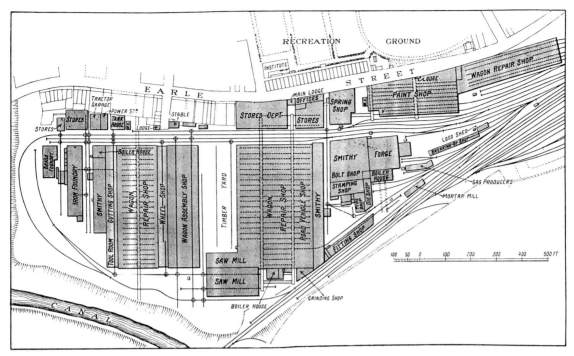

General Layout of Shop.

about 1890 the old Griffin Hotel had been demolished (formerly Mr. Jones's house) and the new Griffin built in 1891. This made way for further development at the extreme eastern end of the Works, where a new wagon shop was added in 1913/14. It was built in reinforced concrete, a break with tradition, for the remainder of the works was built in a dull red brick. The concrete gave it a grey/white appearance and so it quickly became known as the 'White Shop'. It housed two 6-ton and two 20-ton overhead travelling cranes which enabled the repair of bogie wagons, brake vans and special wagons to be concentrated in this building. In 1913 other extensions were made both to the Machine and Fitting Shop and the Brass Foundry.

Facilities at the Viaduct Institute had also been increased in this period, with the addition of three bowling greens, a first-class cricket pitch, three tennis courts and an athletic track. A number of small buildings and pavilions were included to provide amenities. The pensioners' section was furnished with an excellent pavilion built in 1923, named 'Warneford Hall' after the then Works Superintendent.

In 1916 Trevithick moved to Wolverton and W.W.H. Warneford took his place.

Walter Wyndham Hayden Warneford was born in Wiltshire in 1866 the son of the Canon of Salisbury Cathedral. He became an apprentice at the Miles Platting Works of the L&Y in 1882 but transferred to Crewe in 1883. In March 1889 he became an assistant at the steel plant, and rose to Works Manager in 1910. He moved to Earlestown in April 1916 and retired in 1924, two years after the LNWR had become part of the LMS.

At the Grouping in 1923 the LNWR became part of the London Midland and Scottish Railway. But the LMS had inherited a number of wagon works, and rationalisation quickly followed, Earlestown being grouped with Newton Heath Works (L&Y) under Mr. (later Sir) Ernest Lemon as Superintendent. He introduced new methods of construction, and standard wood-framed open goods wagons were produced by mass-production. In 1931 Mr. Anthony became the works Superintendent. He continued to improve the repair of wagons on progressive lines and re-organised the Works to accommodate wagon, lorry and road motor body repair transferred from Newton Heath which took the place of new work lost at Earlestown. The concentration of certain processes at each works continued in the 'thirties. The Iron and Brass Foundries, wheel-making and the stamping and rolling mill were closed and new wagon production finally ceased, Earlestown becoming a heavy repair works for wagons. Its only production were door-to-door containers, 3-link couplings and wagon laminated springs for the whole of the LMS.

In October 1943 hand-forging of 3-link wagon couplings was replaced by an electric flash-butt welding process. Mr. A.E. Bates replaced Mr. Anthony on his retirement in 1946 and made changes to shop layouts, thereby reducing the large number of wagons which were standing idle awaiting repair, and improving facilities for handling steel-frame and all-steel wagons. The number of wagons awaiting repair had swelled dramatically during World War II.

The works passed into nationalisation already on the decline. A firelighter factory was started using its waste tim-

Continued on page 36

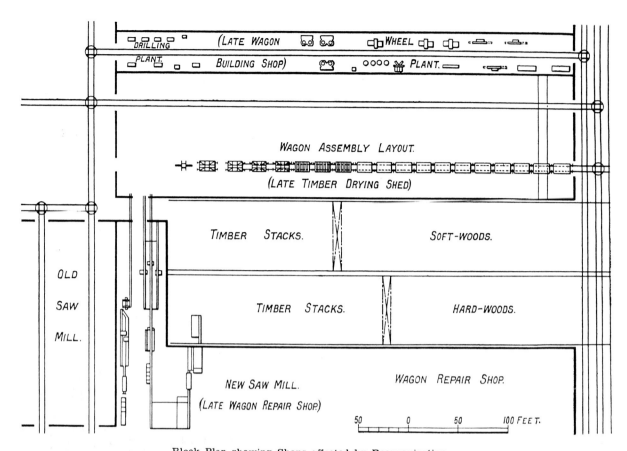

Block Plan showing Shops affected by Reorganisation.

EARLESTOWN WORKS, CARRIAGE AND WAGON DEPARTMENT, L.M.S.R.

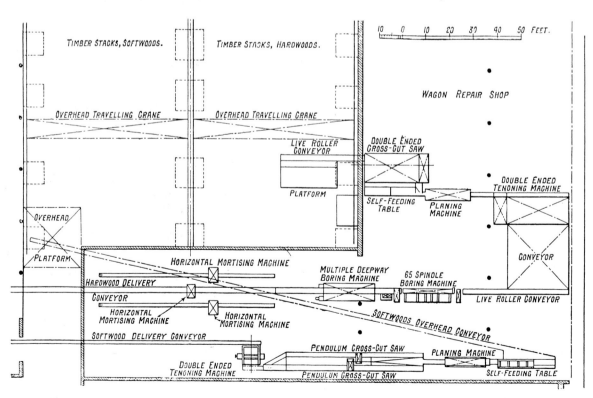

Layout of Sawmill.

General View of Sawmill.

This series of photographs was taken in the Works in the mid-twenties. While this is strictly outside our period, they show interesting aspects in the early LMS days.

This photograph shows the extension to the sawmill, with the final part of the layout of the hardwood section. The wood had been taken from the timber store and had already been cut, planed and tenons made before arriving on the live-roller conveyor, travelling from left to right in front of the wagons. This would deliver it to the 65-spindle multiple boring machine which bored all the holes on the flat in a wagon solebar in one operation. In turn the hardwood was then fed to the multiple deepway boring machine which is in the centre of the photo. It was held in pneumatic cramps and the holes were bored horizontally, first from one side for half the depth, and then from the other so that the holes ran true. It then passed to the mortising machines. The photo also shows the first part of the softwood sawmill. From the top of the right-hand corner of the photo the overhead gravity roller conveyor brought wood from the wood yard direct to the 6-cutter planing machine and then to the pendulum cross-cut saws, which can be seen underneath the conveyor.

NATIONAL RAILWAY MUSEUM (HOR 4174)

From the deepway boring machine the production line split into three, each feeding a horizontal mortising machine with stop bars and pneumatic cramps. In the softwood line on the right we can see the double-ended tenoning machine. The prepared hardwood and softwood parts were then delivered direct to the assembly line.

NATIONAL RAILWAY MUSEUM (HOR 4175)

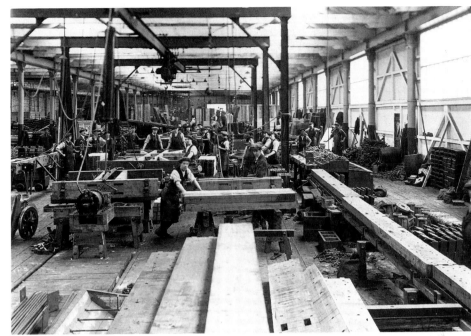

This is the first photo in a set of five showing the assembly line building a 12-ton standard mineral wagon. It shows the assembly of middle bearers and centre longitudinals using pneumatic cramps.
NATIONAL RAILWAY MUSEUM (HOR F3968)

This second shot shows the general assembly of the underframe including fitting the buffers.
NATIONAL RAILWAY MUSEUM (HOR F3976)

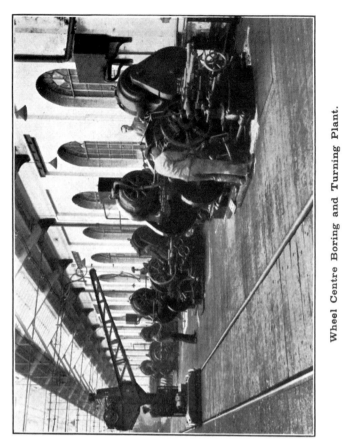

Tyre Boring Plant.

Wheel Centre Boring and Turning Plant.

General View of Wheel Plant.

Tyre Expanding and Fixing Plant.

This view shows the wheels, springs and brake gear being fitted. From this point on, the wagon moved throughout the remainder of the operations on its own wheels. This photo shows the buffer stocks and coupling reinforcement plate extending above the headstock to inhibit body end-movement, as introduced by the RCH 1923 standard. NATIONAL RAILWAY MUSEUM (HOR F3978)

OPERATIONS ON WAGON ASSEMBLY.

Nº 1	Nº 2	Nº 3	Nº 4	Nº 5	Nº 6	Nº 7	Nº 8
ASSEMBLY OF MIDDLE BEARERS AND CENTRE LONGITUDINALS.	GENERAL ASSEMBLY OF UNDERFRAME.	WHEELS, SPRINGS AND BRAKEWORK FIXED.	DRAWGEAR AND BOTTOM DOOR IRONWORK FIXED.	BODY KNEES, DIAGONAL BRACES AND CURB RAILS FIXED.	FLOOR LAID, BOTTOM DOOR AND FAST END FIXED.	QUARTER PLANKS, THROUGH PLANKS AND SIDE DOORS FIXED.	END DOOR FIXED. GENERAL TIGHTENING UP.

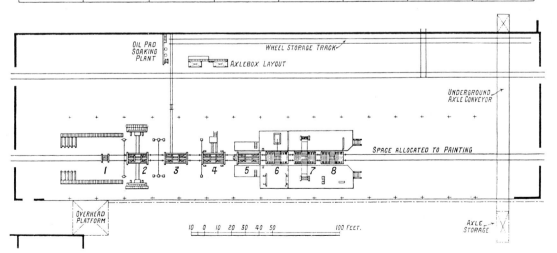

Wagon Assembly Layout, Axle Conveyor, Axlebox Layout, Storage Track and Oil Pad Soaking Plant.

Wheel Assembly.

Axlebox Plant.

Axle Plant.

Axle Conveyor Feeding Wheel Shop.

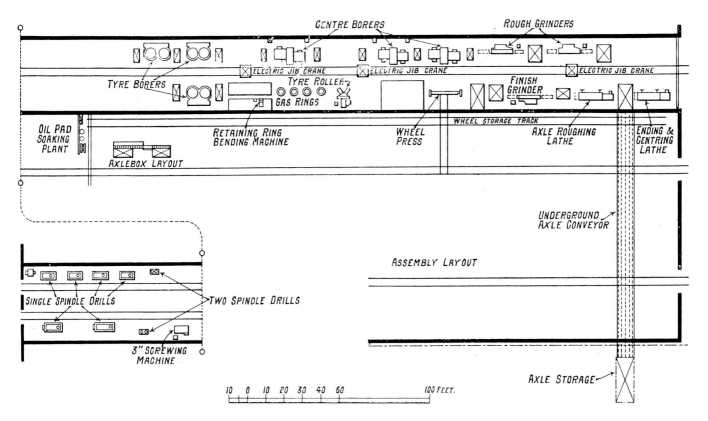

Wheel Plant and Drilling Plant.

A 17in 'Coal engine' passing the Works on a goods train. This view shows crippled wagons on the left awaiting attention in the Works.
HMRS (AAF 932)

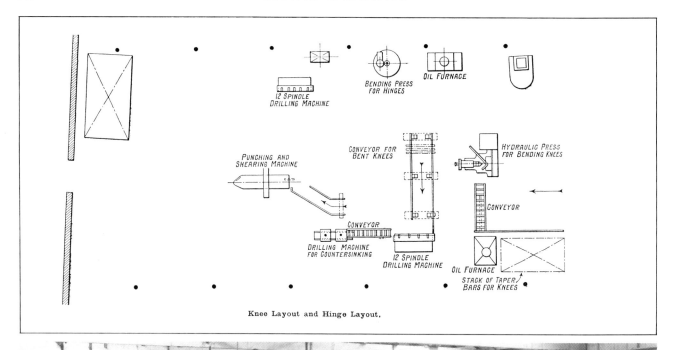

Knee Layout and Hinge Layout.

This view shows the wagons having the drawgear, body knees, diagonal bracing and curb rails fitted. Further down the line, the floor was being laid and the fixed end assembled. The table in the right foreground appears to have been made up of old body-side planks, judging from the '10 TON' lettering still showing. The buffer stocks on the wagon behind were not to RCH standard.

NATIONAL RAILWAY MUSEUM (HOR F3977)

This photo shows the final two stages of fitting the quarter planks, top through planks, side doors and the end doors. The end door was being built up on a jig in the left foreground. The wagon was then complete and moved forward for painting. These 7-plank wagons were again to the RCH standard.
NATIONAL RAILWAY MUSEUM (HOR F3969)

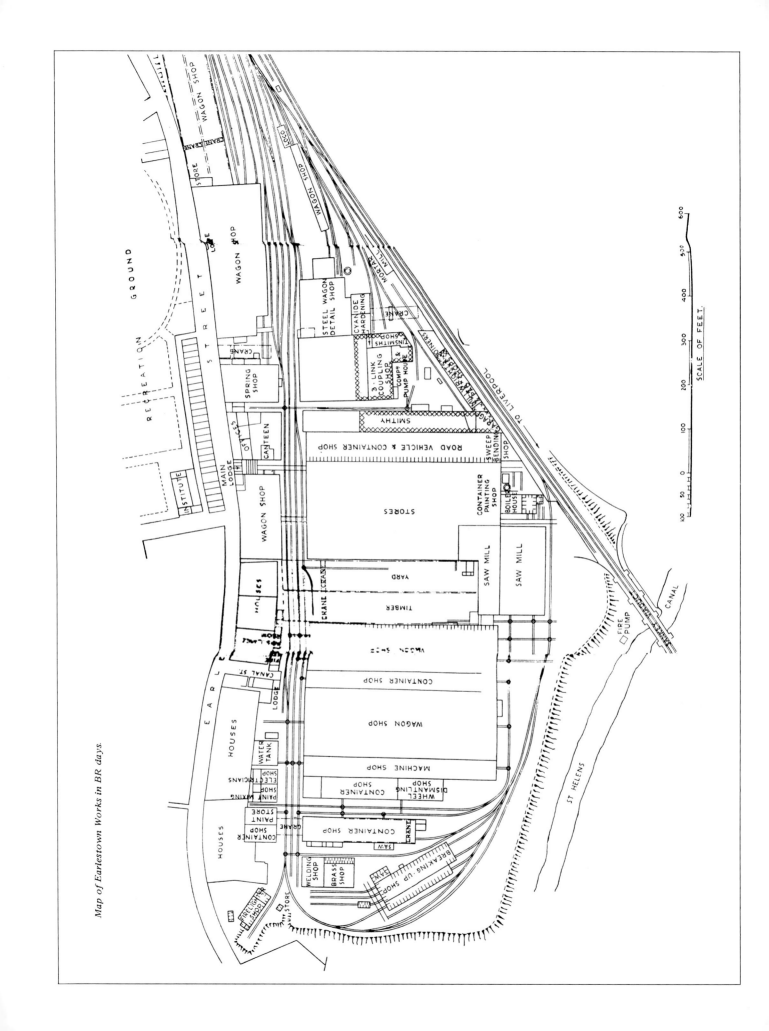

Map of Earlestown Works in BR days.

ber, but with the demise of steam this venture closed. By 1952 workforce levels had reduced to 1,900, of which 1,700 were employed in the workshops. For a brief time it became the repair shop of the three-wheeled Scammell Mechanical Horse, but this also had a short life. The production of containers continued into BR days but the controversial 'Beeching Report' dramatically changed the way freight was carried by rail. The requirement for wagons was drastically reduced and, with its primary *raison d'être* gone, Earlestown Wagon Works closed in 1964. The buildings were revamped and converted into small industrial units and in September 1969 opened as the 'Deacon Industrial Estate'. Rather sadly, that ended a distinguished railway presence of nearly 120 years.

Two views of a Newcastle–Liverpool train heading west past Earlestown Wagon Works in 1959, hauled by 'Patriot' class 4–6–0 locomotive No. 45535 Sir Herbert Walker KCB. *The lower view usefully shows the yard, with the paint shop to the right and the boiler-house chimney prominent on the skyline.*

CTY. E. BELLASS

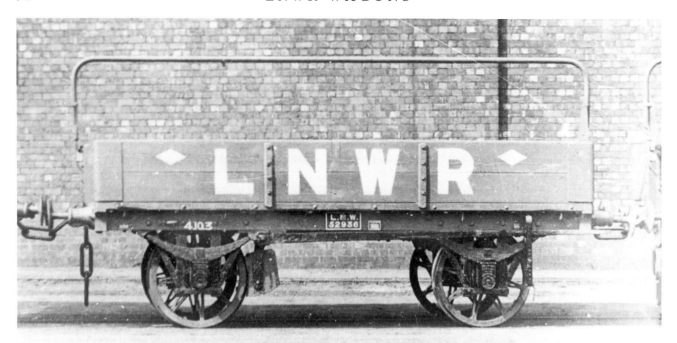

This Diagram 2 wagon, No. 52936, illustrates typical LNWR wagon features. It shows open-spoke wheels running in grease axleboxes, with the earlier type of spring shoe which did not reach up onto the front face of the solebars. The wood-block brake featured here was fitted one side only – a serious risk to shunters and yard staff. The buffers were 10in 3-bolt and the headstock ends are shown cut away more than halfway to the solebars. The Williams automatic sheet support fitted to this vehicle was rare.

A detail view of a 10-ton grease axlebox bearing the legend 'L & NWR Co VIADUCT WORKS EARLESTOWN' together with the journal size code, in this case No. 2, the year of manufacture, 1908, and a great deal of caked dirt.   HMRS (AAG 500)

CHAPTER TWO

CONSTRUCTION & MECHANICAL DETAIL

IN 1859 the LNWR introduced a standard design of merchandise wagon measuring 15ft 0in long by 7ft 1in wide inside on a 9ft 0in wheelbase. This was rather far-sighted since many railway companies were still building smaller wagons than this at the turn of the century. The Lancashire & Yorkshire Railway also pioneered large wagons, as might be expected from a company which was very closely associated with the LNWR.

THE EMMETT PERIOD
1867-1903

When J.W. Emmett took over as Wagon Superintendent at Earlestown, he continued to build wagons to the same dimensions, although his successor at Miles Platting, W. Attock, increased the size of LYR wagons somewhat. Otherwise the wagon-building practice of both remained very similar for many years to come. The detailed study of Emmett's standard merchandise wagon which follows will provide a useful insight into LNWR wagon-building practice.

UNDERFRAME

Constructed from English oak, the solebars were 10½in by 4½in and the headstocks 11in by 4½ in. Behind the headstocks, diagonals 10½in by 4½in ran from each buffer to the transoms, of the same size, which were placed 4ft 6in apart, between the solebars. The dragbox or cradle was made of wood with iron strengthening. A central striking beam, 6½in by 3¼in, ran across between the two longitudinals which were placed 1ft 10in apart. Each of these longitudinals was made up of a 3¼in by 3¼in timber above the striking beam and a 6in by 3¼in timber beneath it. Two spacers, 3¼in by 3¼in, filled in between these two timbers, leaving slots on either side of the striking beam to accommodate the drawsprings.

The whole assembly of longitudinals, spacers and striking beam was fastened by three ⅝in dia. countersunk carriage bolts with square nuts underneath. The lower longitudinals could thus be removed separately whenever the drawgear required attention. The transoms had extensions 2¼in deep by 4½in wide attached underneath them to increase their depth at the centre to match that of the longitudinals.

Instead of fitting a lateral iron tie rod beside each of the transoms, as was the usual practice, the LNWR provided an eye-bolt which ran from one solebar to the other and was fastened to the underside of each transom, thereby forming a truss rod. It was secured to the outside of the solebars by square nuts bearing upon large square washers tapered to match the angle of descent of the bolts. These eye-bolts were a distinctive feature of all LNWR wagons and are easily spotted on photographs.

BUFFING AND DRAWGEAR

The buffer shoes, also referred to as 'sockets' or 'stocks', were 10in long iron castings each of which was fastened by three bolts. The two inner bolts were secured to the U-shaped wrought-iron knee which held the solebar to the diagonal while the outer one was an eye-bolt which fitted into a recess in the outside of the solebar. It was therefore flush with the solebar and indistinguishable from it when the wagon had been painted. Only the nuts can usually be discerned on photographs.

The drawbar was not continuous, the pull being transmitted through the underframe. Each drawbar lay in a guide, at the end of which it was attached to the drawspring buckle by means of a cotter. The drawspring, consisting of seventeen 3in by ⅜in steel plates, rested on a felt pad upon each of the lower longitudinals and, at its extremities, was cottered onto the buffer shanks. Buffing shocks were transmitted through a striking plate, 9in by 3in by ⅜in, onto the striking beam between the two drawsprings. These springs were held in vertical alignment by two 2in by ¼in plates fastened to the top of the striking beam on either side of the spring buckles.

Buffer shanks were 1½in square from the spring to the headstock and 2¼in in diameter through the shoes to the buffer head, which was 12in in diameter and projected 18in beyond the end of the wagon. Headstock and transom were braced together by ⅞in diameter iron tie rods on either side of the drawbar. Similarly, the dragbox was held together by two ⅞in diameter iron tie rods placed diagonally above and below the drawsprings on opposite sides of the drawbars. Standard 3-link couplings, with a gedge on the inner link to facilitate removal from the drawhook, superseded the previous 5-link couplings in about 1875.

RUNNING GEAR

Wheels were fabricated from cast-iron (later cast-steel) centres into holes in which were fitted eight lengths of wrought-iron flat bar, 3in by ⅜in, bent to form, in turn, the right-hand side of one spoke, one eighth, or an octant, of the rim and finally the left-hand side of the adjacent spoke. The whole wheel was drawn together by shrinking on the Bessemer steel tyre in exactly the same manner as a wooden cartwheel was made.

Tyres on all but a few special wagons were 2¼in thick and 3ft 1½in diameter when new. Four 1in securing bolts passed through the rim into the tyre. When the ends of these bolts

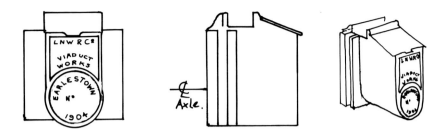

Fig. 1. Grease type. 7-ton and 10-ton versions were similar except for width and numbering.

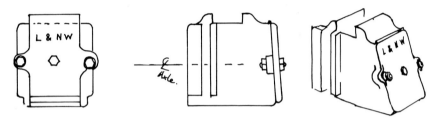

Fig. 2. Flat-fronted — the first oil box.

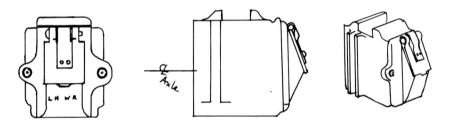

Fig. 3. 'Pointed front' or 'carriage' type.

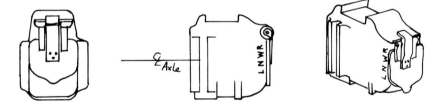

Fig. 4. Bulbous. Note 'LNWR' cast into side.

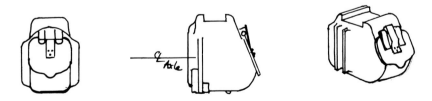

Fig. 5. Bulbous with sloping front. Unusual.

Not to same scale.

became exposed through wear, the tyre was well beyond scrapping limits.

Axles were made of Bessemer steel. In the standard 7-ton wagon they were 4½in diameter over the wheel seats, tapering to 4in at the centre. Journals were 6in long by 3in in diameter. Grease lubricated brass bearings fitted into cast-iron axleboxes, the front of which bore the legend 'L&NWR C° VIADUCT WORKS EARLESTOWN' together with the journal size code and the year of manufacture (see photo, page 36). The 'W' irons were made from wrought-iron ¾in thick. The outer wing continued in a straight line behind the solebar whilst the inner one was angled upright to clear the transoms. In photographs the arrangement of bolts on the solebar indicates this unequal winged 'W' iron. Most other railways angled both wings but the LNWR retained the unequal 'W' iron as standard until the introduction of 18ft 0in long wagons in the twentieth century.

The brake consisted of a simple block of poplar wood in which holes were drilled and filled with a mixture of sand and resin to improve friction (poplar is resistant to burning). The block was fastened to a wrought-iron hanger, 3¼in by 1¼in at the top end, tapering to 2⅞in by ⅞in at the bottom. The brake spindle was 3in in diameter by 8in long and worked in a trunnion bearing made integral with one of the spring shoes. A tapered square section protruded 4in from the end of the spindle upon which the brake hanger and brake lever were force-fitted and cottered.

'Pointed front' or 'carriage' type axlebox (Fig. 3).

'Flat-fronted' axlebox (Fig. 2).

LMS Listing of ex-LNWR Wagon Axleboxes

Type of box	Type of Pad & Drwg. No.	Type & size of Bearing	Size of Journal	Type of Liner	Type of dust Shield	No. of Drawing
No. 2 Grease	nil	No. 2	8in x 3¾in	nil	nil	251
Slate truck (grease)	nil	white metal bush	4in x 2in	nil	nil	no drawing
No. 4, 3in or 4in springs	waste	8in x 3¾in	8in x 3¾in	8in x 3¾in	wood	394
No. 5	waste	8in x 3¾in	8in x 4in	8in x 4in	wood	308
No. 8, 3in or 4in springs	waste	9in x 4in	9in x 4in	9in x 4in	wood	499
No. 9	waste	9in x 4in	9in x 4in	9in x 4in	wood	259
No. 10	AAW149 Drg.E1684A	9in x 4½in	9in x 4½in	9in x 4½in	wood	487
No. 11	10in x 5in Drg.E1707A	10in x 5in	10in x 5in	10in x 5in		329
No. 12	10in x 5in Drg.E1707A	10in x 5in	10in x 5in	10in x 5in	wood	448
No. 14	L&Y B6 modified	11in x 6in	11in x 6in inside	11in x 6in	wood split type	242
No. 15	waste	11in x 6in	11in x 6in	11in x 6in	wood	455A
No. 16	waste	9in x 4in	9in x 4in	nil	wood	926
No. 18	Drg.15/1225F	9in x 4in	9in x 4in	nil	wood	956
No. 20	Drg.15/1225F	9in x 4in	9in x 4in	nil	wood	1119
No. 21	L&Y B6 modified	11in x 5½in	11in x 5½in inside	11in x 5½in	wood split type	439

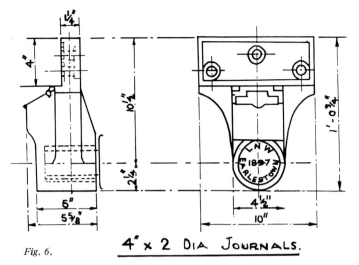

Fig. 6.

4" x 2 DIA JOURNALS.

FESTINIOG SLATE TRUCKS (GREASE)

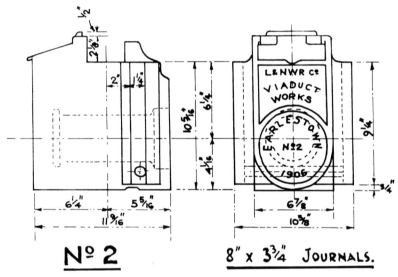

Nº 2

8" x 3¾" JOURNALS.

Fig. 7.   10 TON WAGONS (GREASE)

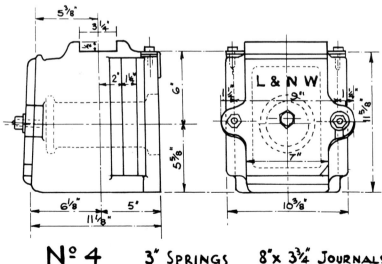

Nº 4   3" SPRINGS   8" x 3¾" JOURNALS.

Fig. 8.   10 TON WAGONS (OIL)

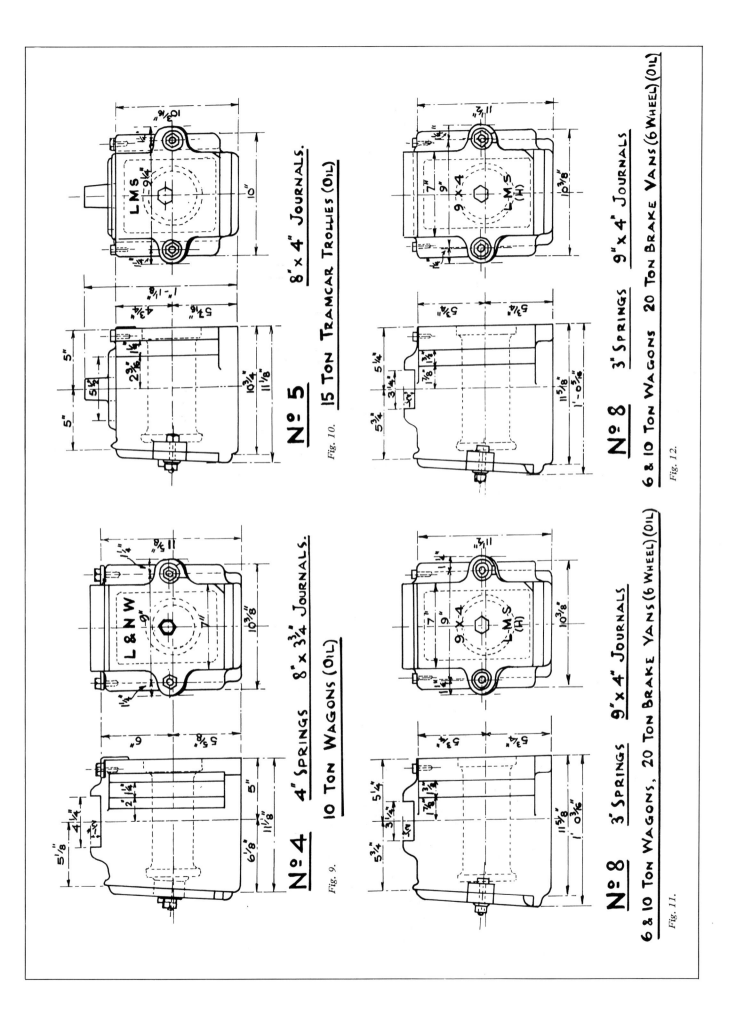

8" × 4" JOURNALS.

N⁰ 5   15 TON TRAMCAR TROLLIES (OIL)

Fig. 10.

8" × 3¾" JOURNALS.

N⁰ 4   4" SPRINGS   10 TON WAGONS (OIL)

Fig. 9.

9" × 4" JOURNALS

N⁰ 8   3" SPRINGS   20 TON BRAKE VANS (6 WHEEL) (OIL)
6 & 10 TON WAGONS

Fig. 12.

9" × 4" JOURNALS

N⁰ 8   3" SPRINGS   20 TON BRAKE VANS (6 WHEEL) (OIL)
6 & 10 TON WAGONS,

Fig. 11.

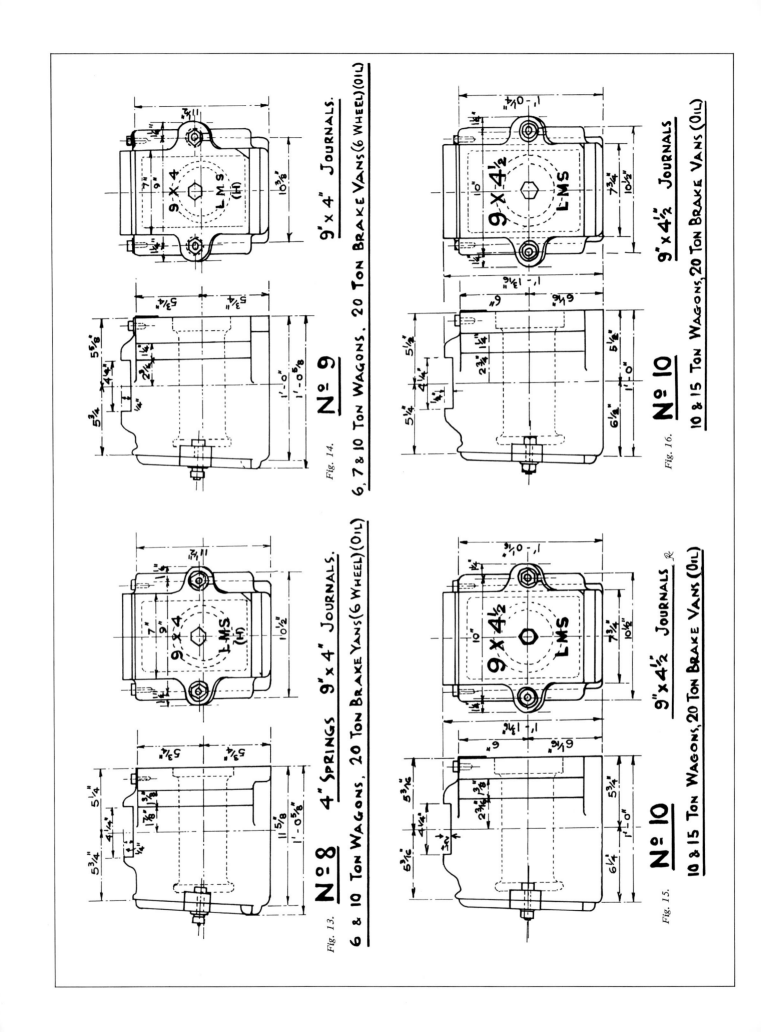

9" x 4" Journals.

Fig. 14. Nº 9

6, 7 & 10 Ton Wagons. 20 Ton Brake Vans (6 Wheel) (Oil)

9" x 4½" Journals

Fig. 16. Nº 10

10 & 15 Ton Wagons, 20 Ton Brake Vans (Oil)

4" Springs 9" x 4" Journals.

Fig. 13. Nº 8

6 & 10 Ton Wagons, 20 Ton Brake Vans (6 Wheel) (Oil)

9" x 4½" Journals

Fig. 15. Nº 10

10 & 15 Ton Wagons, 20 Ton Brake Vans (Oil)

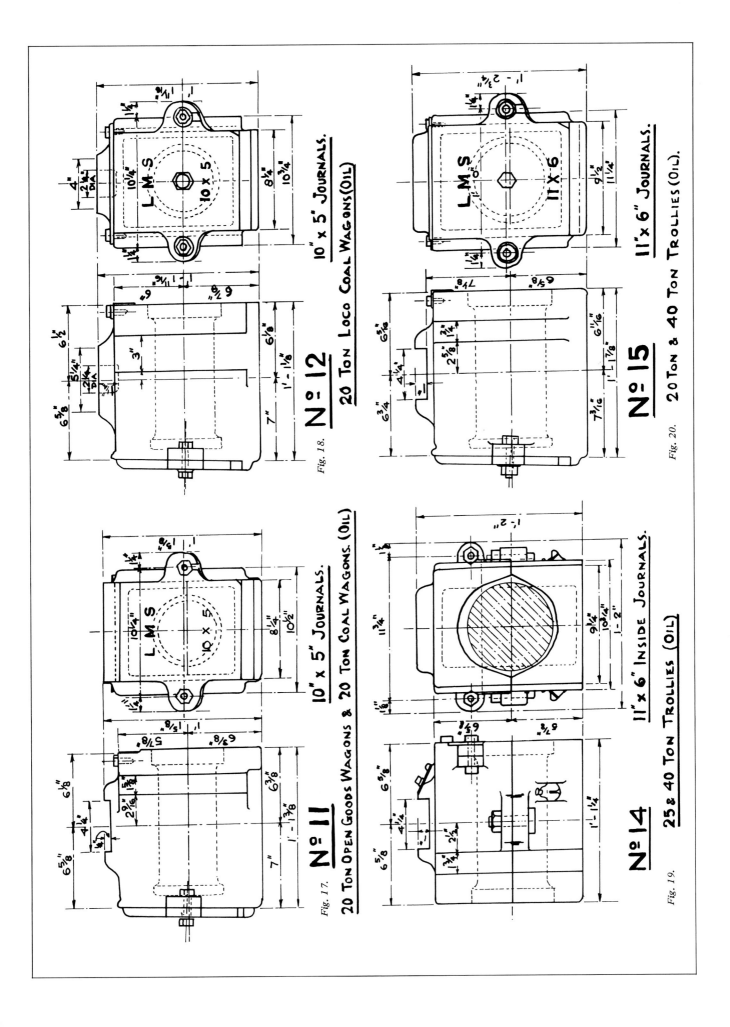

Fig. 18.

No. 12

20 Ton Loco Coal Wagons (Oil)
10" x 5" Journals.

Fig. 20.

No. 15

20 Ton & 40 Ton Trollies (Oil).
11" x 6" Journals.

Fig. 17.

No. 11

20 Ton Open Goods Wagons & 20 Ton Coal Wagons (Oil)
10" x 5" Journals.

Fig. 19.

No. 14

25 & 40 Ton Trollies (Oil)
11" x 6" Inside Journals.

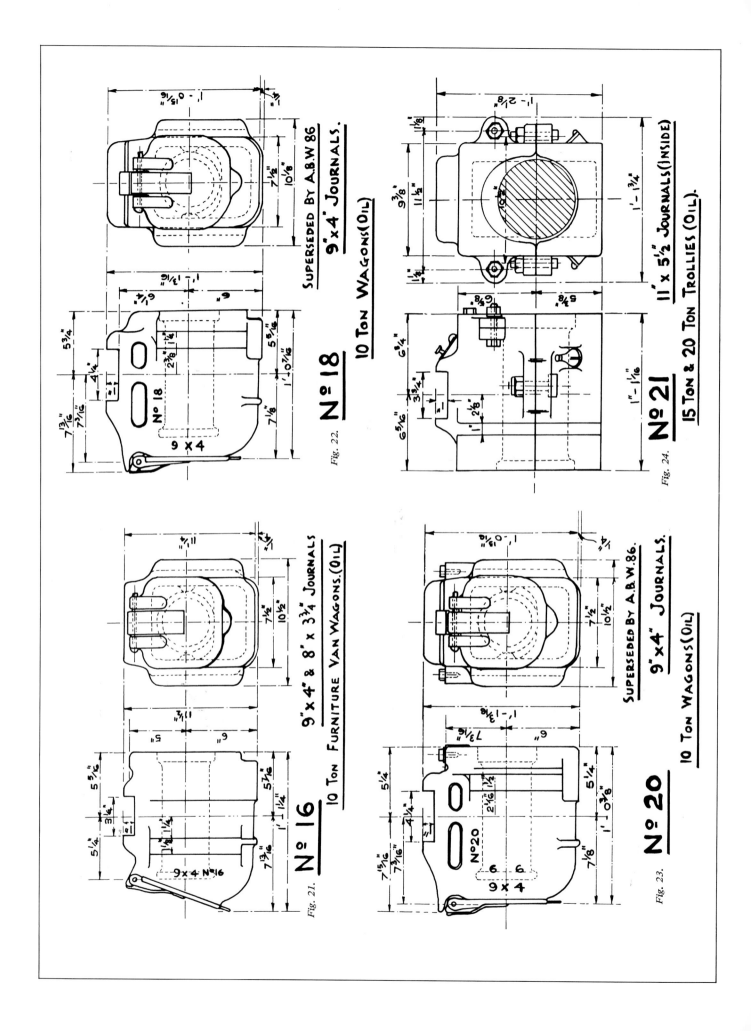

SUPERSEDED BY A.B.W 86.

9" x 4" JOURNALS.

10 TON WAGONS (OIL)

Nº 18

9 X 4

Fig. 22.

11" x 5½" JOURNALS (INSIDE).

15 TON & 20 TON TROLLIES (OIL).

Nº 21

Fig. 24.

9" x 4" & 8" x 3¾" JOURNALS

10 TON FURNITURE VAN WAGONS. (OIL)

Nº 16

9 X 4 Nº 16

Fig. 21.

SUPERSEDED BY A.B.W. 86.

9" x 4" JOURNALS.

10 TON WAGONS (OIL)

Nº 20

Nº 20

9 X 4

Fig. 23.

The wrought-iron brake lever was 3¼in wide and 1¼in thick at the trunnion end, and the handle protruded beyond the headstock to give the maximum leverage. To clear the lever, the headstock was cut away, all four headstock ends being dealt with in the same way. This is another distinctive feature of all standard LNWR wagons. In the running position, the lever rested on a small bracket bolted to the solebar. The pin rack was mounted separately to the right of this bracket.

BODYWORK

The end stanchions of this one-plank wagon were of oak, 4in by 3½in, and spaced 2ft 0in apart. Each was secured to the headstock by two ⅝in carriage bolts, through a wrought-iron strap, 2in by ⅜in, which extended upwards to include the bottom half of the end plank. Teak or pine, 10½in by 3in, was used for the end plank.

The curb rail, also of oak, 3½in wide by 3in deep, was attached through spacer blocks 6in long, 3in deep and 2¼in wide, to the solebar by eight ⅝in carriage bolts, those at either end also securing the frame knee to the solebar.

Two wrought-iron body knees supported each side plank which was fastened with ½in countersunk bolts. Side planking was teak or pine 3in thick like the end plank but 11in deep to allow for the half inch difference between the depth of the headstock and solebars. The lower edge of each plank was rebated in a similar manner to that used today on tongued and grooved 'matchboarding'. Most of the other railways abandoned this practice during the 1870s, preferring to use a simple bevel on the upper edge of their wagon planks, but Earlestown retained the original arrangement almost until LMS days. The LNWR later adopted 9in wide planks for open wagons where other companies preferred to make theirs 7in wide. Note that these plank widths are all nominal, the actual planed size being ⅛in less.

Corner plates were 9in wide and ¼in thick. The planks were fastened to them with ⅜in rivets. The inside edge of the planks tapered to 2½in wide at the top and were capped with 'D' section iron 2½in by ⅝in secured by ⅝in countersunk carriage bolts, eight in each side, which passed through the plank and curb rail, and four in each end which passed through both plank and headstock.

Floor boards were of 2½in thick teak or pine. Twenty-four of these were of 7in nominal width, that is 6⅞in when planed; the two end planks, 7½in wide, had a rebate, 1½in wide by ½in deep, cut in them to accommodate the raised headstock.

This method of construction applied to all the 7-ton wagons built during the Emmett period. Small modifications were made over the years. The larger 10-ton wagons were built in the same way, dimensions being increased where necessary. On some diagrams, iron flitch plates were fitted to the face of the outside of solebars to increase strength and load-carrying capacity, and to locate fixings more rigidly (see the two photographs of Diagram 12 timber wagons on page 147 where the flitch plate is seen particularly clearly).

After some experimental wagons of larger capacity had been built by Emmett, H. D. Earl revised the wagon design to carry greater payloads. A standard 10-ton wagon was produced 18ft 0in long and 7ft 10in wide on a 9ft 9in wheelbase. The increase in length to 18ft was a significant step forward, yet Earl kept the wheelbase to 9ft 9in. It is believed that this was done to avoid replacing the large numbers of 10ft diameter wagon turntables that would otherwise have been required. RCH standard double shoe brakes with 'V' hangers were adopted as well as oil lubrication in the axleboxes. The separate brake lever bracket or 'rest' was abolished and the 'rest' incorporated in the pin rack. Buffer shoes were secured with 4 bolts, and corner plates carried ½in countersunk bolts with square nuts outside instead of ⅜in rivets. Otherwise, construction was very similar to the Emmett wagons.

RUNNING GEAR

BRAKE GEAR

The following is a summary of the types of brake fitted to non vacuum and Westinghouse braked vehicles. Details of brakes on fitted wagons accompany the description of those vehicles. The 'Key:' is a code used in the 'known examples of Diagram' to indicate which type of brake or buffing gear was used on particular examples.

Direct Wooden Brake *Key: Wood 1S Fig. 25*

The earliest type of brake in use on LNWR wagons. Examples survived in traffic use until the 1900s and in internal use until the 1930s. Since it was intended primarily as a stabling brake, only one wooden block per wagon sufficed. The whole range of 7-ton merchandise and livestock wagons, both open and covered, was fitted with this brake until the mid-1880s.

Wooden Pushrod Brake *Key: Wood Pushrod 1S Fig. 29*

This design was originally fitted to heavier wagons, for example trolleys and gunpowder vans, where more leverage was required for an adequate brake application. It was also used in those wagons which were piped for running in passenger trains, such as prize cattle wagons and horse-boxes. A worn block could be taken up by adjustment of the turnbuckle on the push rod.

Direct Iron Brake *Key: Direct 1S or BS Fig. 26*

Originally fitted to Traffic Coal wagons whose payload was 8-tons, this brake, with its iron block, was intended to be pinned down when descending steep inclines. Adjustment was provided by a set bolt at the bottom of the hanger.

LNW Company Drawings of Brake Gear

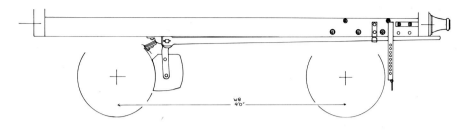

Fig. 25. Year 1870.
WOOD BLOCK & FLAP BRAKE
Used on Open, Covered, Cattle, Hopper, Rail, Meat, Furniture, Ballast, P'Way Stores wagons, etc.
Ratio: 8.4 to 1.
Single brake, 9ft wheelbase, straight lever.

Fig. 26. Year 1883.
IRON BLOCK FLAP BRAKE (no links)
Traffic Coal, West Cumberland Coke Wagons & Refrigerated Vans.
Ratio: 8 to 1.
Single brake, straight lever.

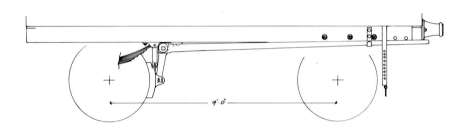

Fig. 27. Year 1897.
IRON BLOCK, FLAP & LINKS BRAKE
Covered Goods Vans, Hopper & Timber Wagons.
Ratio: 8.2 to 1.
Single brake, 9ft wheelbase, straight lever.

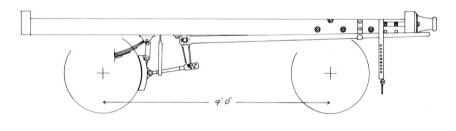

Fig. 28. Year 1895.
IRON BLOCK, FLAP & PUSH ROD BRAKE
Open Goods, Timber, Cattle & Rail Wagons, and Beer Vans.
Ratio: 9.5 to 1.
Single brake, 9ft wheelbase, straight lever.

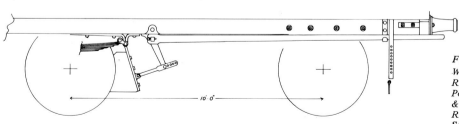

Fig. 29. Year 1875.
WOOD BLOCK & PUSH ROD BRAKE
Powder, West Coast Meat & improved Cattle Wagons.
Ratio: 10 to 1.
Single brake, 10ft wheelbase, straight lever.

Continued on page 49

Ventilated van No. 31292 to Diagram 89 featuring the flat-fronted nearly-vertical type of No. 4 or No. 8 axlebox, pushrod iron brakes with reversible brake blocks, 3-bolt buffers, screw couplings with side chains and square bolts fixing the ironwork.
NATIONAL RAILWAY MUSEUM (ETN 10F)

This picture of special cattle wagon No. 49610 to D23 shows the wood block brake with pushrod. Note the end of the brake lever offset downwards to give added clearance, in contrast to the drawing. The W-irons and grease axleboxes were to the standard Earlestown design but with longer springs and shackles fitted. The wagon label holder plate situated to the left of the tare weight '7.6.2' reads 'TO CARRY 6 TONS' and this was apparently reinforced by the legend 'LOAD 6 TONS' in minute letters to the right of the tare weight. Note also the screw couplings with side chains, and through pipes.
NATIONAL RAILWAY MUSEUM (ETN E76)

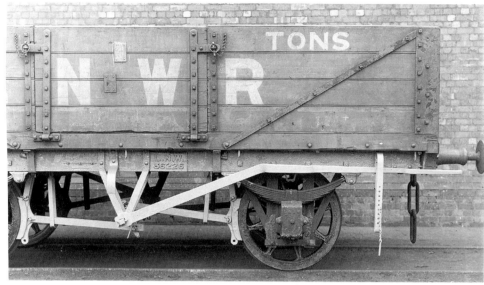

This side view of 10-ton open wagon No. 36226 to D84 illustrates the double brake (highlighted in white) in which the pushrods from the brake shaft to the brake blocks were constructed from twin flat bars, pinned to the blocks by a clevis pin and retained by a split pin. Note the brake shaft terminating in a squared end and the brake lever fixed onto it by another split pin. Whilst the door spring stop had a matching rubbing plate on the door, the second rubbing plate was for the brake shaft end and looks newer. They were not fitted at first. The supports to the curb rail from the solebar, fitted either side of the door, almost hide the trussrod eyebolt ends. The central 'bolt' on the No. 4 axlebox cover was actually part of the casting and turning it with a spanner rotated the entire front cover about the left-hand bolt to reveal the journal, bearing and pad. The right-hand bolt had a spring washer beneath the nut which tightened the sides. The square nuts on the corner plate were a little out of alignment whilst one appears to have fallen off. Four of the five rope cleats can be seen projecting below the curb rail. The texture of the solebar indicates it was surfaced with a steel flitch plate.

NATIONAL RAILWAY MUSEUM (ETN E112)

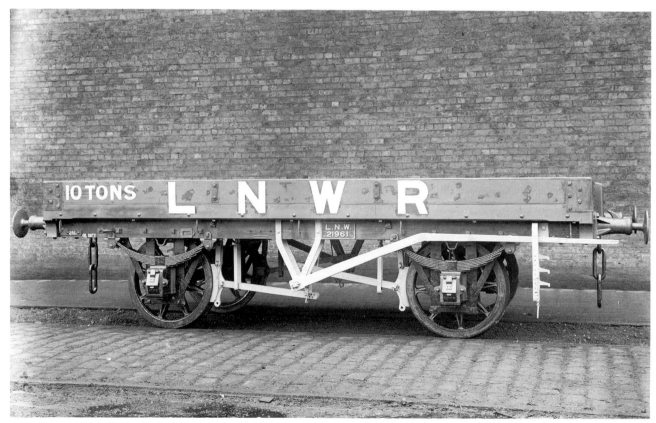

This photograph of 10-ton one-plank wagon No. 21961 to D103 was one of a series taken by the LNWR to illustrate experimental devices under trial to hold the brake lever locked down (without success). The device consisted of the three teeth seen projecting to the right of the brake lever keep. Here, however, we want to point out the 'pointed cover' axleboxes, the compression stops for the springs bent out of iron strip, and the short side straps between the 'L' and 'N', and the 'W' and 'R' fixing the side plank onto the knees, which are inside. The paint date at the left-hand end reads '2/15' but the 'OIL DATE' on its darkened panel looks blank.

NATIONAL RAILWAY MUSEUM (ETN E100)

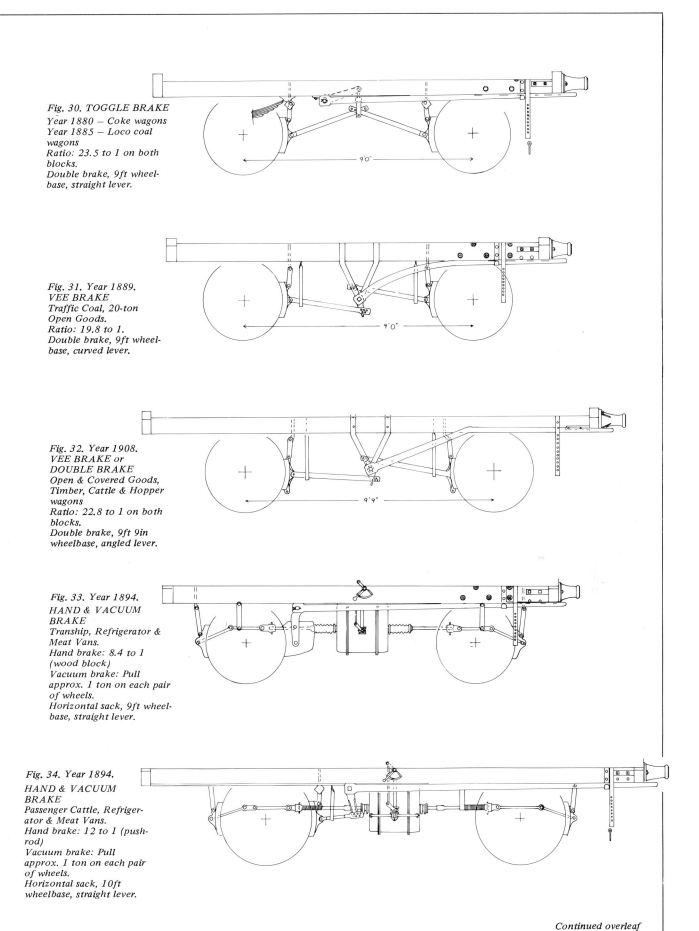

Fig. 30. TOGGLE BRAKE
Year 1880 – Coke wagons
Year 1885 – Loco coal
wagons
Ratio: 23.5 to 1 on both
blocks.
Double brake, 9ft wheel-
base, straight lever.

Fig. 31. Year 1889.
VEE BRAKE
Traffic Coal, 20-ton
Open Goods.
Ratio: 19.8 to 1.
Double brake, 9ft wheel-
base, curved lever.

Fig. 32. Year 1908.
VEE BRAKE or
DOUBLE BRAKE
Open & Covered Goods,
Timber, Cattle & Hopper
wagons
Ratio: 22.8 to 1 on both
blocks.
Double brake, 9ft 9in
wheelbase, angled lever.

Fig. 33. Year 1894.
HAND & VACUUM
BRAKE
Tranship, Refrigerator &
Meat Vans.
Hand brake: 8.4 to 1
(wood block)
Vacuum brake: Pull
approx. 1 ton on each pair
of wheels.
Horizontal sack, 9ft wheel-
base, straight lever.

Fig. 34. Year 1894.
HAND & VACUUM
BRAKE
Passenger Cattle, Refriger-
ator & Meat Vans.
Hand brake: 12 to 1 (push-
rod)
Vacuum brake: Pull
approx. 1 ton on each pair
of wheels.
Horizontal sack, 10ft
wheelbase, straight lever.

Continued overleaf

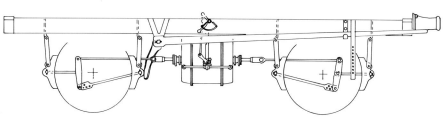

Fig. 35. Year 1896.
HAND & VACUUM
BRAKE
Refrigerator & Meat Vans.
Hand brake: 6.3 to 1.
Vacuum brake: Pull
approx. 3 tons on each pair
of wheels.
Horizontal sack, 9ft wheel-
base, straight lever.

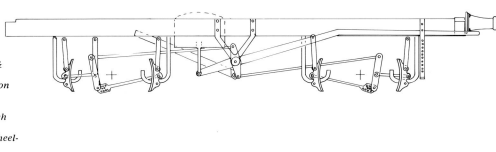

Fig. 36. Year 1904.
HAND & VACUUM
BRAKE
Covered Goods, Fruit &
Refrigerator Vans.
Hand brake: 59.6 to 1 on
both pairs of wheels.
Vacuum brake: Pull
approx. 4.7 tons on each
pair of wheels.
Vertical sack, 9ft 9in wheel-
base, angled lever.

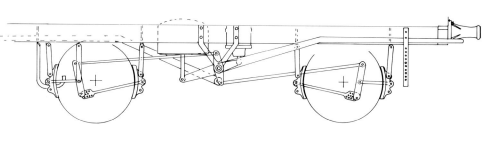

Fig. 37. Year 1906.
HAND, VACUUM & AIR
BRAKE
West Coast Refrigerator &
Meat Vans.
Hand brake: 59.6 to 1 on
both pairs of wheels.
Vacuum or Air brake: Pull
approx. 4.7 tons on each
pair of wheels.
Vertical sack, 9ft 9in
wheelbase, angled lever.

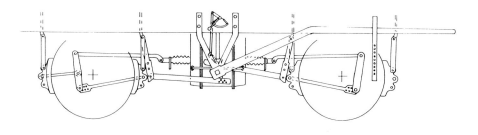

Fig. 38. Year 1917.
HAND & VACUUM
BRAKE
Meat & Refrigerator Vans.
Hand brake: 25.5 to 1 on
both pairs of wheels.
Vacuum brake: Pull
approx. 3.6 tons on each
pair of wheels.
Horizontal sack, 9ft wheel-
base, angled lever.

Direct Iron Replacement Brake *Key: Direct 1 rep. B Fig. 27*
Clearly an improved version of the previous design, adjustment of the block against the tyre was achieved automatically because the former was suspended from a hanger pivoted on a bracket attached to one of the transoms. This brake was most widely used on 7-ton wagons as a replacement for the first wooden type because the same trunnion bearing, in this case combined with the spring shoe, could be used without alteration. Similarly, the pin rack could be left in its original location.

Iron Push Rod Brake *Key: Pushrod 1S or BS Fig. 28*
Introduced in about 1885, this design was applied to newly constructed merchandise and livestock wagons. Wear of the block was taken up by means of the extra pin holes in the push rod. For the first time, a safety loop had to be provided in case the pin fell out of the push rod. This safety loop was attached to the opposite side of the transom to the block hanger by the same two nuts and bolts. Many wagons with this brake had a second set added on the opposite side in the early 20th century.

Iron Double Push Rod or 'Toggle' Brake
  Key: Fulc B Fig. 30
Apparently designed specifically for non-traffic coal wagons, whose capacity was 8 or 10 tons, and so required more braking surface, this brake went out of use around 1900, probably because the long steeply-angled push rods could not be readily restrained from dropping onto the track if an upper pin failed, because a safety loop mounted on the transom would be too close to the other end of the rod to offer it any support. There is no photographic evidence to suggest that safety loops were ever fitted to this brake. It is sometimes referred to as the 'fulcrum' brake.

Curved Lever Double Brake *Key: CLDB Fig. 31*
This was the earliest design of standard double brake with 'V' hanger. It was applied only to Traffic Coal wagons, both as a replacement for the direct iron type and in later construction. It was the only type to use a curved brake lever, except for narrow-gauge slate wagons.

Standard Double Brake *Key: DBBS and DB1S Fig. 32*
The RCH-approved brake with 'V' hanger and cranked lever was adopted as standard for new construction in 1903, although it had been applied to 10-ton merchandise and coal wagons since the late '90s. Many conversions of existing wagons had only one set but, for new construction, two sets were supplied. When the double brake was standardised, a new design of brake block had to be provided. The existing block had only one eye for attachment to the hanger. Early double-block brakes therefore needed a similar block cast with the hanger eye on the opposite side for the right-hand brake. The new standard brake block was provided with two eyes so that the same block was applicable to both left and right-hand wheels.

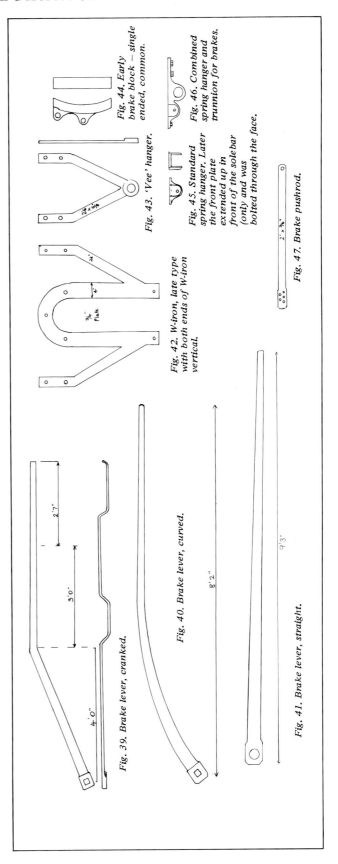

Fig. 44. Early brake block – single ended, common.

Fig. 46. Combined spring hanger and trunnion for brakes.

Fig. 43. 'Vee' hanger.

Fig. 45. Standard spring hanger. Later the front plate extended up in front of the solebar (only and was bolted through the face.

Fig. 42. W-iron, late type with both ends of W-iron vertical.

Fig. 47. Brake pushrod.

Fig. 39. Brake lever, cranked.

Fig. 40. Brake lever, curved.

Fig. 41. Brake lever, straight.

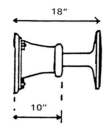

Fig. 48. 10in 3-bolt buffer
of the Emmett period

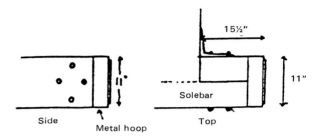

Side

Metal hoop

Solebar

Top

Fig. 49. 'Dumb' buffers

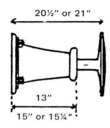

Fig. 50. 13in 3-bolt buffer

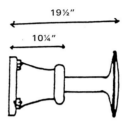

Fig. 51. 4-bolt type
— 20 ton Brake Van

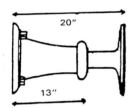

Fig. 52. 4-bolt type
— Meat Van

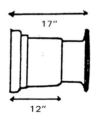

Fig. 53. Single-rib 4-bolt
buffer introduced with
18ft wagons in 1903 by
H. D. Earl

Fig. 54. Self-contained
rubber buffer

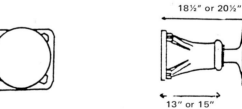

Fig. 55. 2-rib 4-bolt buffer
intoduced 1910 onwards
by Trevithick

Fig. 56. 2-rib base

Fig. 57. Single-rib base

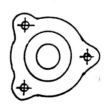

Fig. 58. 3-bolt shoe base

BUFFING GEAR

Dumb Buffers *Key: Dumb Fig. 49*

Even in the earliest days, wagons for livestock and other loads which could be easily damaged by rough shunting, were equipped with a pair of spring buffers at one end at least. From 1859 onwards, all new merchandise and livestock wagons carried spring buffers at both ends.

Spring Buffers in the Emmett Period *Key: 10in 3-bolt, 12in 3-bolt and 13in 3-bolt Fig. 48/50*

The standard wagon buffer, whether with rubber or plate spring, was carried in a cast-iron shoe, 10in long and secured by three bolts. From 1879, when screw couplings were adopted for cattle wagons, these vehicles were provided with buffer shoes of a similar design but 13in long in order to support the longer buffer rods required to suit the longer couplings. The distance from headstock over buffer head became 1ft 8½in (later increased to 1ft 9in) instead of the standard 1ft 6in. A third type of shoe was fitted from about 1890 to certain 10-ton wagons where more support was required for the buffer rods. These were 12in long but the distance over buffer head remained 1ft 6in.

Key: 4 bolt, 4 bolt rect. Fig. 51/52

Brake vans and refrigerator vans were fitted with a pattern of buffer shoe fastened by four bolts. Those on refrigerator vans had a rim with reverse curves around the bolts, similar to the three-bolt types, but brake vans had buffer shoes with a plain rectangular rim. All the Emmett buffers had heads 12in in diameter.

Spring Buffers in the Earl, Trevithick and Warneford Period *Key: 4-bolt 1-rib/2-rib Fig. 53/55/56/57*

Soon after the new standard 18ft 0in wagon was introduced, a new buffer was provided. It had a 13in diameter head and the shoe was 13in long with a strengthening rib cast on the outside and fastened by four bolts. From about 1910 onwards, the shoe had two ribs cast onto the outside.

Self-Contained Buffers *Key: Rubber SC Fig. 54*

Whenever design considerations precluded the use of the usual transverse plate spring for buffing, self-contained buffers were used. For example in a furniture van wagon the load bed was at or below buffer level, requiring a different solution. The first design used Indiarubber cylinders and was fitted to trolleys; furniture wagons; mineral hoppers; loco, carriage and wagon department coal and coke; and ballast wagons. In the case of the last three types, no modification beyond the provision of a full-width headstock was required to the existing dumb-buffered design of these wagons.

Key: RCH(SC)

When dumb-buffered timber wagons were converted, from the turn of the century onwards, recourse was made to the standard RCH pattern of self-contained buffer with helical spring, similar to those used for the same purpose by many other railway companies.

Key: Steel SC

A third pattern of self-contained buffer was used on wagons with steel underframes. In this case the shoe was tapered instead of being parallel-bodied.

3-bolt early buffer.

This plan view blown up from a photograph of Diagram 84 No. 24543 illustrates the thinness and large curve of the corner plates, the short travel of the three-bolt buffers, cross-section of the head, and the bolts fixing down the curved-section iron capping on the sides.

Single rib buffer.

2-rib buffer.

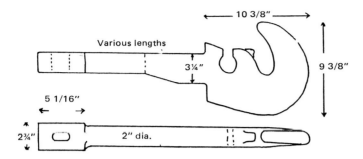

Various lengths

10 3/8"

3¼"

9 3/8"

5 1/16"

2¾"

2" dia.

Fig. 59. Coupling hook, showing gap that gedge fits into.

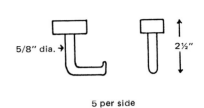

5/8" dia.→

2½"

5 per side

2 per side

Fig. 60. Sheet ties

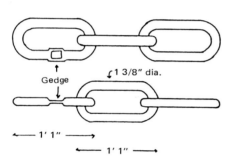

Gedge

1 3/8" dia.

1' 1"

1' 1"

Fig. 61. Standard three-link coupling with gedge to fit into gap in coupling hook.

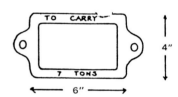

TO CARRY

7 TONS

4"

6"

Fig. 62. Label carrier

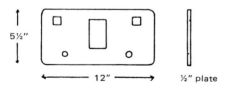

5½"

12"

½" plate

Fig. 63. Coupling hook plate

L.N.W.
4028

6½"

13" approx.

Fig. 64. Standard numberplate to fit on solebar(s)

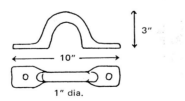

3"

10"

1" dia.

Fig. 65. Horse staple

This photograph of D16 No. 234 in post-1908 livery is included to show the typical construction features of LNW brake vans, with open-spoke wheels, whilst the brakes were a twin version of the wood-block pushrod brake with the brake shaft slung from a substantial central cruciform hanger inset into the solebars. The axleboxes were grease and the springs were mounted on spring shoes made out of a single long iron strip, each end being bent up with shackles to form the mounting itself similar to the Cattle Box on page 47. The top step is shown painted grey whilst the framing was not painted the darker grey or black that it sometimes was before the 'LNWR' lettering was added in 1908. The rivets on the corner plates are visibly very different in size from the bolts along the bottom edge. The numberplate was unusually painted in shop grey, not black, but possibly only for the official photograph. Occasionally, uncommon variants such as grey brake levers were noted in service by some observers.   NATIONAL RAILWAY MUSEUM (ETN E71)

This excellent close-up of a bulbous-shape No. 18 or No. 20 oil axlebox with its vertical 'LNWR' cast onto the box side includes several other features of interest: the open-spoke wheels — in this case with tyres that look brand new, if not thicker than the standard 2¼in; the later type of spring shoe with an extension up outside the solebar for an additional fixing bolt; the curved shape of the typical headstock end; the square nut and angled square seating retaining the eye-bolt end of the lateral truss rod along the underside of the transom — see how distinctive this is. Note the shape of the bottom keep to the W-iron, the reversible-shape brake block of the double brake, and the typical curved top of the brake lever pin rack. The lifting date painted on its black panel has yet to give up its secrets.

NATIONAL RAILWAY
MUSEUM (ETN E114B)

This picture of Diagram 9 No. 44772 showing the result of incorrectly loading barrels, also very nicely shows details of the wagon end. The corners of all LNWR wagons, where the side and ends planks met, were radiused before being covered by the corner plates. On this wagon the plates were originally fixed with rivets, but over the years most had been replaced by bolts, leaving rivets only through the top side plank. The rope cleats on the end show up well; the upper pair, and those on the headstocks outboard of the buffers, were of the self-tightening type. They were probably fitted after the wagon was built, whereas the pair inboard of the buffers were the original simple rings. Note that four still had remnants of rope attached! Buffers were normally fixed using hexagonal-headed bolts with nuts on the inside, whereas most bolts on the wagon were put in from the inside with square nuts on the outside. In this case the nuts on the draw plate were also hexagonal. These were the 7/8in diameter tie rods which extended the full length of the wagon, two from each headstock to each transom and also two more between the transoms. It is very unusual to see hexagonal nuts used here. A correct method of loading barrels is shown by the low-sided wagon beyond, where they had been laid down and tied. An alternative would have been to stand the barrels upright, but tightly pack them together so that they could not fall over.

CHAPTER THREE
OPEN GOODS WAGONS

THE London and North Western Railway was formed by an Act of Parliament dated 16th July 1846. In 1848 a report by Captain Mark Huish commissioned by the LNWR directors showed that on 1st January 1847, the LNWR owned the following open wagons:

	Southern Division	Northern Division	Manchester & Birmingham	Total
6-ton large goods wagons	831	100	29 }	2,745
4¼-ton medium goods wagons		1,593	192 }	
3¼-ton small goods wagons	510	1,077	542	2,129

Open wagons accounted for 4,874 from a total goods stock of 6,236, i.e. 78% of the total. The proportions dropped to 56% in 1902 and 52% in 1923. This was caused by greater specialisation to suit traffic needs, notably covered vans. As can be seen from the table, a great number of different designs of open wagon existed from various sources.

The 3¼-ton designs were probably not built after 1847 and became extinct before 1862. The 4¼-ton designs continued to be built until about 1859 when what was later described as Diagram 1 was introduced. After this their numbers began to decline. They became extinct, at least in revenue service, in 1873.

At a meeting of the Institute of Mechanical Engineers in 1852, Mr William A. Adams of Birmingham presented a paper on the use of wrought-iron for wagon underframes and stanchions. In this paper he stated that he had built about 500 wagons of this construction which were working on the Taff Vale, Monmouthshire, Midland, and London & North Western Railways.

In 1855 *Railway Machinery* by D.K. Clarke was published, including a number of drawings by H. Henson, Goods Superintendent of the Southern Division, and many of these wagons were also made of iron.

A committee minute of December 1862 stated that 'there are 50 iron wagons of a cylindrical shape or form, 13ft long by 8ft diameter, with one sliding door, average tare 4 tons 12 cwt. and from their peculiar construction they are not well adapted for general traffic and it is recommended that to make them more useful the cylindrical part be cut down or reduced to 2ft 2in from the wood floor reducing the tare by 10-cwt making it better adapted for general merchandise or loco coal traffic having sufficient capacity to carry six tons.'

From these fragments it can be seen that several experiments with iron wagons were being made at this time although the vast majority of wagons were made of wood.

A Stores committee minute dated 9th June 1859 stated that the standard wagon was to be of 7-tons capacity and went on to describe what later became known as Diagram 1. However, the valuations at the end of each financial year continued to show 6-ton wagons rather than 7-ton. The number of 6-ton wagons increased to 8,840 by 1861 and

continued to rise. In that year, 646 8-ton wagons appear in the valuations for the first time, but their numbers were in decline and they could well have been inherited from an amalgamated company.

In 1877 over half the 6-ton wagons were reclassified as 7-ton, the remaining 6-ton and 8-ton types being subsequently described as 'miscellaneous of different capacities'. At the end of that year the open wagon stock was:

7-ton	19,186	Probably mostly Diagram 1, built after 1859.
10-ton	50	Diagram 8 wagons built new in that year.
Different capacities	11,044	Including probably under 300 8-ton and various 6-ton built before 1859 as well as absorbed wagons to various designs.

The stock of 7-ton wagons increased rapidly and had reached 33,389 by 1885. These were mostly Diagram 1 although Diagram 2 had also been built from 1870. It is thus likely that the earliest Diagram 2 wagons were also rated at only six tons when built. Both these diagrams appear to be to the standards described later except that they had tie rods and the axleboxes were smaller overall, with 6in by 3in journals. New construction excluded tie rods, at least by 1884.

The number of wagons of different capacities declined equally fast, reducing to below 1,000 in 1884, and below 500 in 1886. Of course, the capacities of these wagons do not tell us very much about their appearance or how they were built and, unfortunately, very little else is known about them. We do know that some were 12ft long, some 13ft 6in and some 15ft.

In spite of the tremendous rate of building, in the early 1880s there was a shortage of goods wagons and some coal and coke wagons were borrowed from other departments and used for general merchandise.

SUMMARY

Diagram	Introduced	Description
1	1859	9in sides, to carry 7-tons
2	1870	20in sides, 7-tons
3	1879★	20in sides, fall doors, 7-tons
4	1893	36in sides, door on each side, 7-tons
5	1902★	20in sides, fall doors, 10-tons
6	1886	20in sides, 10-tons
7	1885	Slate truck wagon (fall doors), 10-tons
8	1877	22in sides (West Cumberland), 10-tons [door one side only]
9	1884	36in sides, door each side, 10-tons
10	1901	42in sides, door each side, 20-tons
11	1903	High-sided open goods wagon, 10-tons
84	1904	36in sides 18ft, 10-tons
84a	?	36in sides 18ft, 10-tons [may be LMS]
103	1910	9in sides 18ft, 10-tons

NOTE:
★ indicates earliest date wagons were known to be in service.

DIAGRAM 1 – OPEN GOODS WAGON WITH 9in SIDES

As already mentioned, the Stores Committee minuted in 1859 that the standard wagon capacity was to be seven tons and the internal dimensions of the body were 15ft x 7ft 1in with a depth of 9in and wheelbase of 9ft. The timber for the body was 3in thick, so the external dimensions can easily be calculated. The sides were single planks 11in x 3in plus a ⅜in capping, giving a nominal inside height of 9in allowing for a 2½in floor of 7in wide boards, rebated ½in over the buffer plank which was ½in deeper than the solebars, the end plank being 10½in deep. They had grease type axleboxes and 6in x 3in journals. The springs were 3ft 6in long and had seven plates 3in x ½in. The external width was soon increased from 7ft 7in to 7ft 8in and wagons of similar design were still being built at the turn of the century.

These wagons were built in large numbers until 1889, by which time about 20,000 were in use. Those built after June 1889 were 16ft long outside including a batch of 100 built as late as 1904. It is recorded that this batch was especially for meat traffic from Birkenhead but quite how this was carried is uncertain as contemporary accounts of that traffic make no mention of these wagons. It is possible that containers were used.

Until 1883 they had a single wooden brake block acting on one wheel. The last 1,000 or so built after 1883 probably had a cast-iron block with direct action, whilst the 100 built in 1904 had a similar arrangement but with a pushrod, and probably on both sides from new. From 1896, a start was made to replace the brakes on earlier wagons with the pushrod type. As some wagons were scrapped, the brakes were often salvaged and re-used on the second side of other wagons being repaired. Very few received the more modern double brakes on one or both sides. Buffers were also rarely

This official Crewe photograph is useful because it shows a typical Diagram 1 (No. 31446) in everyday working condition and dated precisely to 27th July 1896. The picture was taken within Crewe Works and the wagon is seen loaded with what appears to have been sand for casting. The two diamonds of the pre-1908 livery are just discernible directly above each axle. Note that two horse hooks were provided, one at either end of the solebar, except where the brake lever was fitted. The wheel tyres appear thin, but at this period most wagons (and locomotives) had thinner tyres, even when new. Locomotives acquired steel tyres (3in or 2½in) from 1885 onwards. The date on the left-hand axlebox appears to read 1876 or 1878, so it must have been a replacement, since the wagon is thought to have been built in 1872 or 1873.
NATIONAL RAILWAY MUSEUM (CRA 312)

Diagram 1 No. 11821 photographed at Earlestown when brand new in August 1885. Compared with the picture above, the diamonds are further apart, showing how such things varied over the years. The entire wagon including all ironwork was painted grey and this is thought to have been for photographic purposes, although the amount of black did vary from time to time anyway. Some wagons received grey brake levers, for example, and J. P. Richards recalls occasional examples where all the running gear was grey. That apart, the livery details are typical. The label holder is seen over the left-hand axle, an alternative (and perhaps more common) position being just to the right of the numberplate. Square nuts on the strapping (actually the body knees) and round-headed coach-bolts in the curb rail contrast with the tiny 3/8in rivets in the corner plates. A. G. ELLIS (23990)

updated and were of the standard 10in stock, 3-bolt pattern. However, the earliest wagons of this type were built with dumb buffers and these were rebuilt with sprung buffers of the self-contained type.

Some Diagram 1 wagons were modified in 1894-1910 to have steps and handrails as shunters' trucks to Diagram 51. It is possible that as many as 75 were so modified. From the late 1890s others had upright iron frames added to carry cases of sheet glass, and thus modified became Diagram 39 (see Chapter 6). A large number were modified in this way and the population of Diagram 39 wagons eventually totalled 146.

In 1909 the Goods Traffic Committee decided to 'replace them by standard 36in side 10-ton wagons until the number of 9in wagons reduces to 6,000', i.e. Diagram 1 wagons were to be replaced by Diagram 9. Diagram 1 wagons were never fitted with uprated journals or oil type axleboxes and were consequently never rated at more than seven tons. Indeed, as they became older and the axles wore, most, probably all, were downgraded to six tons, which is, of course, the capacity their predecessors started at in 1859. This happened from 1911 onwards.

One 16ft wagon was transferred to the Engineering Department Eastern Division in 1915 as ballast stock No. 2208 and fitted for gauging tunnels. At least one other 16ft wagon was fitted with side loading platform for interchange traffic with the Grand Union Canal at Rickmansworth in 1922.

Only six survived to pass into LMS stock in 1923, one of which was 15ft 6in long, the remainder being 16ft.

This picture of an unidentified Diagram 1 open has been included to show a typical load, in this case a furniture pantechnicon. The location was Shallcross, Cromford & High Peak Railway. One might have expected some securing ropes at the ends as well as the sides, but perhaps the pantechnicon was blocked out from the end of the wagon, or perhaps loading (or unloading) had not been completed. Rings or cleats for securing ropes were provided on all open goods wagons, on the headstocks and beneath the curb rails.
REAL PHOTOGRAPHS (C9122)

Known examples of Diagram 1:
Diagram book tare for type: 4.4.2

Number	Tare	Buffers	Brakes	Axleboxes	Notes
1563	4.13.0				
11821	4.10.0	10in 3-bolt	Wood 1S	Grease	15ft 6in
31446	4.3.1	10in 3-bolt	Wood 1S	Grease	15ft 6in
24945	4.4.1	10in 3-bolt	Wood 1S	Grease	15ft 6in
29747	4.12.1				
68123	4.10.0	10in 3-bolt	Pushrod 1S	Grease	16ft 0in

Diagram 1 No. 24945 is the subject of this official Earlestown photograph and the paint date 8/09 at the left of the solebar gives a good indication of the date, since the photograph was clearly taken to show the new LNWR lettering which was introduced in the previous year. The label holder 'TO CARRY / 7 TONS', immediately to the right of the numberplate, is the most reliable method of determining the capacity of an LNWR wagon, the only other difference being the size of journals and axleboxes. Standard features include the 10-inch buffer stocks, wooden brake block and split spoke wheels. Inside the rim of the nearest wheel can be seen the square head of a bolt, four of which fixed the tyre to the centre and was the method preferred by the LNWR for most of its separate existence. The grease axleboxes both carry a 1902 date and, since this was a 15ft 6in example built before 1889, were probably replacements. Axleboxes were often replaced and hence are not a reliable indicator of the date a wagon was built. The corner plates were held on by countersunk bolts (or possibly coachbolts) with square nuts on the outside. It is likely that these were new; when repair work was necessary, the original rivets were often replaced by bolts.
(NATIONAL RAILWAY MUSEUM (47A))

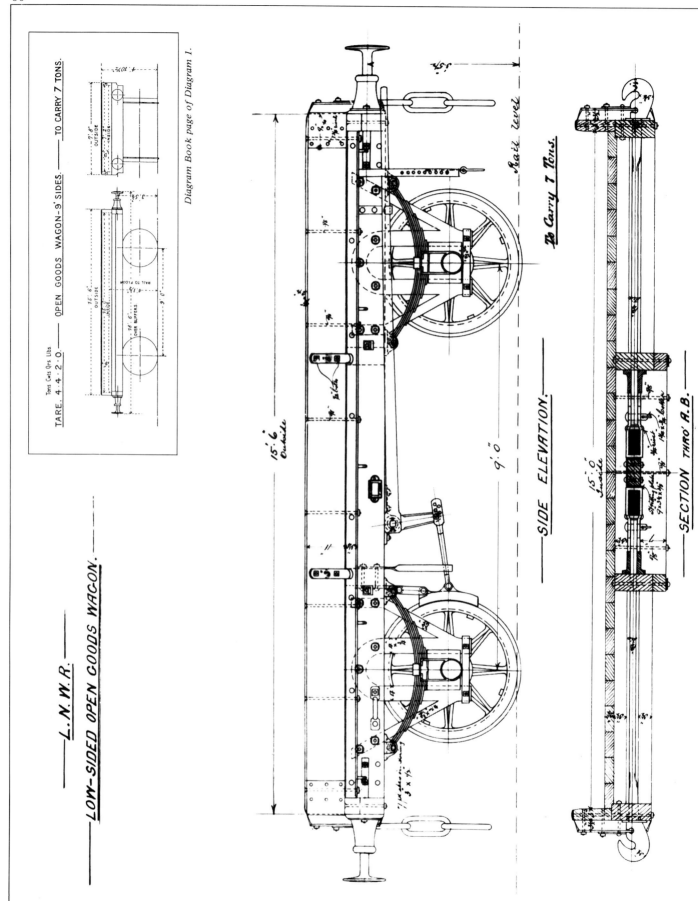

Diagram Book page of Diagram 1.

— L.N.W.R. —

— LOW-SIDED OPEN GOODS WAGON. —

— SIDE ELEVATION. —

— SECTION THRO' A.B. —

To Carry 7 Tons.

Rail level

15' 6"
Outside

9' 0"

OPEN GOODS WAGON—9' SIDES. — TO CARRY 7 TONS.

TARE. 4·4·2·0.

Tons Cwts Qrs Lbs

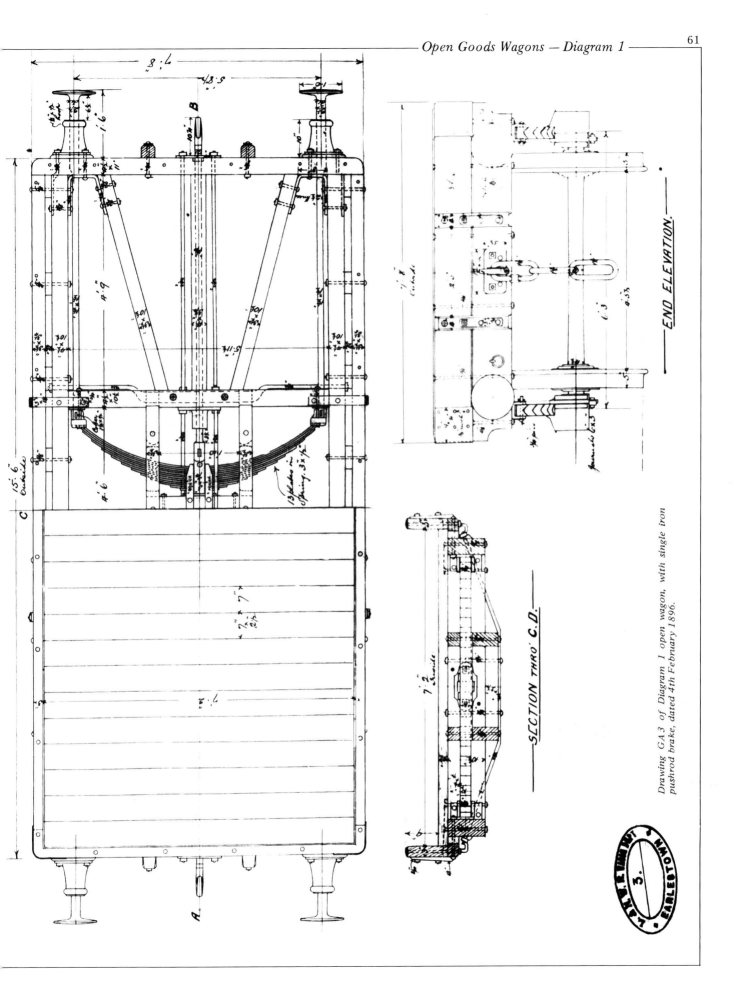

SECTION THRO' C.D.

END ELEVATION.

Drawing GA3 of Diagram 1 open wagon, with single iron pushrod brake, dated 4th February 1896.

Although poor photographically, this picture by Jim Richards, taken c.1923, nicely shows the final LNWR livery, after diamonds had been deleted. Notice that the tare was painted on the curb rail rather than the solebar by this late date and the capacity could appear at either end. The wagon was originally built with the iron pushrod brake, the second set having been added later. The vast majority of Diagram 1 wagons were 15ft 6in long. This wagon was one of the 100 late-built examples which had the iron pushrod brake from new and were 16ft long. Such a difference in length should be noticeable in photographs, but in fact can be quite difficult to judge. The most reliable method is to look at the distance between the bolts fastening the inner knee and the spring shoe. They were almost adjacent on a 15ft 0in wagon; approx 5in apart on a 15ft 6in vehicle and approx 8in apart for 16ft 0in examples. Built with a capacity of 7 tons, it had been downgraded to 6 tons sometime after 1911. We are fortunate to have this photographic record, since although over 20,000 wagons were built to Diagram 1, only six survived to 1923.

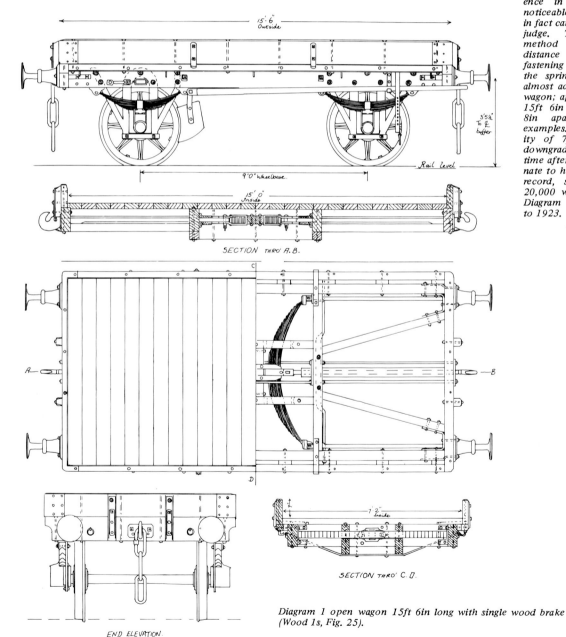

Diagram 1 open wagon 15ft 6in long with single wood brake (Wood 1s, Fig. 25).

DIAGRAM 2 – OPEN GOODS WAGON WITH 20in SIDES

The Diagram 2 wagon was introduced in 1870. The design was as Diagram 1 in all respects except that the sides were formed of two 11in x 3in planks plus ⅝in capping, giving an inside height of 20in after allowing for the usual 2½in floor rebated ½in over the buffer plank, which was ½in deeper than the solebars as before. The ends were constructed of one 11in and one 10½in plank. Both side and end planks were of 2¾in timber. The width appears to have been 7ft 8in from the start. The drawings show springs with twelve plates 3in x ⅜in but these are thought to have been interchangeable with the seven-plate type.

Approximately 14,000 of these 15ft 6in wagons were in service by the time the standard length was changed to 16ft for wagons constructed after mid-1889. The population then began to decline even though approximately 4,700 16ft long examples were built before production ceased in 1906. Those built prior to about 1883 had the single wooden brake block. Later examples had the brakes current at the time. They could thus be seen with single cast-iron block with or without pushrod. Apart from receiving a second set of brakes as described for Diagram 1, when older wagons were scrapped, the brakes on Diagram 2 wagons were normally not updated. All appear to have had grease-type axleboxes and, except for very early examples, three-bolt buffers.

In the early 1900s some were fitted with 8in x 3¾in journals, still with grease-type axleboxes but with more modern brakegear, and upgraded to ten tons. These wagons thus became Diagram 6 whilst those remaining in Diagram 2 were downgraded to 6 tons capacity from 1911 onwards. A total of 453 wagons to Diagram 2 passed into LMS ownership in 1923, of which at least 400 were 16ft long.

Known examples of Diagram 2:
Diagram book tare for type 4.6.1

Number	Tare	Buffers	Brakes	Axleboxes	Notes
849	4.12.3	10in 3-bolt	1S	Grease	
910	4.10.0	10in 3-bolt	Wood 1S	Grease	15ft 6in
1919?		10in 3-bolt	Pushrod 1S	Grease	16ft
36134		10in 3-bolt	1S	Grease	
36277		10in 3-bolt	Wood 1S	Grease	15ft 6in experimental tarpaulin bar
42024		10in 3-bolt	Wood 1S	Grease	15ft 6in
52936	4.10.3	10in 3-bolt	Wood 1S	Grease	15ft 6in experimental tarpaulin bar
53625	4.11.0				

Diagram 2 No. 42024 photographed at Earlestown when new in 1878. The wagon had yet to be painted, the wood being untreated and the ironwork in an 'as cast' or 'as forged' state, and probably 'japanned' before storage. The diamonds appear to have been paper or card tacked on. The photo on page 19 was taken on the same occasion and was reproduced in the Souvenir Booklet published by BR (LMR) to mark Earlestown's centenary in 1953. It was then described as 'a low-sided open wagon with single hand-brake of the wood brake-block type', which was built in 1 hr 41 mins on 8th March, 1878. COLLECTION A. G. ELLIS

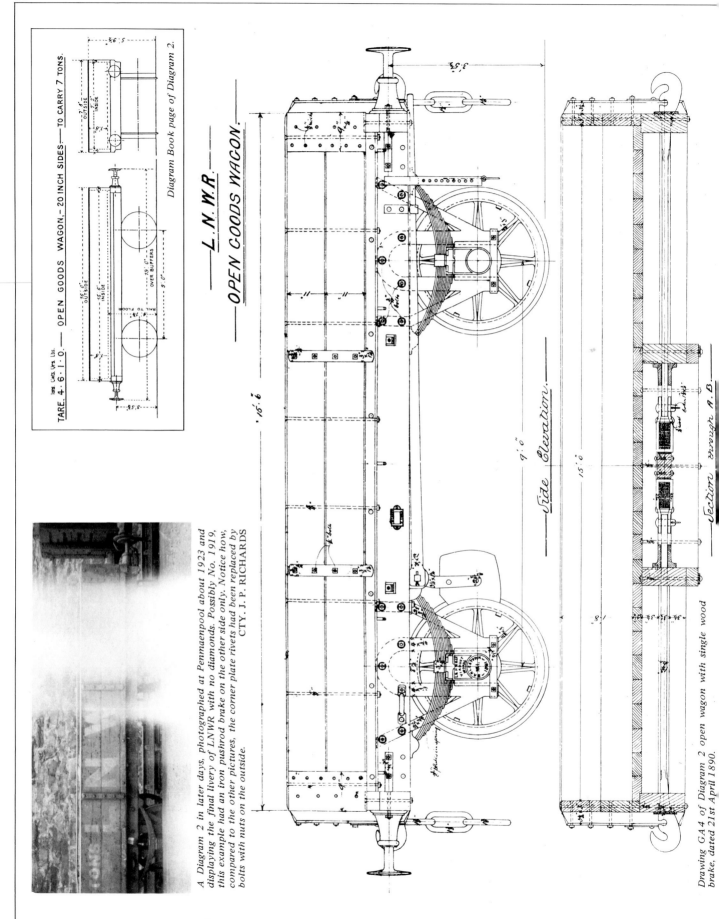

Diagram Book page of Diagram 2.

TARE. 4 . 6 . 1 . 0. — OPEN GOODS WAGON. – 20 INCH SIDES – TO CARRY 7 TONS.

— *L.N.W.R.* —
— *OPEN GOODS WAGON.* —

— *Side Elevation.* —

— *Section through A . B.* —

A Diagram 2 in later days, photographed at Penmaenpool about 1923 and displaying the final livery of LNWR with no diamonds. Possibly No. 1919, this example had an iron pushrod brake on the other side only. Notice how, compared to the other pictures, the corner plate rivets had been replaced by bolts with nuts on the outside.
CTY. J. P. RICHARDS

Drawing GA4 of Diagram 2 open wagon with single wood brake, dated 21st April 1890.

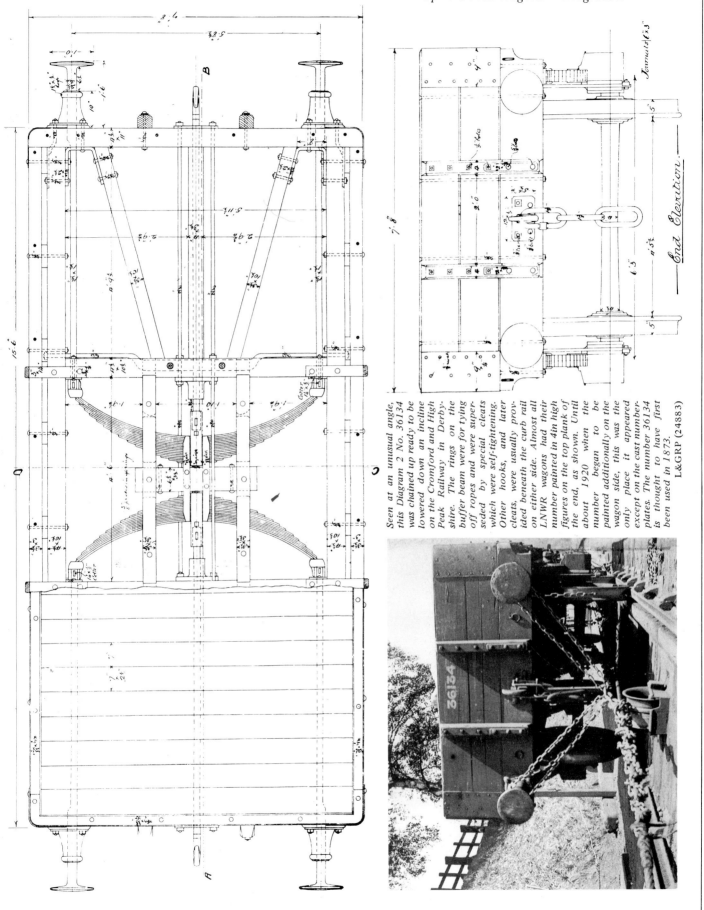

End Elevation.

Seen at an unusual angle, this Diagram 2 No. 36134 was chained up ready to be lowered down an incline on the Cromford and High Peak Railway in Derbyshire. The rings on the buffer beam were for tying off ropes and were superseded by special cleats which were self-tightening. Other hooks, and later cleats, were usually provided beneath the curb rail on either side. Almost all LNWR wagons had their number painted in 4in high figures on the top plank of the end, as shown. Until about 1920 when the number began to be painted additionally on the wagon side, this was the only place it appeared except on the cast number-plates. The number 36134 is thought to have first been used in 1873.

L&GRP (24883)

DIAGRAM 3 – OPEN WAGON WITH 20in SIDES AND FALL DOORS

The Diagram 3 wagon was introduced at least by 1879. Once again the design was identical to Diagram 1 except for the sides and ends. The floor was again 2⅓in thick but in this case the curb rail was made deeper to bring the top flush with the floor, enabling the contents to be shovelled out more easily when the side was dropped. The sides and ends were two 10in x 2¾in planks (some accounts give 10½in), and because the curb rail and floor were flush, this gave an internal height of 20in (or 21in). An insert 2¾in x 2in was therefore visible across the end of the wagon between the end planks and the buffer plank.

Iron strapping fixed to the sides protruded beyond the ends and engaged with a hinged hasp. The hasps had to be raised at both ends of the wagon to allow the side to drop down. In LNWR terminology these drop sides were referred to as fall doors. The ends of the buffer planks, instead of having the familiar curved shape, were cut off square and acted as a stop for the side. This presented a problem because the brake lever was usually curved in plan so as to set out past the end of the beam. This would have interfered with the falling doors and so the set was made in elevation instead, the lever protruding beneath the beam.

The exact dates of construction and number built are not easy to determine because there also existed a ballast wagon to Diagram 62 which was almost identical to Diagram 3, the main difference being the end stanchions which protruded above the tops of the ends to locate lengths of rail when being transported. The square-ended buffer planks must have put a great deal of strain on the side and those built to Diagram 62 received proper curved steel solebar-mounted springs in three places to soften the blow. Some of these were provided with canvas flaps over the springs and axleboxes to prevent dust from the ballast entering the bearings.

Because of the similarity of these two types, some Diagram 3 wagons were used for ballast work and some of these had the canvas flaps added. This includes a batch of about 300 which were transferred to the Permanent Way Department on its formation in 1912–13. Similarly, one or two Diagram 62 wagons could be seen on normal duties not associated with permanent way use. The quantity of Diagram 3 wagons therefore varied somewhat, particularly in later LNWR days.

To make identification more difficult, dirt sometimes rendered the lettering illegible and at least one ballast wagon had raised end stanchions at one end only, probably as a result of repair. Identification from a photograph can thus be almost impossible unless the number plate is readable. Diagram 3 wagons were often seen on other departmental duties. For example, they were particularly suitable for carrying ash and cinders from loco sheds. Ten were especially built for this purpose as late as 1909, although these could have been to Diagram 5. Twenty others were built to carry cinders for the Wagon Department at Earlestown in 1892.

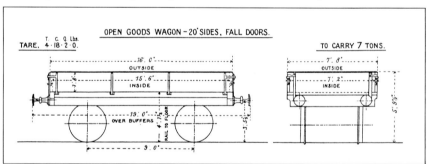

Diagram Book page of Diagram 3.

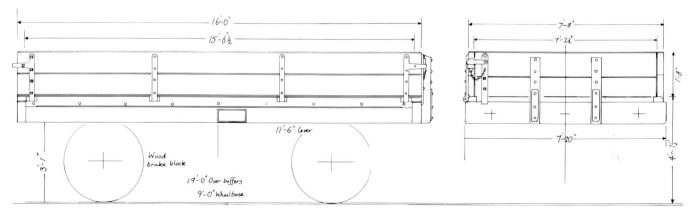

Line drawing of body of Diagram 3 open wagon with fall doors.

At least 80 were lettered 'Birkenhead & London only' and used for meat traffic until 1905. Another was noted being used to carry coal for the Carriage Department in 1902 and some were allocated to the Garston, Widnes and St Helens area.

From the building dates, early examples would have been 15ft 6in outside although most, including a large batch of 150 built in 1892, would have been 16ft long. All were 7ft 8in wide. The standard grease-type axleboxes were used throughout their lives with a rated capacity of seven tons, but they were downgraded to six tons after 1911.

Probably all were built with single brake blocks, either of wood or iron, depending on the date built. Service vehicles generally were slow to receive updated brakegear and it is likely that Diagram 3 wagons also remained with single brakes all their lives. Certainly some retained one wooden block into the mid-1920s. Of the 71 which remained to pass into LMS ownership in 1923, seven were of 15ft 6in length and 64 were 16ft long.

Known examples of Diagram 3:
Diagram book tare for type: 4.18.2

Number	Tare	Buffers	Brakes	Axleboxes	Notes
41724	4.14.0	10in 3-bolt	Wood 1S	Grease	All
57905	4.10.2	10in 3-bolt	Wood 1S	Grease	believed
57959	4.10.1	10in 3-bolt	Wood 1S	Grease	to have
58047	4.15.0	10in 3-bolt	Wood 1S	Grease	been 16ft.

A Diagram 3 open wagon with fall doors, photographed by Jim Richards at Earlestown in about 1923. No. 58047 was built in about 1892 and is shown carrying the late standard livery of LNWR with no diamonds, although, surprisingly, there is no sign of '6 TONS' lettering. Conceivably this example had not been back to works for repainting, and therefore still carried a 7 tons plate. The wooden brake block, almost worn out, was very unusual for so late a period and suggests that the wagon was allocated for internal use, something which would also explain the absence of '6 TONS' noted above. The wagons on either side were 18ft Diagram 103 open wagons.

A lovely photograph, again by Jim Richards, this time of Diagram 3 No. 57959 in about 1923. Clearly for departmental use, the lettering reads 'CINDER WAGON TO BE RETURNED TO EARLESTOWN WAGON WORKS', where the photograph was taken. The tare weight painted above the left-hand axlebox reads 4.10.1, whilst the lettering on the painted black square above the right-hand axlebox reads '16–4–23 / LIFTING DATE'. Such lifting dates were applied very late in the LNWR period, probably from 1921. The wagon was built in about 1892 and appears totally as built. Note the typical LNWR recessed shape to the headstock ends had given way to plain square ends which acted as crude stops for the drop side, there being no separate sprung steel door stop. When built the wagon would have had a capacity of 7 tons, being downgraded after about 1911.

DIAGRAM 4 – OPEN GOODS WAGON WITH 36in SIDES & DOORS EACH SIDE

COLLECTION E. TALBOT

Taken at Stafford, this is one of a series of photographs taken to illustrate incorrect loading of wagons. In this case Diagram 4 No. 8155 was loaded very high with sacks and sheeted over, but poor roping down had enabled one sheet to blow off, leaving the sacks exposed. The size of the load was not at all unusual for an open wagon, provided it was correctly sheeted over. The wagon is seen in pre-1908 livery of diamonds only, but subsequently downgraded from 7 tons to 6 tons, the number 6 being clearly brighter, indicating that a full repaint was not considered worthwhile. A 'NOT TO GO' label can be seen pasted in the centre of the side door due to the unstable load.

This rather dark photograph of Diagram 4 No. 49448 was taken by Jim Richards in 1922 and apart from the livery was probably in as-built condition, with a single iron, pushrod brake on one side only. Note that, unlike most examples of Diagram 3, Diagram 4 wagons had a sprung door stop on the solebar and a striker plate on the door itself.

The first Diagram 4 was a solitary wagon built in 1893. This apparently proved successful, for volume production started in 1894 and over 15,000 had been built by the time they were discontinued in 1903. The design was very similar to Diagrams 1 and 2. The floor was from 7in x 2½in timbers but, as with Diagram 3, the curb rail had to be increased in depth from 3in to 5½in to bring it level with the top of the floor. The sides were four 9in x 2¾in planks, giving a height of 36in both internally and externally. Unlike Diagram 3, the bottom plank on the ends was widened to 11½in, so dispensing with the separate 2½in insert plank. This is clearly discernible in photographs because the lower edge of the corner plate lines up with the bottom of the side but not with the bottom of the end boarding. The springs had seven plates 3in x ½in.

All Diagram 4 wagons were 16ft long by 7ft 8in wide. The door opening extended for the full height of the side, and was tapered in plan, being 4ft 7½in on the outside face and 4ft 6½in on the inside. The door edges similarly tapered, of course, to give a tight joint when closed. They were initially built as replacements for ageing Diagram 1 and 2 stock but some were built to the capital account.

All the wagons were built with 6in x 3in journals, grease-type axleboxes and were rated at seven tons. In later life this was reduced to six tons. 10in 3-bolt buffers and a single iron brake block operated by pushrod were fitted from new to all examples. Wagons built after 1898, and some passing through works for repair, had a similar brake fitted to the other side. Few Diagram 4 wagons appear to have received double brakes one side, or indeed double brakes both sides.

At first the corner plates had three bolts through the centre two planks, and four through the upper and lower planks. Final batches had three bolts through each plank. A total of 3,601 survived to pass into LMS ownership in 1923. The reason for their apparently rapid decline is that many were later fitted with larger bearings and uprated to ten tons, in which form they became Diagram 9.

Known examples of Diagram 4:

Diagram book tare for type: 5.6.3

Number	Tare	Buffers	Brakes	Axleboxes
187	5.10.1		? BS	Grease
623	4.16.2		SB1S	Grease
7308	5.4.3			
8155			Pushrod BS	Grease
10912	5.3.2		SBBS	Grease
19689	5.2.0		SB1S	Grease
23968	6.4.1			
25681		10in 3-bolt		Grease
25734	5.7.2		SBBS	Grease
28744	5.14.1		SBBS	Grease
32959	5.5.2		SB1S	Grease
33021		10in 3-bolt		Grease
34286	5.2.3		SB1S	Grease
36934	5.13.0	3-bolt	Pushrod	Grease
38496				
41888	5.15.0		SBBS	Grease
49448	5.1.0	10in 3-bolt	Pushrod 1S	Grease
53603		10in 3-bolt	Pushrod BS	Grease
57912	6.12.0			
66396	5.7.2		DBBS	Grease
68410	5.7.0	10in 3-bolt	Pushrod BS	Grease
70228	6.5.2			

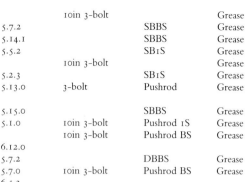

Diagram 4 wagons were sometimes used for departmental work, as witnessed by this example whose lettering reads 'CREWE WORKS PURPOSES ONLY NOT TO GO ON MAIN LINE'. The steel striker plate on the door is seen more clearly in this view and was fixed by four small screws. The corner plates, however, were fixed with bolts and square nuts, as was usual after about 1902. Three tarpaulin cleats can be seen below the curb rail, one almost in the centre and one just outboard of the door opening. No horse hook can be seen on the right-hand end even though brakes are fitted to the far side only. It is possible that one set of brake gear became damaged and, bearing in mind the internal usage, was removed and discarded. On the solebar can be seen an oval plate. Other Crewe Works internal user wagons had these plates which read 'LOCO WORKS CREWE / number / LNWRY', but since these wagons were not revenue-earning vehicles, it is thought that these oval plates indicated their attachment to the Loco Works plant and bore their number within the plant.
COLLECTION G. H. PLATT

Yet another Jim Richards photograph taken c.1923, this time of Diagram 4 No. 68410 built in about 1900 with pushrod brakes on both sides. Painting the wagon number on the side of most wagon types was introduced very late in LNWR days, probably 1921 or 1922. The tyres on this example must have been close to their wear limit.

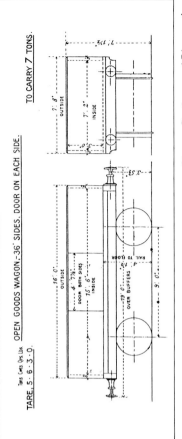

NATIONAL RAILWAY MUSEUM (843/2/63)

This photograph of D4 No. 53603 is not included to show the presumably experimental coupling aid, but to illustrate the script lettering on the lower plank and the less-common lettering on the top plank above it. It also shows the brake lever resting in a hook rather than a notch in the pin-rack. It can be seen that the three upper nuts on the end verticals had separate washers under them, whereas the domed heads were outside on those bolts that went through the solebar.

OPEN GOODS WAGON.—36" SIDES. DOOR ON EACH SIDE.

TO CARRY 7 TONS.

TARE. 5 · 6 · 3 · 0.

Diagram Book page of Diagram 4.

Drawing GA6 of Diagram 4 open wagon with single iron pushrod brake, dated 19th December 1895. Note the brake pushrod safety strap was twisted through 90° so it could be bolted to the wood crossmember.

— *L. N. W. R.* —

— DEEP-SIDED OPEN GOODS WAGON. —

— SIDE ELEVATION. —

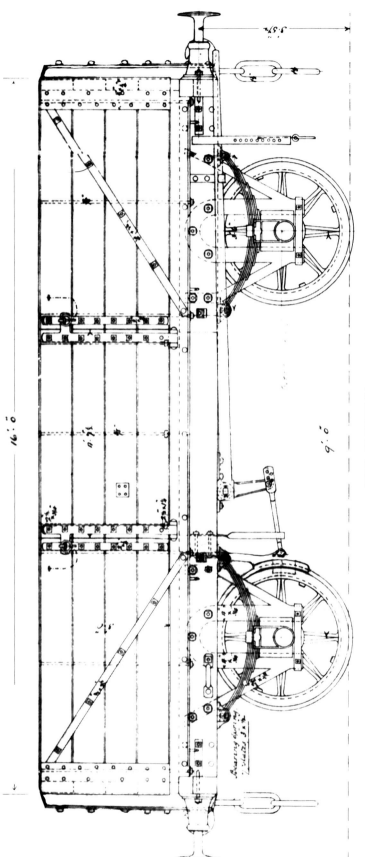

TO CARRY 7 TONS.

PLAN

END ELEVATION.

CROSS SECTION at A.B.

DIAGRAM 5 – OPEN WAGON WITH 20in SIDE AND FALL DOORS

These wagons had varying origins and were to three different lengths but were basically a ten-ton version of Diagram 3, with fall doors. The construction details were the same but they were fitted with the larger 8in x 3¾in journals still in grease-type axleboxes and heavier springs. The building dates are uncertain and it is quite possible that none were constructed new to this diagram, all being conversions from 15ft 6in Diagram 7, 16ft Diagrams 3 and 62, and 18ft Diagram 62A.

As described under Diagram 3, there was very little difference between this design and ballast wagons. The total number built to this Diagram was always small, the highest stock reaching 94 in 1912. At times, ballast wagons appear to have been released by the Permanent Way Department and used in general service. Most of these would have conformed to Diagram 5. Some of the larger 18ft ballast wagons were also released and incorporated into general stock, the additional size apparently not being important as both 16ft and 18ft were classified as Diagram 5. The longer length was handwritten onto page 5 in most copies of the Diagram Book.

It is likely that, as with Diagram 3, these were mostly used for departmental duties. In 1902, there were only twelve wagons and all were described as being for 'Staffordshire'. It is possible that they were used to carry clay for brickmaking, their fall doors and large payload being particularly suited for this traffic. It is also recorded that some were built as early as 1884, but this is likely to be the date of building as a seven-ton wagon rather than the date of conversion to Diagram 5, which probably occurred in the mid 1890s. When modified they retained grease axleboxes, but some were fitted with pushrod brakes on both sides whereas the 18ft examples always had double brakes on both sides. The 18ft wagons are more fully described under Diagram 62A ballast wagons in a later volume of this book. By 1911 slate traffic from Blaenau Festiniog had declined and in that year twenty-eight Diagram 7 wagons had their rails removed, thus conforming to Diagram 5 although only 15ft 6in long. It is thought that other wagons to Diagram 7 were similarly converted later. Some Diagram 5 wagons were transferred to the newly formed Permanent Way Department in 1913 and 61 passed into LMS ownership in 1923. From their building dates it is likely that all but about fifteen of these were 18ft versions by then.

Known examples of Diagram 5:
Diagram book tare for type: 5.0.0

Numbers:

2173	8892
2835	18334
3282	18661
7100	19734
8144	24844
8233	26349

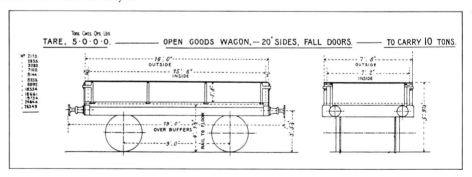

Diagram Book page of Diagram 5

DIAGRAM 6 – OPEN GOODS WAGON WITH 20in SIDES

These were indistinguishable from Diagram 2 except for uprated grease axleboxes carrying 8in x 3¾in journals, solebar flitch plates and heavier springs, giving a capacity of 10 tons. Initially, four were converted from 15ft 6in Diagram 2 wagons in 1886, followed by six more between 1894 and 1902 which had been built as Diagram 2 between 1873 and 1883. These early Diagram 6 wagons were used to carry vitriol between Birkenhead and Warrington, vitriol being a distillate of copper sulphate, transported in large carboys, hence the necessity for the larger payload of ten tons.

Four of these ten wagons were scrapped before 1902, another in 1903, and three more soon after, leaving just two examples. However, fifty-two more conversions from Diagram 2 wagons took place between 1907 and 1913. These appear to have been mostly 16ft wagons and were for general use. What became of them is uncertain because by 1914 only two remained and they were being used for sand at Earlestown. In July 1915 these two were transferred to the Wagon Department for transporting coal and thus Diagram 6 became extinct.

It is likely that the bulk of them were transferred to the new Permanent Way Department when it was formed in 1913. Certainly some were used for ballast work and received canvas flaps over the axleguards like ballast wagons.

The 15ft 6in wagons were probably fitted with the then current iron block pushrod brakes on one side only when converted. The 16ft wagons had double brakes both sides, still retaining grease-type axleboxes and 3-bolt buffers.

Known examples of Diagram 6:
Diagram book tare for type: 4.12.2

Number	Tare	Buffers	Brakes	Axleboxes	Notes
543					16ft
7483					16ft
24381			SB1S		15ft 6in
34783			SB1S		15ft 6in
38909	5.12.0	10in 3-bolt	DBBS	Grease	16ft
46494					–
52114	4.10.2				16ft

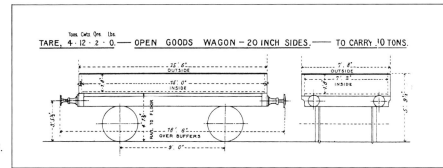

Diagram Book page of Diagram 6.

TARE, 4 · 12 · 2 · 0. — OPEN GOODS WAGON — 20 INCH SIDES. — TO CARRY 10 TONS.

This official Earlestown photograph has appeared in print before, described as a Diagram 2, but the label holder above the left-hand axlebox clearly reads 'TO CARRY / 10 TONS', so this must have been one of the rare Diagram 6 wagons. The centre of the axleboxes both read 'No. 2' which is believed to indicate larger journals, those on 7-ton wagons generally reading 'No. 1' or the journal size itself. For 10-ton wagons the whole axlebox was larger, but this is surprisingly difficult to see in photographs. The paint date is 8/09 and the picture was clearly taken at about that time to illustrate the new LNWR livery. The side planks look in pristine condition, the brake gear had been altered to double shoes, spring buckle stops had been bolted under the solebars and the corner plates were fixed with bolts and square nuts, all of which suggests that the wagon had been substantially rebuilt, rather than just repainted. It was thus probably newly converted from Diagram 2 to Diagram 6 when the photograph was taken. Quite possibly the second set of brakegear was added at the same time. One feature of most 10-ton wagons was the steel flitch plate on the solebars which is identifiable in a number of ways: firstly, the general appearance is very smooth with slight pitting from rust, quite unlike a wooden beam; secondly, the square nuts had no washers behind them. In addition, when a flitch plate was fitted, the eye-bolts attaching the 3-bolt buffer shoe to the solebar, normally cranked outwards, recessed into the outer face of the solebar and fastened by two bolts with square nuts, were not used. Instead, a straight bar, threaded at both ends was inserted into a hole in the solebar accessed by a slot or mortice on the underside of the solebar for fitting the inner washer and nut. Since this arrangement merely secured the buffer shoe without adding to the strength of the headstock to solebar joint (through which part of the drawbar load was often transmitted), extra straight eyebolts were added outside the flitch plate and fastened with the usual two bolts through the solebar with square nuts on the outside. This was either done at the top and bottom of the solebar or, as in the case of the above wagon, at the bottom only. These eye-bolts became standard for all new wagons with flitch plates after 1903 and a stronger 4-bolt buffer shoe was soon designed with a larger square flange to incorporate them. The five tarpaulin cleats beneath the curb rail are easily seen. The grey brakegear and lever were probably as used in traffic, rather than being specially painted for the photograph, although the black lever rack looks out of place. Notice the bolt heads all squarely aligned — the practice of good craftsmen.

NATIONAL RAILWAY MUSEUM (48A)

DIAGRAM 7 – SLATE TRUCK WAGON WITH FALL DOORS

The LNWR had a branch from Llandudno Junction to Blaenau Festiniog and interchange facilities with the 1ft 11½in gauge Festiniog Railway were opened there in 1881. At first, coal, minerals and general goods were transhipped, slate being carried by the Festiniog Railway itself to Portmadoc where it was loaded direct into waiting ships. The importance of the traffic at the time may be judged by a statement in a Government report from H M Inspector of Mines, who said in 1882 that, 'After coal and iron, slate is the most valuable mineral raised in the U.K.'

In 1885 the LNWR built 150 1ft 11½in gauge slate wagons based on a Festiniog Railway design which was 6ft 2in long, 3ft 2in wide with 1ft 6in high sides on a 3ft 2in wheelbase. The intention was to load these miniature wagons onto a standard gauge six-wheeled transporter wagon. A general arrangement drawing of the transporter survives, but none were ever built. They would have carried six small wagons in two parallel rows but the design was rejected due to the difficulty of arranging docks for the end loading required. Ironically, the idea was revived and adopted by the GWR a few years later. Instead, fifty Diagram 7 slate truck transporter wagons were built in 1885 which were very similar to Diagrams 3 and 5, and were 15ft 6in long with fall doors.

Each wagon could accommodate three narrow gauge wagons loaded transversely, for which purpose lightweight bridge rails were laid on the floors. As was common at the time, no door stops were provided for the opening sides, they merely banged against the end of the buffer plank, as on early wagons to Diagram 3.

They had a capacity of ten tons from new which was unusual for that period. This was necessary, of course, because each narrow gauge wagon could weigh as much as three tons when loaded. Standard grease-type axleboxes were used whilst brakes of the iron block, direct-action type were fitted to one side only. They probably remained like that until scrapped. The width over the sides was unusually narrow at only 7ft 5in in order to hold the slate wagons securely in place. Blocks were bolted to the inside of the sides to bear against the central buffer/coupling.

It is also believed that there was a fixing through the floor of the transporter wagon which located in the heavy angle brackets which were fixed to the solebars of all LNWR 1ft 11½in gauge wagons. Buffers were standard three-bolt with 10in stocks.

No further wagons to Diagram 7 were built but in 1887 a hundred further narrow gauge slate wagons were built exactly as the previous batch but with the addition of brakes which had not been fitted to the first batch. The fifty transporter wagons each held three slate wagons, a total capacity of 150, but presumably the small wagons were delayed at

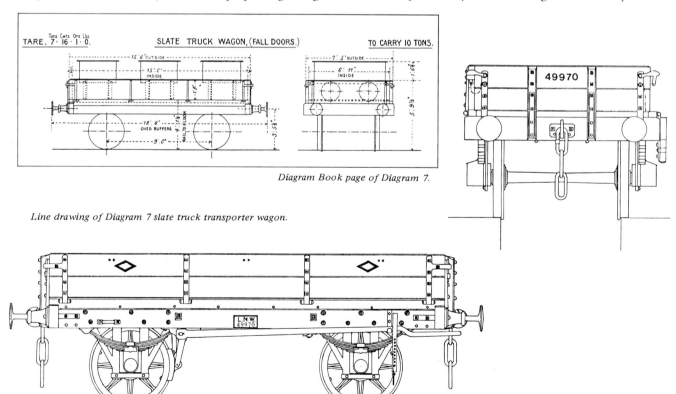

Diagram Book page of Diagram 7.

Line drawing of Diagram 7 slate truck transporter wagon.

each end of the journey by loading and unloading whereas the standard gauge wagons merely went down the line to Deganwy near Llandudno, where the slate in the small wagons had to be painstakingly loaded into waiting ships. In 1898 a further batch of fifty small wagons was made, but this time with wood sides to carry coal to the quarries in the Blaenau Festiniog area.

On the narrow gauge wagons the number plates were of similar style to the standard LNWR wagon number plate but were only 5 inches long by 3½ inches high. They were usually riveted to the solebar, the numberplate being on one side and the builders plate normally on the other. The LMS replaced both plates by new castings to the same design and with the same details, but replacing 'LNW' with 'LMS'. Thus the builders plates proclaimed 'LMS EARLESTOWN 1885'!

Another interesting feature of these plates is that the LMS apparently renumbered the wagons in the 284,000 series, after the LNWR brake vans; ordinary LNWR stock numbers were incremented by 200,000. Because of the batch building, the numbers would almost certainly have run in blocks. There are, however, discrepancies: when the LMS came to apply the renumbering to all 300 wagons surviving at the grouping, many of the wagons were in use at various quarries and some were never found. A few therefore survived with LNWR numberplates. It would appear that the LMS numbers bore no resemblance to the LNWR numbers. The only LNWR number known with any certainty is 158, on a wagon now preserved at Llechwedd Slate Caverns. An example at Padarn has 82 painted on it but this must be subject to doubt. The LMS numbers known are 284465 from the 1887 batch (now in the Talyllyn Railway museum at Towyn); 284526 from a photograph; and 284436, from a privately preserved plate. There is documentary evidence that the full range was numbered 284301–284600 as below.

The late J.P. Richards recalled that when the LMS took over in 1923 all the wagons had migrated onto the Festiniog Railway, so the LMS did not actually have them. Slate from France became cheaper than the Welsh variety in the 1890s and so many of the wagons were never used for their intended traffic over the LNWR but remained in use within the Blaenau Festiniog area for many years.

Illustrations in Appendix 5 show narrow-gauge slate wagons No. 158 and another unnumbered example, both at Llechwedd. This appendix also includes illustrations of the wagons built at Earlestown to carry loco coal for the narrow-gauge locos. They have a single end door for unloading. The underframe is pure LNWR and the side diagonal and vertical straps have a distinctive footing which is identical in design to the slate wagons. Two examples are known to exist in preservation but no running numbers are known.

Known examples of Diagram 7:
Diagram book tare for type: 7.16.1

Number	Buffers	Brakes	Axleboxes
49970	10in 3 bolt	1S	Grease

Known examples of slate wagons:
LNWR numbers: 158
LMS numbers: 284301–284451 built 1887
                     284551–284600 built 1898

An official LNWR photograph of Blaenau Festiniog station and yard, showing a line of Diagram 7 slate truck wagons, each with one side dropped ready to load with slate wagons. The three empty slate wagons in the sixth wagon suggest that the train had arrived from Deganwy and had not yet been fully unloaded. What is not clear from this angle is that raised loading platforms with ramps between the standard gauge tracks brought the narrow gauge wagons up to standard gauge floor level. Since all fifty Diagram 7 wagons were built together as a batch, it is assumed that their running numbers were consecutive, but it is not known whether 49970 was near the start or end of the sequence. From this angle the narrow body, only 7ft 5in wide, is quite obvious. Just visible inside are the tops of some sort of timber to hold the narrow gauge wagons in place, together with pairs of bolts on the outside.

DIAGRAM 8 – OPEN GOODS WAGON WITH 22in SIDES (WEST CUMBERLAND)

Fifty of these were built in 1877 and a further forty followed between then and 1881 for granite sett traffic in the West Cumberland district. They were 16ft long, which was unusual for the period, 7ft 8in wide, and carried ten tons which was also unusual. Indeed, they were the first ten-ton open wagons on the LNWR.

The construction followed that of the Diagram 3 with a 5½in curb rail and a 2½in x 2¾in insert visible at the ends between the end planking and the buffer plank. The sides and ends were two 11in x 3in planks, giving both an internal and external height of 22in. Unique so far as LNWR open wagons are concerned was the 4ft 4in wide door which was fitted to one side only. This may seem a peculiar thing to do, but it must be remembered that at that time most of the company's covered vans (which were the only goods vehicles they had with doors) had doors one side only and goods staff were used to turning individual wagons so that they approached the loading platform the right way round. This is typical of the economical but logical practices of the period adopted throughout the company during the chairmanship of Sir Richard Moon. It was based on the wide availability of wagon turntables and the large, very cheap labour force of the time – circumstances very different to the present day. The Lancashire and Yorkshire followed similar practices.

In the West Cumberland area, many chaldron wagons were still in use in the 1870s. About 1,000 were owned by

Photographs of Diagram 8 wagons are rare and poor in quality. This and the following illustrations have had to be copied from prints and greatly enlarged. Here we see the body of a Diagram 8 photographed at Harrington Ironworks, on the Cumbrian coast between Whitehaven and Workington. This was very much in the working area for this Diagram. It was taken across a stone wall which unfortunately blocks off everything below the curb rail. The enlargement is indistinct but does at least show the door and strapping. Note the 'For Works to Works Traffic' in script on the single side fall door.
CTY. RON ALLISON

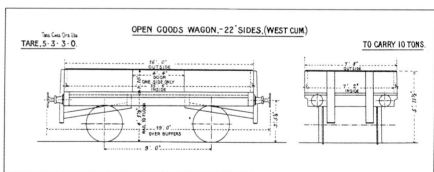

Diagram Book page of Diagram 8.

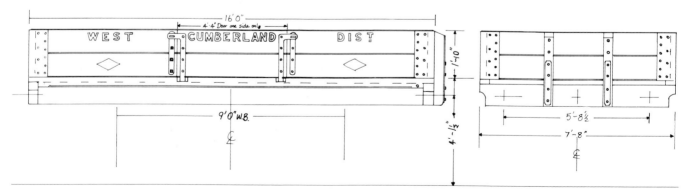

Line drawing of Diagram 8 open wagon.

the LNWR itself. Indeed, the initial batch of Diagram 8 wagons was built to replace 100 ageing chaldrons. In common with other railways, these wagons had larger section end stanchions which were extended downwards below the buffer plank and strengthened by diagonal timbers back to the central transoms. These acted as buffers for the small chaldron wagons, but as they fell out of use, so the extensions were removed. A single wooden brake block was fitted, probably not upgraded throughout their lives. Scrapping

began in the mid-1890s and the last one went in 1918. Because of this, alas, there is only the one photograph positively identified (page 76, left) or an official drawing of a Diagram 8 wagon.

Known examples of Diagram 8:
Diagram book tare for type: 5.3.3

Number	Tare
1234	5.3.3

The second wagon in this shot of Low Gill station, looking north in 1898, is believed to have been a loaded stone wagon to Diagram 8. The Webb 0–6–0 engine was photographed before leaving the low-level platform with an Ingleton branch freight. Notice the framing of the D32 van, fifth behind the engine, was clearly a darker grey than the body sides, as sometimes then seen on brake vans. Note also the monstrous load under the tarpaulin on the third wagon.   CTY. MIKE WILLIAMS

This over-enlargement is believed to show a Diagram 8 stone wagon, which had 22in sides and doors on one side only. The white mark on the side certainly looks like an LNWR diamond symbol, and the buffer stocks look like LNWR three-bolt, although the photograph is not very clear. The lack of number on the end is, however, curious and casts a little doubt on our identification.
CTY. H. GORDON TIDEY
(T5007)

DIAGRAM 9 – OPEN GOODS WAGON WITH 36in SIDES & DOORS EACH SIDE

The first Diagram 9 wagons were a handful built in 1884 for the Garston, Widnes and St. Helens area. The exact purpose for these 36in-side, 10-ton wagons is unclear but it seems that at least some were used to carry cloth from Leeds and surrounding areas to the docks. Others were probably used to carry sand.

A further fifty were built in 1885 and they continued to be built in small numbers until superseded by specially built Diagram 84 wagons in 1907. In 1920 the remaining 300 or so were integrated with the standard Diagram 9 wagons described later. By that date, cloth was presumably being carried in covered vans. It must be remembered, of course, that the original 1884 examples pre-dated Diagram 4 by nine years. The main dimensions and construction methods were the same as Diagram 4 but they had longer journals of 8in x 3¾in, needed to allow loads of ten tons.

Forty-five more Diagram 9 wagons were built in 1896, followed by fifty-five in 1897, all specifically for stone traffic in the Yorkshire district.

By 1902, the seven-ton payload of the standard Diagram 4 wagon was becoming inadequate for general merchandise and 262 more wagons to Diagram 9 were built in the second half of that year. These were the same as described above and no further seven-ton Diagram 4 vehicles were built after 1903. Production of Diagram 9 wagons continued at a similarly fast rate as had those to Diagram 4, and by the time they were superseded by the 18ft Diagram 84 in 1907, over 9,000 had been built.

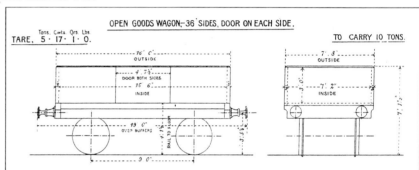

Diagram Book page of Diagram 9.

Diagram 9 No. 49311 is shown here in typical working condition. In this view the grease axleboxes, with 'No. 2' in their centres and dated 1904, are noticeably wider than those used on 7-ton wagons, which presumably had the No. 1 axlebox. This vehicle evidently had the usual 10in buffer stocks whilst the brake lever, vee hanger and brake rack had been outlined with chalk, most likely to make the photograph clearer. Perhaps the figures on the number plate were painted for the same purpose. The pre-1908 livery of diamonds only has almost disappeared beneath the dirt, suggesting the wagon had not been repainted for some time. Indeed, one cannot even see where the tare weight was, let alone read it! In spite of the wooden brake block on the D32 roof door van in the left background, the photograph was probably taken just postwar. NATIONAL RAILWAY MUSEUM (ETN 92)

Diagram 9 wagon No. 19162 was one of many seconded to the Army during the First World War, who had allocated it WD No. 36374. The additional 'tent' had been built on low triangular end planks bolted above the normal end top plank. The blocks on the roof doors supported it flat when open. The tare was 5.16.1 and other features to note are the possibly superfluous sheet ties on the ends, second plank from the top; horse staple, on the solebar under the tare; grease boxes; cranked brake lever, with the grip painted a lighter colour; double brakes; screw couplings and 3-bolt buffers with wooden pads to match the extra length of screw couplings, but no brake piping. Note the front face of the spring hanger blocks were painted body colour.
NATIONAL RAILWAY MUSEUM

From the early 1900s the remaining Diagram 4 wagons began to be upgraded to Diagram 9 and this added a further 9,000 to stock by 1920. In 1911, with so many 10-ton wagons available, it became unnecessary to segregate those earlier examples built for stone traffic and all became available for general merchandise. The Diagram 11 vehicle described later in this chapter was also rebuilt into a Diagram 9.

It is likely that all Diagram 9 wagons including the earliest had an iron pushrod brake from new. Most would have had them fitted to both sides. Some of the later conversions received oil-type axleboxes with 9in x 4in journals and springs with eight plates 4in x ½in. These later conversions probably always had double brakes, often on both sides.

The history of Diagram 9 became more interesting during the war. A total of 950 were modified to have pitched roofs with doors, rather like a salt wagon, and were used to carry grain. These and a number of standard open wagons, including more to Diagram 9, were sent overseas. These and all the War Department vehicles will be more fully described in the appropriate volume. The number left to pass into LMS ownership in 1923 was 18,159.

Finally, there are some wagons which, whilst not strictly to this Diagram, were not listed separately in the 1903 Diagram Book and it is convenient to deal with them here. In late 1904, sixty-six 'Express Traffic' wagons were built. They were similar to a Diagram 9 except for longer 4ft springs with shackles and flat-fronted oil axleboxes. Twenty-two of them were fully fitted with a horizontal vacuum cylinder, and eight had block clasp brakes and screw couplings. The other forty-four were similar again, but through piped rather than fully fitted. Piped-only wagons had their stand pipes painted red. All sixty-six were still in service on formation of the LMS in 1923.

WD No. 36369 shows an Army D9 with the tent roof raised, showing internal partitioning inside. The pin rack was of the type bent up from a single strip, and shaped to form a hook for the brake lever. **NATIONAL RAILWAY MUSEUM (ETN 111A)**

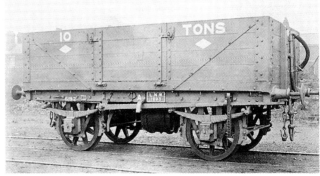

A fully-fitted Diagram 9 wagon, captured by the official Earlestown photographer when brand new in 1904. Points of note include screw couplings, solebar flitch plates, 3 x 3 corner plates, small V-hangers instead of cast trunnions, side chains, 4ft springs with shackles, 8-block clasp brakes, double-acting horizontal vacuum brake cylinder with lever and quadrant on the solebar. The handbrake was operated by simply bearing against the back of one brake block. Both axlebox covers bore the date 1904 and the paint date reads 8/04. By this date several of the new 18ft wagons had been built and would soon become the standard size for LNWR wagons.
REAL PHOTOGRAPHS (R8418)

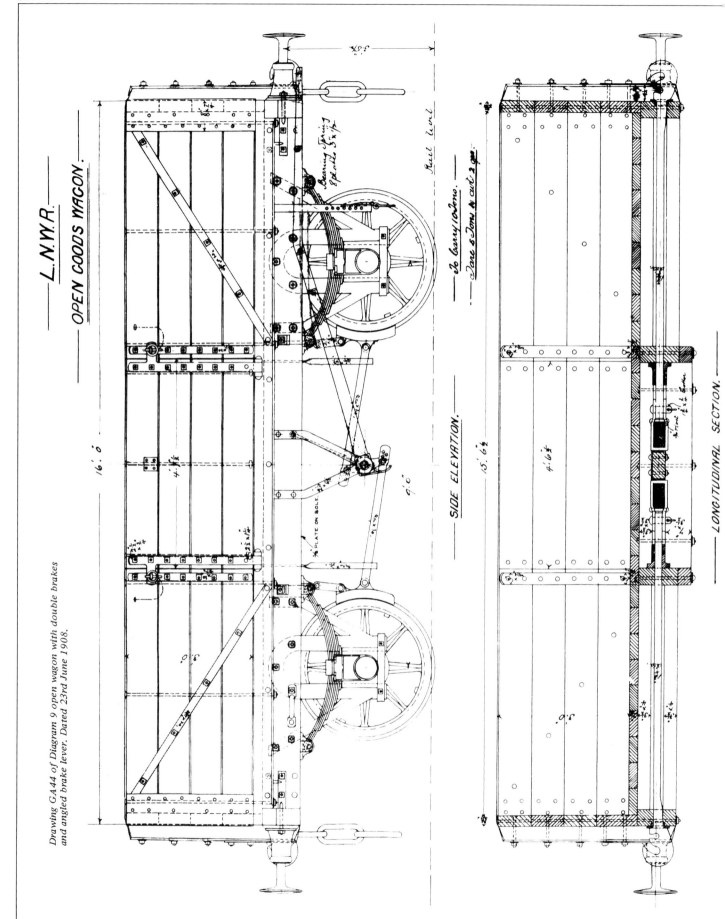

L.N.Y.R.

OPEN GOODS WAGON.

SIDE ELEVATION.

LONGITUDINAL SECTION.

Drawing GA44 of Diagram 9 open wagon with double brakes and angled brake lever. Dated 23rd June 1908.

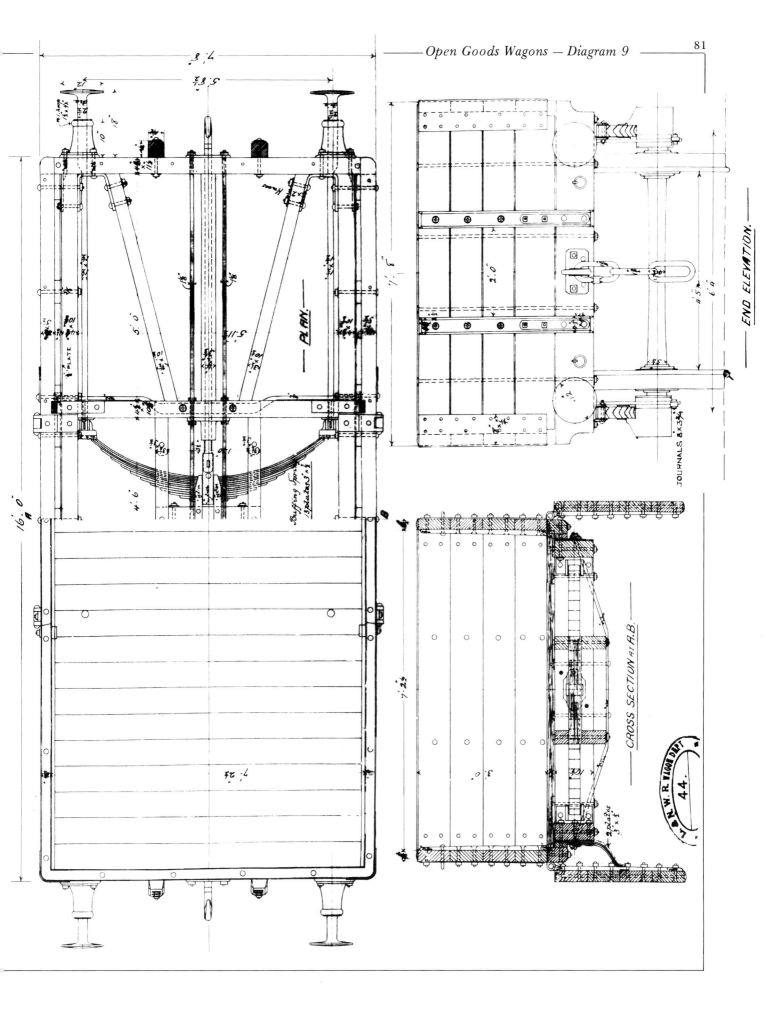

PLAN.

END ELEVATION.

JOURNALS 8×3¾

CROSS SECTION AT A.B.

L&N.W.R. WAGON DEPT.
44.

An interesting development took place in July 1904 when plans were drawn up for an open wagon with steel underframe. This was not a new concept, for the LNWR had built 20-ton steel wagons in 1902, albeit for special traffic (loco coal). The Southern Division had had various iron wagons in the 1850s including gunpowder vans.

The new drawing was for a merchandise wagon and the body was identical to a Diagram 9. All the running gear was also the same including axleboxes, journals, 10in buffers, wheels, springs and double brakes both sides. The underframe had 9in x 3in channel solebars and buffer beams, with 3½in x 6in angle cross members and diagonals. The drawing is very detailed *but it is not known whether any were actually built.* No separate diagram number was allocated, but so far as the traffic departments were concerned, they would have been identical to Diagram 9 and probably included within that number.

No. 4076 was one of only forty-four Diagram 9 wagons built with a through vacuum pipe. The springs were clearly longer than those on a standard Diagram 9 and were mounted on hangers. Although the axleboxes were dated 1895 and 1904, we know that all of these wagons were built in 1904 so presumably a secondhand axlebox cover had been fitted at some time. This shows why these covers cannot be relied upon to correctly date a wagon. The paint date reads 8/09. It had 3 x 3 corner plates and, presumably, solebar flitch plates. The reason for double striker plates being fitted to the door is nicely shown here. If the door had been dropped smartly enough, the sprung door stop would have flexed sufficiently for the door planks to strike the brake cross-shaft — which has left a dent between the first and second planks. In spite of the vacuum pipe, screw couplings and side chains, the buffer stocks were still only 10in long. When 18ft wagons were introduced a few years later, the fitted versions were given longer buffers.
NATIONAL RAILWAY MUSEUM (ETN 50)

This photograph is from a series taken at Stafford to illustrate how not to load a wagon. In this case the load of steel round bar or tubes, although perhaps not above the permitted payload of ten tons, had been loaded in such a way that their entire weight was taken at the very ends of the wagon, which had consequently broken its back. Presumably the wagons at either end were acting as runners. A special flat wagon should have been used instead, something like a Diagram 14, or even a pair of timber wagons. Diagram 9 No. 68533 was built in about 1900 and is probably shown here in as-built condition unless it had been uprated from Diagram 4. The livery was post-1908 LNWR with diamonds. The low tare weight of 5.5.3 reflects the simple pushrod brakes fitted to both sides and the lighter grease axleboxes. The left-hand axlebox had been overfilled, leaving fat marks down the front. Details of the three-bolt buffer stock show up well, as do the corner plate rivets, quite different from the bolts with square nuts seen on the wagon to the left (a Diagram 84). This picture nicely shows the different pattern of the rivets/bolts which is a good rule of thumb to help identification of the wagon length: older wagons had four bolts through the top and bottom planks, three on other planks, whereas generally 18ft wagons had three bolts to each plank. Notice the striker plates screwed to the door, one for the sprung door stop bolted to the solebar and the other for the brake cross-shaft which, most unusually, was riveted over in place of the usual square shaft with split pin, or was possibly a bolt with square shank, rather like a coach bolt. Due to the unstable load, a 'not to go' label had been pasted at the left of the bottom plank.

Known examples of Diagram 9:

Diagram Book tare for type: 5.17.1

Number	Tare	Buffers	Brakes	Axleboxes	Notes
1893	6.19.2	1oin 3-bolt	SBBS	Flat	Vac fitted
4076	6.10.2	1oin 3-bolt	DBBS	Flat	Piped
4853	5.9.2		SBBS	Grease	
5034		1oin 3-bolt	DBBS	Grease	W.D.Grain
8087	6.3.7	1oin 3-bolt	DBBS	Grease	
19162		1oin 3-bolt	DBBS	Grease	W.D.Grain
21371	5.12.2	1oin 3-bolt	DBBS	Grease	
21379		1oin 3-bolt	DBBS	Grease	
23959	6.4.1		DBBS	Bulbous	
23968	6.4.1	1oin 3-bolt	DBBS	Bulbous	
33526					used for sawdust
37153	5.11.0	1oin 3-bolt	DBBS	Grease	
43649	5.19.1		DB1S	Grease	
44772	5.13.0	1oin 3-bolt	DBBS	Carriage	
49311		1oin 3-bolt	DBBS	Grease	
67773	6.2.0		DBBS	Oil	
68553	5.5.3	1oin 3-bolt	Pushrod BS	Grease	
68921	5.12.3		SBBS	Grease	
70228	6.5.2		DBBS	Bulbous	

This picture shows how difficult it can be to guess the date of a photograph. Double brakes both sides, bulbous axleboxes of the final pattern, most corner plate rivets replaced by bolts, spring hangers of the final type bolted through the face of the solebars and very late 'dropped' keeper plates all suggest that this photograph of No. 23959 (tare 6.4.1) was taken in the 1920s, and indeed we know that it was taken in 1923. The surprise is that in spite of all these alterations, it still carried pre-1908 livery and had presumably been only patch-painted for at least 15 years. CTY. J. P. RICHARDS

A typical Diagram 9 as running in the later LNWR period. This picture of No. 37153, with a tare of 5.11.0, shows the final livery of 'LNWR' with no diamonds, but with '10 TONS' painted on the side. Since all lettering looks equally clean, it is likely that the wagon was repainted when the load capacity was painted on, c.1920-23. This wagon retained grease axleboxes, although many had oil boxes by that date.
CTY. J. P. RICHARDS

A companion view to that on page 56, showing bad loading of wagons, but also conveniently showing details of the wagon concerned. In this case it appears to have been a set-piece, perhaps arranged and photographed for staff training purposes. Diagram 9 No. 44772 is shown here with barrels loosely standing on the floor and not restrained in any way. The view through the open wagon door shows how rough the floor planking had become. The heads of bolts holding the strapping on can be seen countersunk into the boards forming the door. This was usually the case in order to present a smooth inside face to the entire wagon. Protruding bolt heads and nuts could cause damage to fragile packings, collect the residue of loose loads and jar the arm of anyone shovelling out the contents if caught with the blade of a shovel. Oil axleboxes with pointed covers can be seen, with brakes both sides. The tare is 5.13.0.

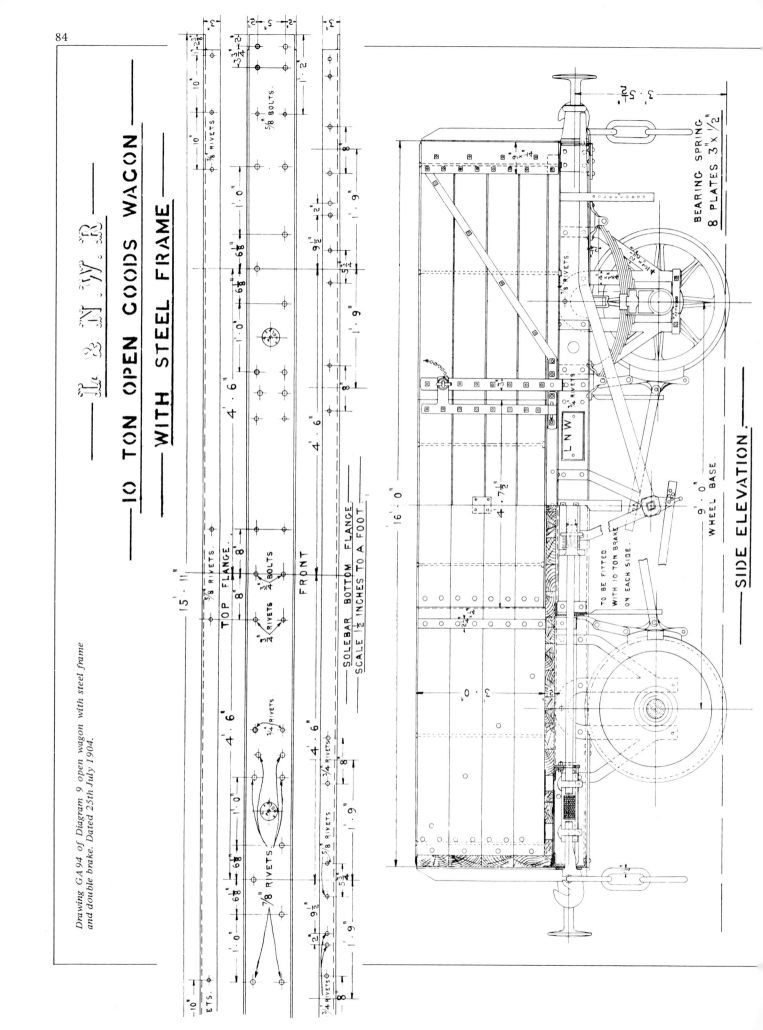

L & N W R

— 10 TON OPEN GOODS WAGON —

— WITH STEEL FRAME —

Drawing GA 94 of Diagram 9 open wagon with steel frame and double brake. Dated 25th July 1904.

SOLEBAR BOTTOM FLANGE.
SCALE 1½ INCHES TO A FOOT.

FRONT

BEARING SPRING
8 PLATES 3" x ½"

— SIDE ELEVATION. —

9' 0" WHEEL BASE.

TO BE FITTED
WITH 10 TON BRAKE
ON EACH SIDE.

L N W R

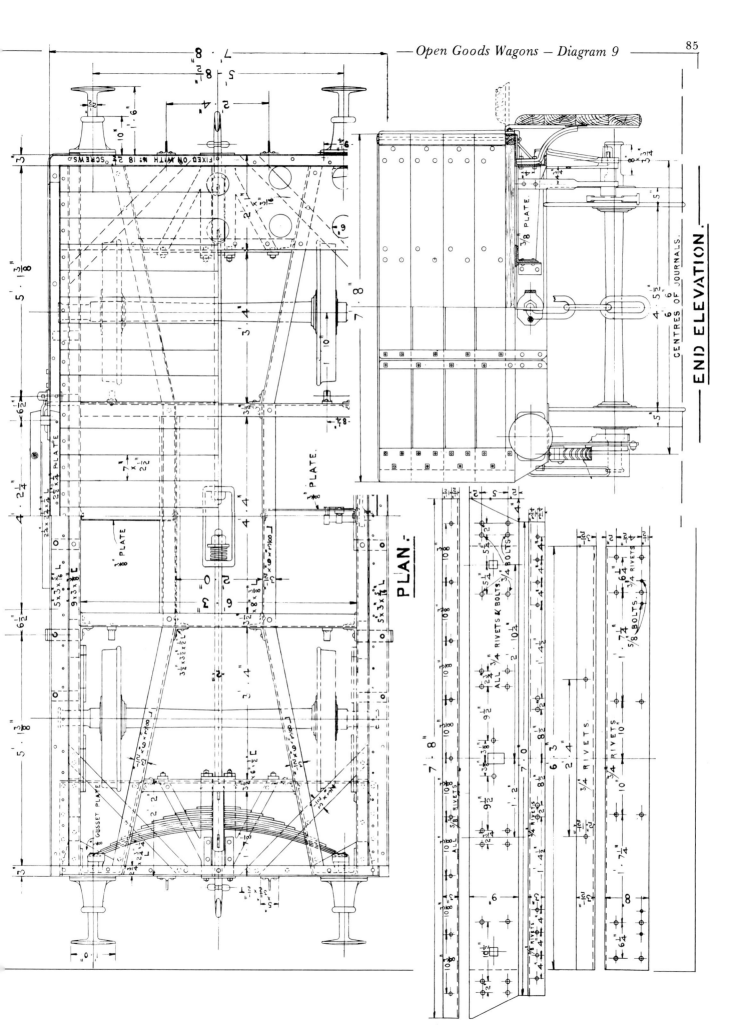

PLAN.

END ELEVATION.

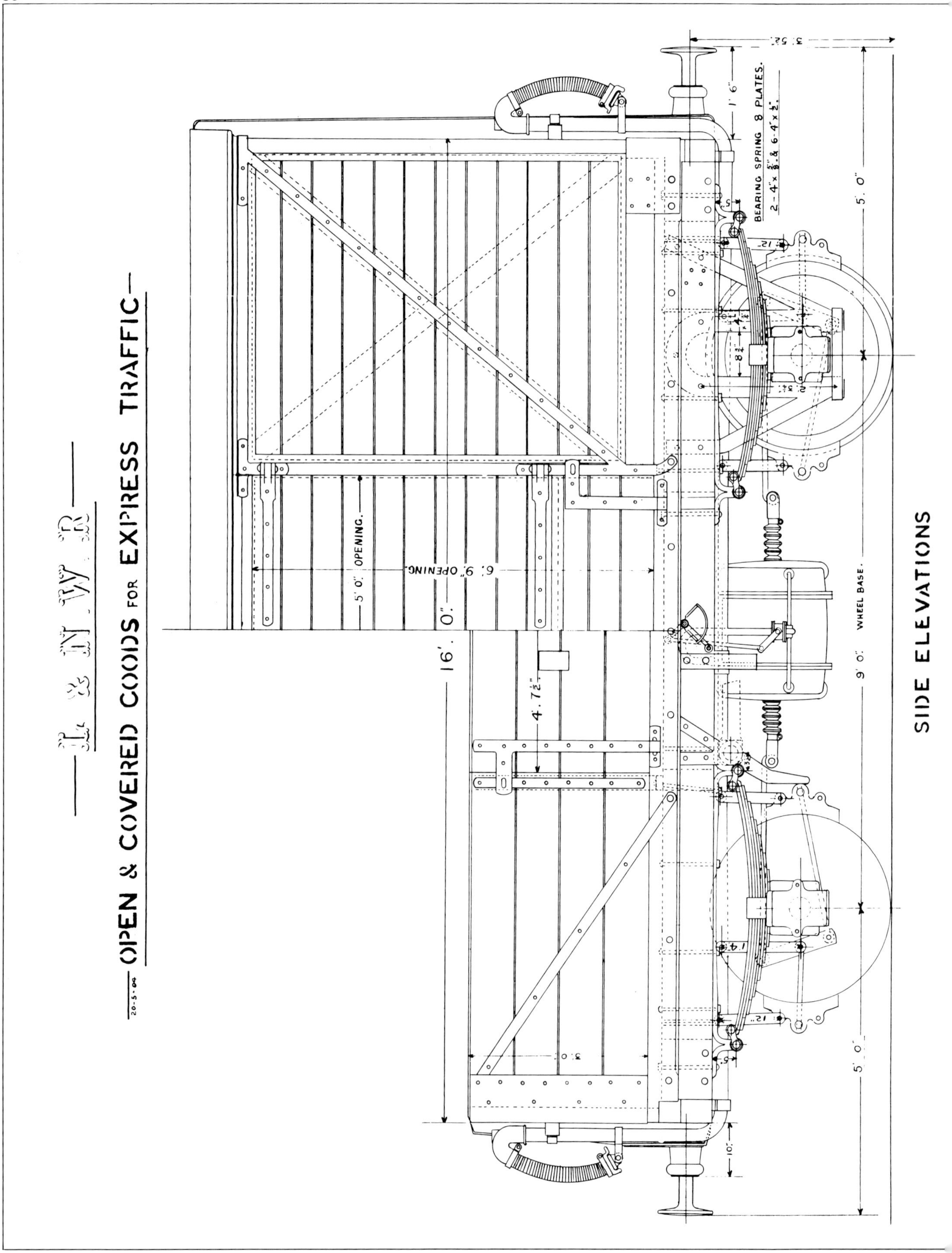
L & N W R
OPEN & COVERED GOODS FOR EXPRESS TRAFFIC
20-5-04
SIDE ELEVATIONS
BEARING SPRING 8 PLATES.
2 - 4" x 5/8" & 6 - 4" x 1/2"
16' 0"
6' 9" OPENING.
5' 0" OPENING.
4' 7 1/2"
9' 0" WHEEL BASE.
5' 0"
5' 0"
1' 6"
3' 5 1/2"
10"

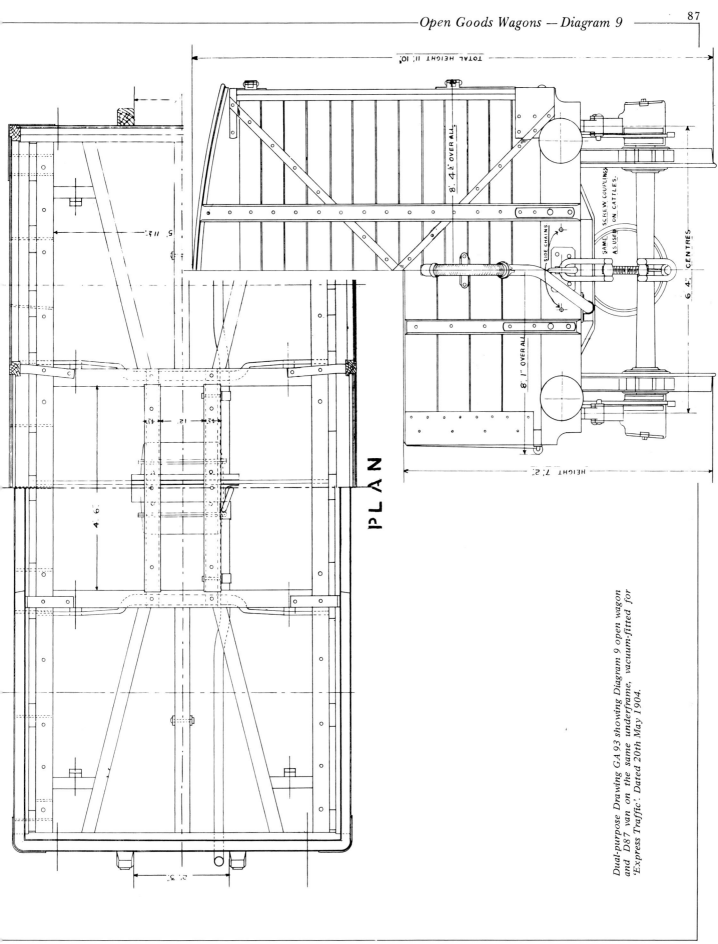

TOTAL HEIGHT 11' 10"

8' 4½" OVER ALL

5' 11"

SIDE CHAINS

SAME SCREW COUPLINGS AS USED ON CATTLES.

6' 4" CENTRES

8' 1" OVER ALL

HEIGHT 7' 2"

4' 6"

12"   4½"

5' 3"

PLAN

END ELEVATIONS

Dual-purpose Drawing GA 93 showing Diagram 9 open wagon and D87 van on the same underframe, vacuum-fitted for 'Express Traffic'. Dated 20th May 1904.

DIAGRAM 10 – OPEN GOODS WAGON WITH 42in SIDES & DOORS EACH SIDE

Encouraged by their larger loading gauge, the American and Continental railways built larger wagons. By the turn of the century, forty-ton bogie wagons had appeared in large numbers and four-wheelers of twenty and twenty-five tons were in use abroad. In Britain, some railways began to experiment with larger wagons for special traffic, notably the GNR with bogie brick wagons, the MR and the GCR, but also the North Eastern Railway who were leading advocates of the 'ton mileage' system.

From the railways point of view, larger wagons meant the same load could be carried by less tare weight and on fewer axles. The traders had other views. Many of them had yards and unloading facilities laid out for six- and seven-ton wagons and they did not want larger vehicles. The matter was even raised at the half-yearly meeting of shareholders in February 1903 where Lord Stalbridge was pressed to extend the use of larger capacity wagons and adopt the 'ton mileage' system. The LNWR eventually did this from 1st January 1913.

Diagram 10 was introduced with two experimental wagons built in late 1901. Forty-eight more were built in 1902 for sand traffic in the St. Helens area and thirty-eight more in 1903, of which at least five were for limestone traffic and six for the West Cumberland District. They were 18ft long,

7ft 8in wide, as before, but with a 10ft wheelbase. The sides and ends were from three 11in x 3in planks with the top, fourth, plank being 9in x 3in. Both upper frame knee bolts continued onto the curb rail.

This gave a nominal height of 42in, and was thus almost one third larger in cubic capacity than a standard 16ft wagon. The floor of 7in x 2½in boards extended over the buffer planks and was covered by the usual 2¾in x 2½in strip. Doors, 4ft 10½in wide outside, 4ft 10in clear opening, were fitted each side and 10in x 5in journals running in square, flat-fronted oil axleboxes gave a payload of 20 tons. The springs were stiffened up to eleven plates 4in x ⅛in. The solebars were faced with a ⅛in flitch plate to add strength and this feature was subsequently used on all 18ft wagons.

To cope with the extra load, the usual split spoke wheels were replaced by 10-spoke wrought-iron ones, still 3ft 1½in diameter. They had 3-bolt buffers with 10in stocks. Brakes were on one side only and similar to the double brakes of the earlier 15ft 6in coal wagons (Diagram 53) with curved handles.

These were unusual in having round-section pushrods, no doubt developed from the single brakes which always had round pushrods. They proved to be too weak and were soon replaced by the later, double flat pushrods.

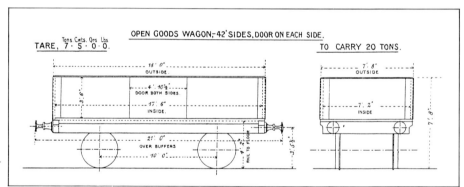

Diagram Book page of Diagram 10.

No. 71604 was one of the first fifty Diagram 10 wagons built, and was photographed at Earlestown when new in 1902. Features of this era, and this batch in particular, include corner plate rivets in 4, 3, 3, 4 formation, 10in buffer stocks, square-fronted axleboxes (bearing the date 1902), short-lived round brake pushrods and handed, single-ended brake blocks. The wheels had ten solid spokes, whereas generally wagons of ten tons capacity or less had wheels with eight split spokes. The positioning of the diamonds and script giving the payload were entirely normal for the period.

REAL PHOTOGRAPHS
(R8403)

A further batch of twelve were built in 1910 incorporating many detail changes which had been introduced during the intervening seven years. These included thinner, 2⅜in timber for the sides and ends with a 7ft 10in outside width, self-contained buffers, brakes both sides with later-type cranked handles as Diagram 84, and other minor details. It is thought that this batch had springs with only seven plates 4in x ⅜in.

A final batch of fifty was built in 1912 to the later design except that 13in single-rib buffers were used instead of the self-contained type.

The St. Helens sand traffic for glassmaking had been carried by 10-ton Diagram 9 wagons and it was logical that the new wagons to Diagram 10 should be used for this traffic too. Some received canvas flaps over the axleguards to keep dirt and grit out of the bearings. They were also used, as mentioned above, for limestone from Buxton and in the West Cumberland District. One early casualty from the 1912 batch was scrapped in 1921 but the remaining 149 still existed in 1923.

Known examples of Diagram 10:
Diagram book tare for type: 7.5.0

Built on Revenue A/c in 1903, no further details known:

2331	10780	23402
2891	16288	33490
5105	18425	35678
6182	18429	36778
7174	21709	36930
9266	22035	46498

Number	Tare	Buffers	Brakes	Axleboxes	Notes
26579	7.15.0	Self cont.	DBBS	Flat	Canvas flaps
47418	7.9.2	1 rib	DB??	Flat	
71331–71332	–	–	–	–	built 1901 Capital A/c
71595–71603	–	–	–	–	built 1902 Capital A/c
71604	7.6.0	10in 3-bolt	DB1S	Flat	built 1902 Capital A/c
71605–71614	–	–	–	–	built 1902 Capital A/c
72340–72367	–	–	–	–	built 1902 Capital A/c
72378–72397	–	–	–	–	built 1903 Capital A/c

No. 26579 is believed to have been from the small batch of ten Diagram 10 wagons built in 1910. It shows many changes from the previous picture: corner plate bolts are now in the 3, 3, 3, 3 formation; self-contained buffers; canvas flaps for keeping ash and dirt from the springs; and normal double brakes both sides. The paint date reads 4/13, but the reason for taking a photograph three years after the wagon was built is unclear. By this date the flat-fronted axleboxes were soon to be superseded, and the last examples carried no date, as seen here. Notice also the flat steel brackets appearing beneath the solebar just outboard of the door and fixed beneath the curb rail close to the body knees. These brackets were first introduced on the new 18ft wagons about 1907.

NATIONAL RAILWAY MUSEUM (ETN 91A)

Diagram 10 No. 47418 photographed c.1923 at Earlestown displays what appears to have been newly-applied LNWR lettering and enormous '20 TONS'. This was from the final batch with single-ribbed buffer stocks. The steel plate on the bottom plank at the right was lettered 'To be returned to / Port ??? Liverpool' and this was therefore presumably one of the many Diagram 10 wagons allocated for sand traffic to St. Helens. The photographs give little indication of the size of these 20-ton wagons, but note that the sides were almost as high as the 'Andrew Knowles' private owner wagon next to it, even though the latter had six planks!

CTY. J. P. RICHARDS

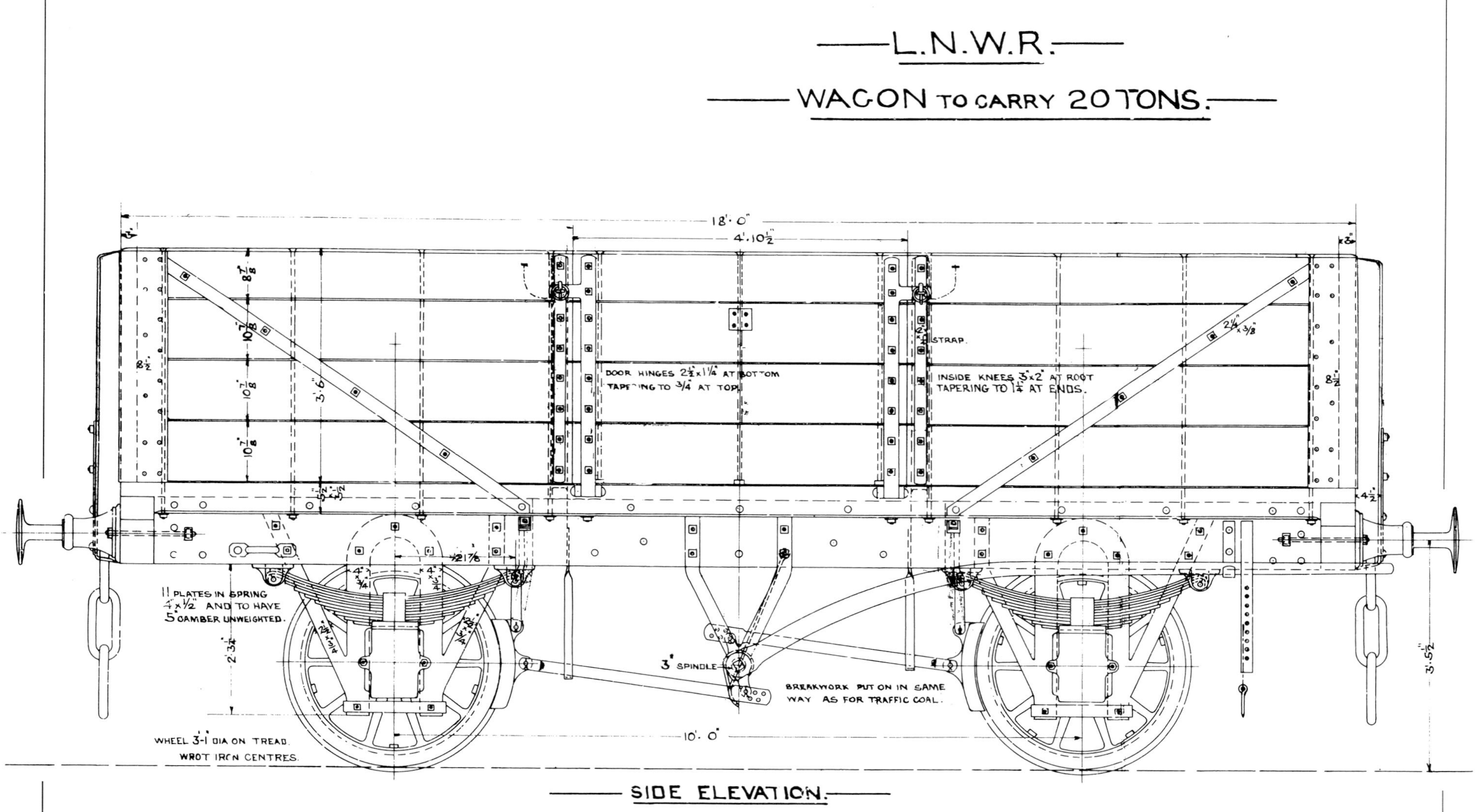

L.N.W.R.

WAGON TO CARRY 20 TONS.

Drawing GA63 of Diagram 10 20-ton open wagon, with double brakes and curved brake lever, dated 20th August 1901.

SIDE ELEVATION.

INSIDE KNEES 3×2" AT ROOT TAPERING TO 1¼ AT ENDS.

DOOR HINGES 2¾×1¼ AT BOTTOM TAPERING TO 3/4 AT TOP.

BREAKWORK PUT ON IN SAME WAY AS FOR TRAFFIC COAL.

3" SPINDLE

11 PLATES IN SPRING 4"×½" AND TO HAVE 5 CAMBER UNWEIGHTED.

WHEEL 3'-1 DIA ON TREAD.
WROT IRON CENTRES.

18'.0"

10'.0"

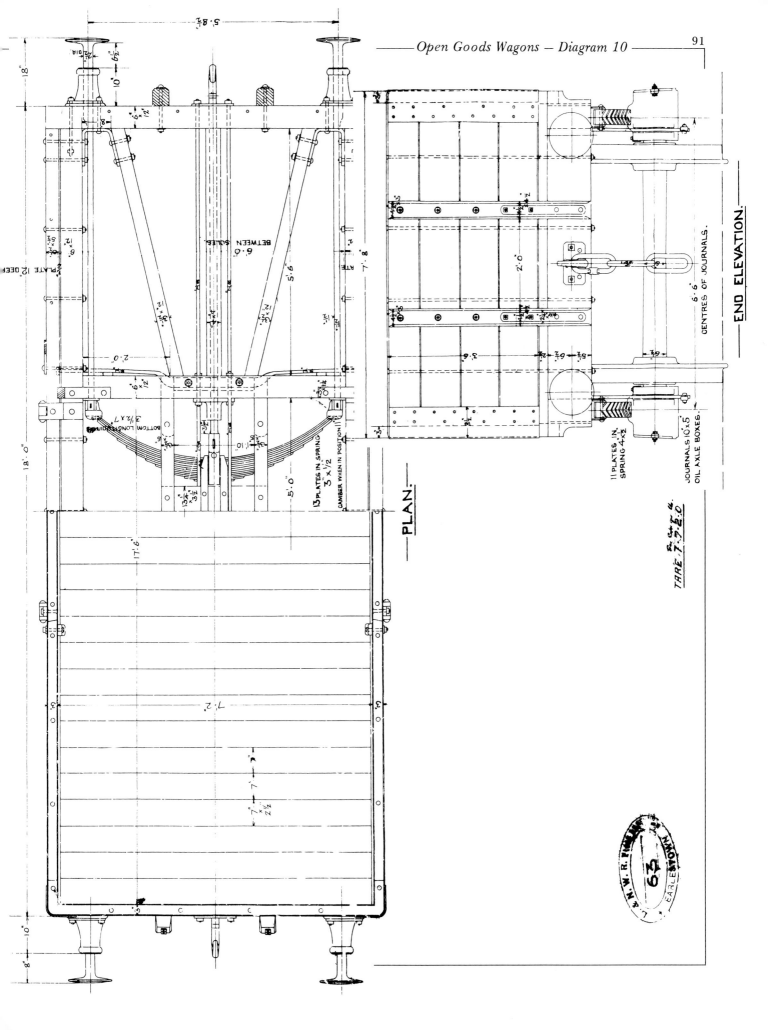

—END ELEVATION.—

—PLAN.—

TARE. 7. 7. 2. 0

Drawing GA85 of Diagram 11 open wagon, dated 27th October 1903.

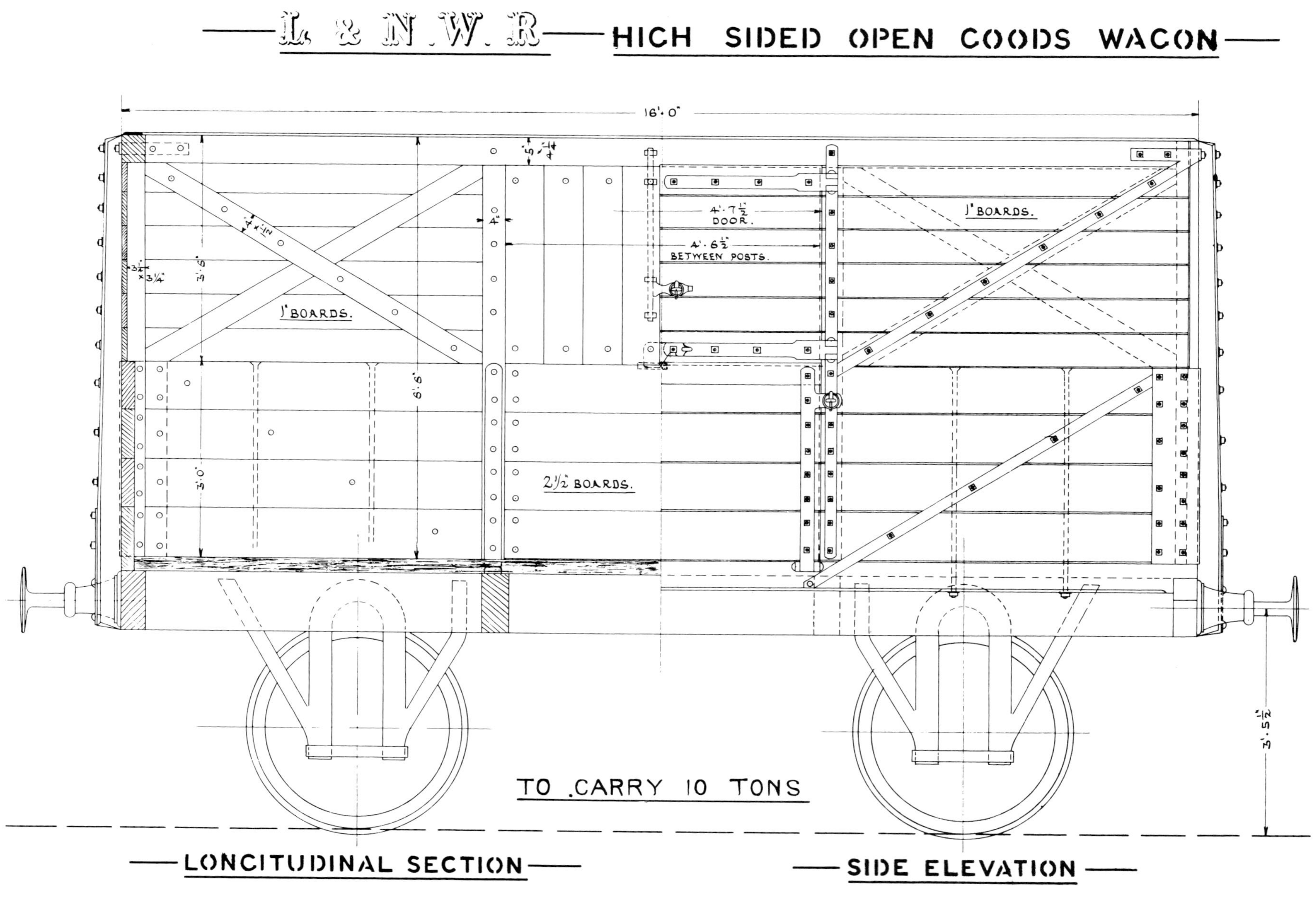

L & N.W.R — HIGH SIDED OPEN GOODS WAGON —

— SIDE ELEVATION —

TO CARRY 10 TONS

— LONGITUDINAL SECTION —

1' BOARDS.

2½ BOARDS.

4'.7½" DOOR.

4'.6½" BETWEEN POSTS

1' BOARDS.

16'.0"

3'.5½"

DIAGRAM 11 – HIGH SIDED OPEN GOODS WAGON

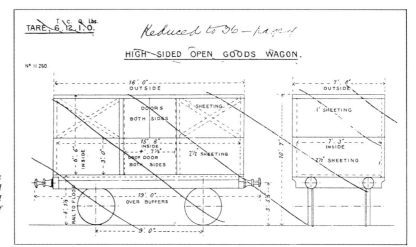

Diagram Book page of Diagram 11. This shows the page after the wagon was reduced to 36in sides, becoming a Diagram 9, and this Diagram deleted. The original is, of course, seen as struck out.

Diagram 11 consisted of only one wagon, No. 11260. It was a 16ft x 7ft 8in 10-ton, four-plank wagon with 36in sides, apparently just like a Diagram 9 except that for an unknown reason, the sides were only 2½in thick. On top of the sides and ends six 6in x 1in boards were supported by 3¼in square framing in the corners and 4in x 1½in criss-cross framing inside with diagonal strapping outside. This gave an overall height of 6ft 6in inside. A conventional 4ft 7½in door was fitted each side. It had 10in 3-bolt buffers and almost certainly grease type axleboxes with 8in x 3¾in journals. The brakegear is unknown.

Very little else is known except that it was probably used to carry empty barrels. Other railways, including the Midland, built wagons especially for empty barrels which were carried in two layers. Competition for the Burton traffic may have persuaded the LNWR to try the idea itself, but this is unproven. This would explain why the tops of the doors were radiused from the inside, so that a barrel would not have to be lifted over the thickness of the door when open, but could be rolled up the slope. The top of the door was wrapped in steel for protection.

No. 11260 was built in late 1903 and before 1909 the upper boarding had been removed, making it into a standard Diagram 9 except for the slightly thinner boarding. Its short life has all the appearance of a trial or prototype that proceeded no further. Regrettably, we have no information to do other than speculate on why this came to be the case.

Only example: No. 11260, tare 6.12.1

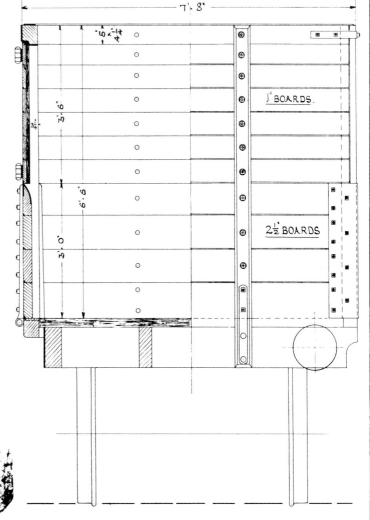

CROSS SECTION —END ELEVATION

DIAGRAM 84 – OPEN GOODS WAGON

The next step in the quest for increased payload came in 1904 when, following the retirement of J.W. Emmett the previous year, the new wagon superintendent, H.D. Earl, increased the standard length of goods stock to 18ft. The width was also increased to 7ft 10in and the wheelbase to 9ft 9in. It is believed that the wheelbase was kept at this figure and not increased to 10ft or more to avoid replacing the many wagon turntables then in use. The wagons still carried ten tons. Two experimental wagons were built early in 1904 and were followed by batches of twelve later that year, then sixty-six early in 1905. These appeared on the first available page of the then new wagon Diagram Book, becoming known as Diagram 84.

They closely followed the design of Diagram 9, with four 9in x 3in planks forming the sides. The ends had the bottom plank increased in width to 11in to mask the 7in x 2½in floor planking which was rebated ½in over the buffer planks. The side doors were increased to 4ft 9½in external width with the angled opening previously described. All had double brakes both sides, grease-type axleboxes and 3-bolt buffers possibly with 10in stocks at first, but certainly 13in later. The journals were the standard 8in x 3¾in. The springs had eight plates, 4in x ½in, and the corner plates always had three bolts in each plank.

In 1907, building of new wagons to Diagram 9 finally ceased and Diagram 84 wagons began to appear in volume

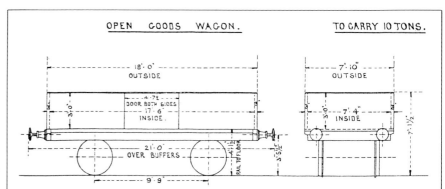

Diagram Book page of Diagram 84.

Diagram 84 was a logical development of the 16ft predecessors and the last high-sided open wagon design of the LNWR. They were built in vast quantities over a period of almost 20 years, yet detail differences were minor. Here we see No. 33550, photographed to show the new livery which, in this case, was painted in 8/09. Oil-filled axleboxes, double brakes both sides, solebar flitch plates and three bolts in each plank at the corner plates were to remain standard features throughout, continuing to the end of the company's separate existence. The axleboxes read 'LNWR', although others of the type read 'L&NW', whilst some early examples also included a date. The wagon appears to have been new and the original print reveals the LNWR's affinity for stamping or casting its initials into everything possible, including the brake blocks, brake lever and rack, axleboxes, and indeed probably every other metal component. LNWR SOCIETY (106)

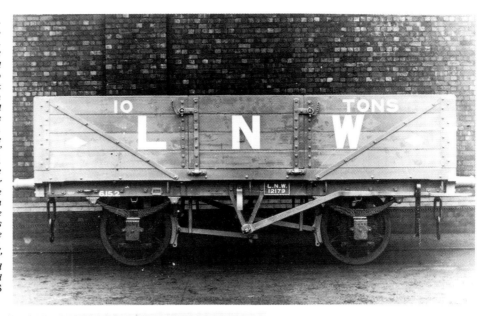

*This curiosity has caused heated discussion amongst LNW enthusiasts for many years. The wagon was a Diagram 84 bearing a paint date of 12/07. Prior to 1908 the standard LNWR livery for high-sided open wagons was '10 TONS' on the top plank and two diamonds on the plank below, which can still be made out on the photograph. It has been suggested that the official photographer, who was very experienced at 'doctoring' negatives, painted out the diamonds and added the lettering in order to seek the Directors' approval. However, the edges of the 'N', in particular, can be seen to waver at the joints between the boards in a manner consistent with parallax, whilst the striker plate on the door has cast a shadow across the letter which would be difficult and unnecessary to fake. It is the opinion of the authors that the wagon was actually painted as shown, probably for the purposes of Directors' approval, but perhaps never entered traffic until repainted in the revised LNWR style.*COLLECTION A. G. ELLIS

No. 75919 was built by C. A. Roberts & Co. of Wakefield in 1912, as part of an order of 100 which in turn was part of an order for a thousand built by five different contractors. This was the first time that the company had purchased a large order from external contractors. It is a later example of Diagram 84 with pointed axlebox fronts and single-rib buffer stocks. The axlebox casting appears to have been the same as that used for the flat-fronted type, but the pointed-front casting incorporated a spring-loaded lift-up lid which made access for oiling easier, cleaner and faster. Access to the bearing and pad necessitated removal of the entire front. The white-painted tyres were, of course, only for the photograph. Perhaps less obvious are the spring shoes which were to a later pattern, now bolting through the face of the solebar. The drawplates changed at about this time also, becoming more square and with a steel bracket to prevent the coupling links being lifted off. Perhaps theft or borrowing and misplacing of coupling links had become commonplace. The tare weight was 6-14-3.

right up to 1921, but these differed slightly from the 1904-05 examples. The main difference was in the design of the underframe which included increasing the width between solebars from 5ft 11½in to 6ft 1in. This was probably to provide clearance for larger, 9in x 4in journals with oil-type axleboxes which were used from late that year and became the standard thereafter. The payload remained at ten tons. The other main difference was an increased door width to 5ft outside, 4ft 11in clear opening.

From 1907, the new 18ft wagons began to replace those Diagram 9 examples attached to the Garston, Widnes and St. Helens area and as before they were kept separate from ordinary stock. This practice ceased in 1919 when approximately 100 of the 18ft wagons then in that area were integrated with the normal Diagram 84 stock.

Diagram 84 wagons were built right through the periods of 13in 3-bolt, single-rib and two-rib buffers; flat, carriage-type and bulbous oil-type axleboxes. They were never rebuilt or altered to or from any other diagram.

A minor detail change occurred in 1918 when the diagonal side strapping, instead of being cut off flush with the corner plates, was made longer and set to rest on top of the plates. Some received a door of different design: the top and bottom boards were chamfered and wrapped with steel plates so that trucks could be wheeled from platforms, over the lowered door and into the wagon without bumping up the full 3in thickness of the planks, a design pioneered on Diagram 11 in 1903 (q.v.). Also a 2ft length of strapping was added vertically in the centre of the door, probably to provide, with the hinges, three points of contact with a loading platform when lowered. These doors appear to have been an LNWR modification, although most may have been carried out after 1923. Some 16ft Diagram 9 wagons are believed to have received similarly modified doors.

L & N W R

10 TON OPEN GOODS 18 FT LONG

CAPACITY 385 CUBIC FT $\frac{20 \cdot 2 \cdot 04}{}$

A useful close-up shot of Diagram 84 No. 36226 showing many of the early features such as 3-bolt buffer stocks and axleboxes (this time branded L&NW). The central 'bolt' on the No. 4 flat-fronted axlebox cover was actually part of the casting and turning it with a spanner rotated the entire front cover about the left-hand bolt to reveal the journal, bearing and pad. The right-hand bolt had a spring washer beneath the nut which tightened the cover (which had a slotted hole) against the box. All 18ft 10-ton wagons and vans had a steel strip fixed beneath the transoms, protruding beneath the solebars and bolted beneath the curb rail. Modellers may delight in the gap between the solebar and the buffer-beam at the right-hand end, probably caused by shrinkage on this clearly far from new wagon. The second striker plate on the door was soon applied to some wagons, but strangely never adopted for new ones. It is worth noting that the diagonal strapping butts against the cornerplate, finishing flush with it.

NATIONAL RAILWAY MUSEUM (ETN 112)

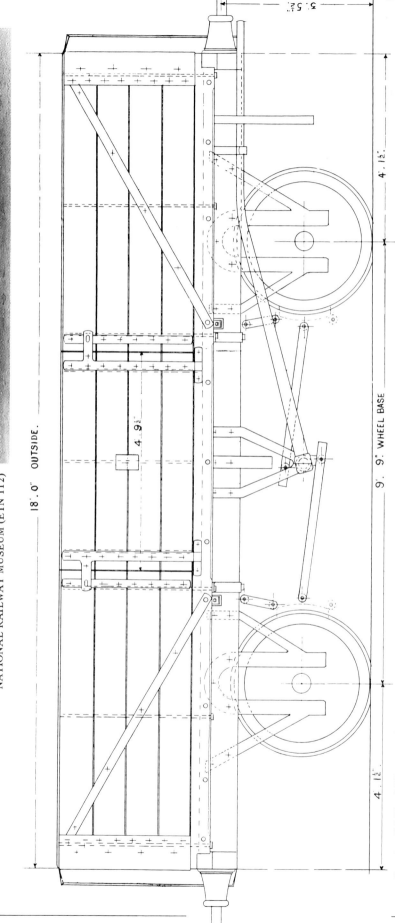

SIDE ELEVATION

18'.0". OUTSIDE.

9'. 9". WHEEL BASE

4. 1½".

4. 1½".

4. 9½".

5. 5½".

Drawing GA 91 of Diagram 84 open wagon with 5ft 11½in frame and double brake. Dated 20th February 1904.

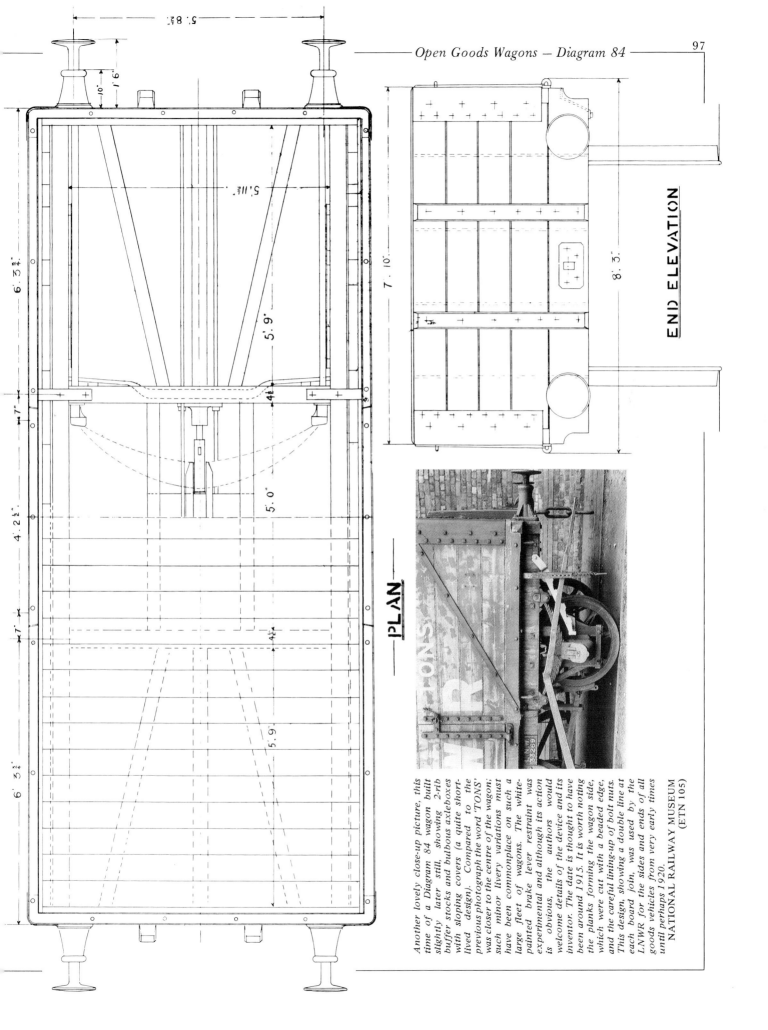

5. 8½"

1' 6"

10"

6' 3¾"

5' 11¾"

5' 9"

7"

4' 2¾"

7"

4¼"

5' 9"

6' 3¾"

4½

5. 0"

—PLAN—

7' 10"

8' 3"

END ELEVATION

Another lovely close-up picture, this time of a Diagram 84 wagon built slightly later still, showing 2-rib buffer stocks and bulbous axleboxes with sloping covers (a quite short-lived design). Compared to the previous photograph the word 'TONS' was closer to the centre of the wagon; such minor livery variations must have been commonplace on such a large fleet of wagons. The white-painted brake lever restraint was experimental and although its action is obvious, the authors would welcome details of the device and its inventor. The date is thought to have been around 1915. It is worth noting the planks forming the wagon side, which were cut with a beaded edge, and the careful lining-up of bolt nuts. This design, showing a double line at each board join, was used by the LNWR for the sides and ends of all goods vehicles from very early times until perhaps 1920.

NATIONAL RAILWAY MUSEUM (ETN 105)

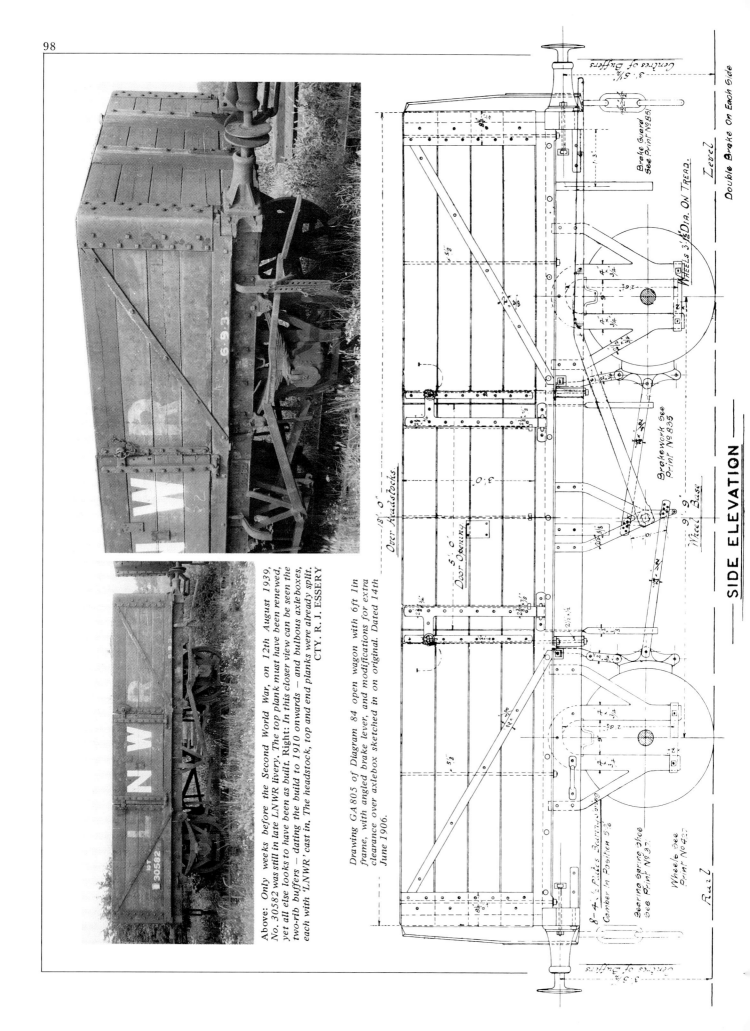

Above: *Only weeks before the Second World War, on 12th August 1939, No. 30582 was still in late LNWR livery. The top plank must have been renewed, yet all else looks to have been as built. Right: In this closer view can be seen the two-rib buffers — dating the build to 1910 onwards — and bulbous axleboxes, each with 'LNWR' cast in. The headstock, top and end planks were already split.*
CTY. R. J. ESSERY

Drawing GA 805 of Diagram 84 open wagon with 6ft 1in frame, with angled brake lever, and modifications for extra clearance over axlebox sketched in on original. Dated 14th June 1906.

SIDE ELEVATION

Double Brake On Each Side

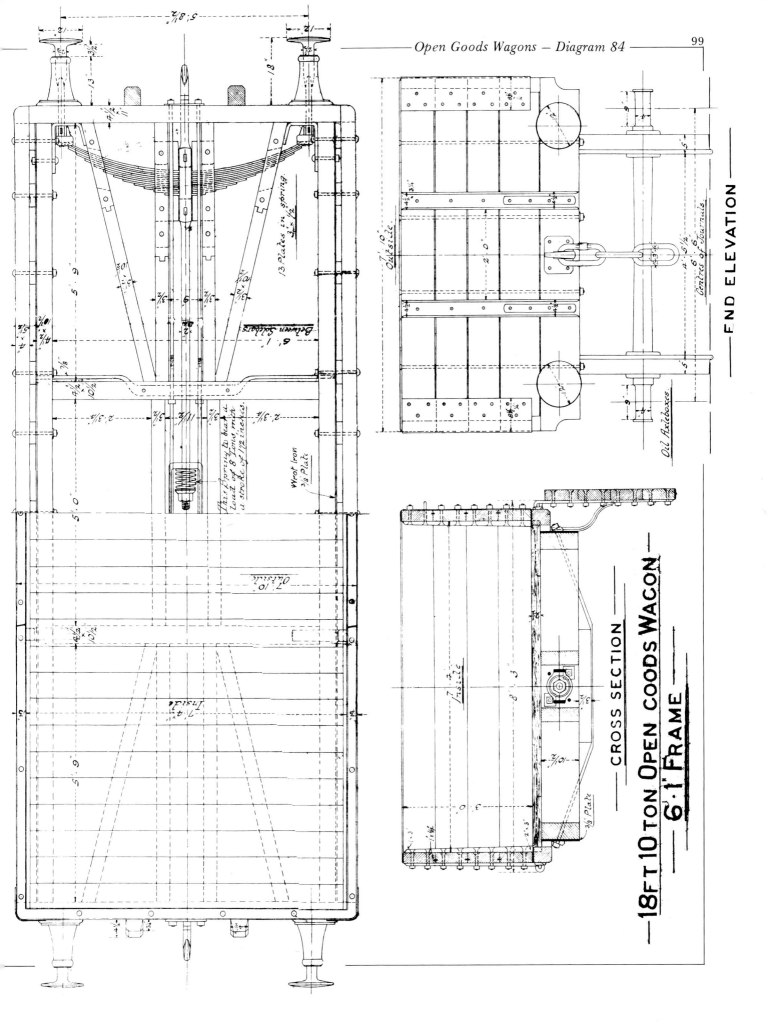

END ELEVATION

CROSS SECTION

18 FT 10 TON OPEN GOODS WAGON

6'.1" FRAME

This picture shows No. 70138, a very late example of Diagram 84, when new in 1921. The paint date reads 5/21, oil date 14/5/21 and lifting date 4/5/21. As this was clearly a brand new wagon, it is interesting to see that very few details had changed, even from the earliest examples. The major differences were the bulbous, flat-fronted axleboxes, planking cut with a straight bevelled edge and diagonal strapping which now joggled over the corner plate and was held by the corner plate bolts.

A handful were scrapped, probably as a result of accidents, leaving 15,040 to pass into LMS hands in 1923. More were built after the grouping but may have begun to incorporate standard LMS features (see Diagram 84A). It is interesting to note that when the design was finally replaced by the LMS's own Diagram 84 equivalent, in spite of the wider use of steel, the outside length was reduced to 17ft 6in, although capacity was increased to 12 tons.

In late 1910, sixty 'Express Traffic' wagons were built along the lines of those based on the Diagram 9, but this time to Diagram 84 dimensions. The new wagons had 4ft springs with shackles, twenty being fully vacuum-fitted with eight-block clasp brakes. The remaining forty were through piped and all sixty survived to pass into LMS ownership in 1923.

In the spring of 1945, as war in Europe was drawing to a close, HM Government put pressure on the railways of Britain to help Belgium by providing wagons for the Belgian Railways. It was agreed that 2,000 wagons, all of the same type, would be shipped via Zeebrugge loaded with coal. In the end the LMS supplied all 2,000 and selected ex-LNWR Diagram 84 wagons. They were sold on the dockside – the SNCB inspected them and if they were satisfactory the LMS were paid there and then. Those purchased were taken into SNCB stock and gave several years of valuable service.

Known examples of Diagram 84:
Diagram book tare for type: 8in journals 6.11.0
                             9in journals 6.15.2

Number	Tare	Buffers	Brakes	Axleboxes	Notes
10170	6.15.1	13in 3-bolt	DBBS	Flat	Tarpaulin bar
11254	6.6.17	13in 3-bolt	DBBS	Flat	
12179	6.15.2	13in 3-bolt	DBBS	Flat	
17985	6.8.2	13in 3-bolt	DBBS	Bulbous	
21176		13in 2-rib	DBBS	Flat	
25649	6.10.1	13in 3-bolt	DBBS	Bulbous	
26127	6.4.0	13in 2-rib	DBBS	LMS/bulbous – one pair each end	
29413	6.11.0	13in 2-rib	DBBS	Bulbous	
30481		13in 2-rib	DBBS	B.R.	
30582	6.9.3	13in 2-rib	DBBS	Bulbous	
33269		13in 2-rib	DBBS	Bulbous sloping	
33550	6.13.0	13in 3-bolt	DBBS	Flat	
34049	6.5.0	13in 1-rib	DBBS	Carriage/Bulbous – one pair each end	
36226		13in 3-bolt	DBBS	Flat	
37065	6.5.0	13in 1-rib	DBBS	Bulbous	
44157		13in 2-rib	DBBS	LMS	
44597	6.16.1	13in 2-rib	DBBS	Bulbous	
46597	6.8.2	13in 1-rib	DBBS	Bulbous	
49856	7.10.0	13in 2-rib	DBBS	Bulbous	
54363			DBBS	Bulbous	
60549	6.13.0	13in 2-rib	DBBS	Bulbous	
70138	6.18.0	13in 2-rib	DBES	Bulbous	
75919	6.14.3	13in 1-rib	DBES	Carriage	
78832	6.5.1	13in 2-rib	DBBS	Bulbous	
211173★		13in 2-rib	DBBS	Flat	
224433★	6.6.0		DB?S	Bulbous	
226127★		13in 2-rib	DBBS	Flat	
230481★			DB?S		
244157★					
251942★		13in 2-rib	DB?S	Bulbous	
275209★				Flat	

★indicates LMS Nos.

By 1930 No. 49856 was a post-1909 Diagram 84 still in LNWR livery. Note the number was now on the side plank, together with the label holder and the tare of 7.1.0. An unusual part repair had been carried out to a plank in the centre of the door and the brake lever pin rack was bent askew. The sole-bar numberplate had by now not been painted white.

LENS OF SUTTON

No. 54363 is another post-1909 wagon still in LNWR livery in LMS days, this time in 1930. Most unusually the brake shaft rubbing patch on the door had been fitted in diamond orientation — not so wise when it brought the middle screws right to the plank edge. The chalk marks were quite typical of a wagon in service.

LENS OF SUTTON

By May 1938 No. 29413 was also in LNWR livery after sixteen years of LMS ownership. The '10T' symbol had been moved to the lower side plank but the '10' on the top still remained, with the label holder below the number. Two-rib buffers and bulbous axleboxes date the build to 1910 onwards. The top door plank had been renewed and the brake lever pin rack again on the skew.   CTY. R. F. ROBERTS

No. 244157 is seen in LMS livery in company of Manger's Salt wagons in this view. The tare reads '6.6.2'; the label holder can be seen at the right on the bottom plank; buffers were two-rib and axleboxes flat-fronted.
CTY. HMRS (H1829)

These two Diagram 84 wagons were seen at Kinnerley on the Shropshire & Montgomeryshire Railway on 6th October 1931. Both had bulbous axleboxes but, incongruously, the nearer on No. 275209 was the angled No. 16 variety (Fig. 21). The nearest wagon had the extra vertical strap on the door, whilst the LMS livery on the nearest had faded almost beyond recognition.
CTY. R. H. CARPENTER (RKL R19)

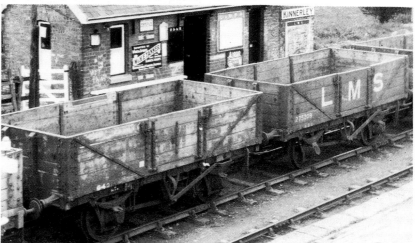

No. 248149 showed signs of incompleted repair work when photographed in LMS days. The top of the 'M' had not been painted on the replacement door plank — an omission not unknown. The tare of 6-5 had been moved to the right-hand side of the curb rail. Buffers were single-rib (Fig. 53); axleboxes bulbous Nos. 18 or 20; and door vertical strapping added.

This picture of No. 224433 was taken at Skelton Junction on the CLC lines in 1939. The tare was 6.6 and it had bulbous axleboxes, two-rib buffers and the vertical strap on the door which also acted as a rubbing plate for the end of the brake cross-shaft. The small-style LMS lettering was at left.
CTY. G. H. PLATT

No. 251942 was a Diagram 84 design seen in LMS days. It has double brakes both sides but the brake lever pin rack had already got bent askew. Buffers were 13in 2-rib and axleboxes bulbous. Repairs must have been carried out for one end and two side planks were lighter. Note the brake gear drop straps were not parallel but angled in a narrow 'vee' shape.
HMRS (ABJ 212)

D84 10-ton open wagon No. 226127 was photographed in LMS livery at Renfrew on 17th February 1946. It shows signs of wear and much graffiti, including a chalked 'Chad' symbol and an allusion to King George IV which is probably best left unexplored. Notice how one axlebox was flat-fronted, the other bulbous, and the two-rib rectangular base buffers. The two replacement door planks look to have been much thinner, from the thick inserts under the strapping, and the lower two end planks appear to have been replacements, being lighter in colour. A. G. ELLIS
COLLECTION (4498)

Looking its age, Diagram 84 open LMS No. 211173 loaded and coupled to other RCH-specification wagons. It had already had a patch panel on the lower end and two thin planks where the 'L' of 'LMS' should have appeared. Note the wooden spacers used under the strapping to compensate for the differing dimensions. The side door was bowing out under the load.

HMRS (AAT 719)

This photograph of No. 60549 was taken in the 1930s. The number had been added to the side but removed from the end. Most lettering was barely visible although the tare was clearly 6-13. The '10 tons' legend appeared twice and the label holder had been moved up to beside the door. Two-rib buffers, dating the build to 1910 or after (Fig. 55) and bulbous No. 18 or 20 axleboxes (see left) complete the picture.

CTY. R. J. ESSERY (LW377)

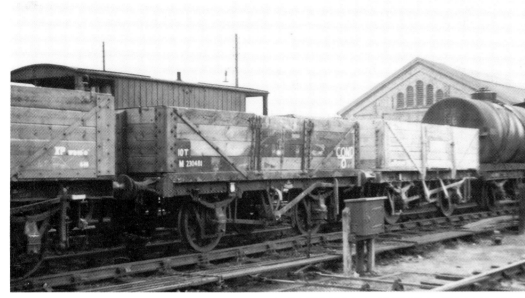

Seen at Bletchley on 12th July 1958, No. 230481 was in BR livery but labelled as 'condemned'. The sides already showed a lean outwards. RCH axleboxes, square-ended headstocks and an LMS numberplate had been fitted.

No. 021439 was in a parlous state when photographed on 17th July 1965, and the 'condemned' lettering confirms the near end of its days. Just about all the paint had worn off yet it was lettered to return to Belgrave Road Goods Depot, Leicester. Several changes had been made from as built' brake lever cut short and wrapped round to form a grip; square-ended headstocks; flat-fronted LMS axleboxes and the curb-rail support brackets had gone.
CTY. R. J. ESSERY (AE53/1)

DIAGRAM 84A – OPEN GOODS WAGON

This diagram is something of a mystery. It differed from the standard Diagram 84 only in having 2½in thick planks instead of 3in, and being 8ft wide over the sides, instead of 7ft 10in. The reason for this is unknown and the difference is probably not sufficient to identify in a photograph. The number built is also unknown, but the fact that a diagram was produced (rather than just a drawing) suggests that they did exist albeit possibly after 1923. One theory is that a new design of hinge was tried, thus allowing a wider wagon to remain within the 8ft 3in maximum overall width.

A drawing dated 1919 shows a wagon to the same overall dimensions as D84 (except the width) but has five planks instead of four. Presumably after the First World War timber was more difficult to obtain, so narrower planks were tried, as other companies had found necessary.

The LMS built 250 10-ton open wagons of 'LNW design' at Earlestown in 1924 as LMS Lot 24. The company's records state 'No Diagram', i.e. no LMS Diagram was issued, but this Lot may well have had its origin in LNW Diagram 84A.

No photographs, dates or further information are currently known.

DIAGRAM 103 – OPEN GOODS WAGON WITH 9in SIDES

There remains just one major development in LNWR open goods wagons. In 1909 the Goods Conference Committee recommended that the number of wagons with 9in sides should not fall below the then current stock of 6,000. Since nearly all Diagram 1 wagons had been built prior to 1887, and some were nearly forty years old, many were in urgent need of replacement.

Diagram 103 was introduced in 1910 and continued to be built up to 1921, leaving 5,964 to pass to the LMS in 1923. The dimensions followed the pattern established with Diagram 84 and were 18ft long by 7ft 10in wide. The wheelbase was 9ft 9in. Unlike Diagram 1 which it superseded, the later standard methods were used including the 5½in curb rail, set flush with the top of the floor.

The sides were built of 9in x 3in planks and the ends of 11in x 3in. The internal height remained at 9in, as on Diagram 1. The wagons are easily distinguished from Diagram 1 in having five bolts in each corner plate as against six on the shorter wagons. The floor was of 7in x 2½in

planks, rebated ½in over the buffer planks. The springs had eight leaves 4in x ½in, still 3ft 6in long and, so far as is known, they all had the wider underframe with flitch plates, 6ft 1in between solebars, and 9in x 4in journals. Because the majority replaced elderly Diagram 1 open wagons, many Diagram 103 wagons took their low running numbers.

They were all rated at ten tons and had double brakes both sides. The building dates covered the periods of flat-fronted, carriage type, and bulbous oil axleboxes, and all three types could be seen. The buffers were always of the 13in single- or double-ribbed types.

In 1917-1918, 1,000 Diagram 103 open wagons were built for the War Department and sent overseas. Their ultimate fate is unknown.

A number were rebuilt by the LMS with drop sides and fitted with vacuum brakes to work on express freight trains with container traffic. As this occurred after 1923, it is beyond the scope of this book and readers are referred to *The LMS Wagon* by Essery & Morgan.

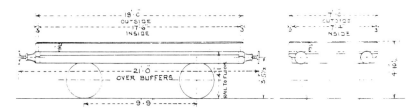

Diagram Book page of Diagram 103.

One of the earliest Diagram 103 open wagons, bearing a paint date of 2/10. Since D103 wagons were built on revenue account to replace ageing Diagram 1 vehicles, and since Diagram 1 wagons originated in the very early years of the LNWR, the running numbers allocated to D103 wagons included some very low numbers. Apart from the length, other details which distinguish these from the smaller wagons are the 5-bolt cornerplates instead of 6 and shorter side strapping which no longer extends down over the curb rail. Here we see No. 6950 featuring square axleboxes and single-rib buffers.
NATIONAL RAILWAY MUSEUM (ETN 78)

Known examples of Diagram 103:
Diagram book tare for type: 6.1.2

Number	Tare	Buffers	Axleboxes	Notes
426	6.0.2	13in 2-rib	Bulbous	
1485		13in 2-rib	Carriage	
2440	6.2.0	13in 1-rib	Carriage	
4127		13in 1-rib	Flat	May 1937
4706	6.0.0	13in 1-rib	Carriage	
6437	5.15.0	13in 2-rib	LMS	
6808	5.18.0	13in 2-rib	LMS	
6950	6.1.2	13in 1-rib	Flat	
7503	5.11.1	13in 1-rib	Flat	(as 207503)
7802	5.15.0	13in 2-rib	LMS	(as 207802)
9346	6.1.1	13in 2-rib	LMS	
9531	5.12.0	13in 2-rib	Bulbous	Nov. 1946 (as 209531)
9980	5.18.2	13in 2-rib	Bulbous	
10062	6.1.2	13in 2-rib	Bulbous	
10401	6.0.1			Drop sides; vac brake (as 210401)
12437	5.14.0	13in 2-rib	Bulbous/LMS	(as 212437)
19905	5.15.2	13in 2-rib	Bulbous	
20984	5.18.0?	13in 1-rib	Bulbous	
21847	5.12.0	13in 1-rib	Bulbous	Nov. 1933
22039		13in 1-rib	Bulbous	
22882	6.3.0	13in 1-rib	Carriage	
24594		13in 1-rib	Flat/LMS	BR, Feb. 1978 (as M224594)
24797	5.16.0	13in 1-rib	Flat	
26223	5.17.2	13in 2-rib	Carriage/bulbous – one pair each end	

No. 4706, with a tare exactly 6 tons, was slightly later than the previous photograph because it had received pointed fronts to the axleboxes which incorporated a spring-loaded lift-up lid to aid oiling. All other details appear to be the same. Note there was no number painted on the end of No. 4706. 'George the Fifth' class No. 1394 Harrier was built in July 1911, which helps to date the photograph. The vehicle to the right was a tranship or tool van, fitted with self-contained buffers.

A similar Diagram 103 at work in 1913 at Wantage, Berkshire. This picture of No. 22882 shows pointed axlebox fronts and the later livery, diamonds having been discontinued and 10 TONS added.
COLLECTION
R. S. CARPENTER

Although this Diagram 103 No. 20984 was very similar to those depicted in the previous photographs, this picture illustrates another of the uses for low wagons. Exactly what the load was we do not know, but the photograph is from a Crewe negative showing a very long pressure vessel mounted on a bogie bolster wagon. At each end the overhang required a runner wagon, at the near end No. 20984, which usefully also carried the domed ends. The lettering painted or chalked onto the pressure vessel reads 'Nottingham end' and appears to have contained narrow gauge rails, so we believe it may have been for the pressure creosoting of sleepers. The load could have been bound for the Beeston Sleeper Depot, on the Midland main line between Nottingham and Derby.
COLLECTION R. J. ESSERY
(Crewe MC 891)

Although fitted with bulbous axleboxes, the single-rib buffers show that No. 22039 was still not one of the last of the type built. All other details remained the same. The board on the end of the load reads: SANDBERG 'INSITU' PROCESS. CONTRACTORS SCHOLEY & Co. Ltd. 56 VICTORIA ST. WESTMINSTER. LONDON S.W.1. The reason for the photograph was, of course, to record inadequate securing of the load which had broken through the end plank of the wagon. Not only that, the truck which resembles a platelayers' trolley, had been damaged and may well have damaged the adjacent wagon as well. The 'NOT TO GO' label can be seen nailed to the side, above the left-hand axle.
LNWR SOCIETY (9587)

As wagons passed through the shops for repair, it was customary to salvage as many components as possible, hence the piecemeal replacement of corner plate rivets by bolts on the earlier wagons, for example. Mechanical components were replaced individually too, hence the unreliable dates on grease axleboxes, but by the Warneford period this included components of quite different appearance, and this photograph by Jim Richards shows how dangerous it can be to date wagons by such features alone, since one axlebox had been replaced by one of more modern design. Of course, this was only possible because of the LNWR's policy of standardisation which applied to all three major workshops and lasted throughout the company's separate existence. Such mismatched axleboxes became common, although, for some reason, Diagram 103 wagons seem to have been particularly susceptible to this practice! This wagon was No. 26223 and had a tare weight of 5.17.2.

Despite the late date — November 1933 — No. 21847 was yet another wagon in late period LNWR livery when photographed at Swindon. Inevitably LNWR livery surviving so late would be something to be photographed. It can be seen that the brake gear safety straps twisted through 90 degrees just below the transoms. The tare was 5.12 (in italics); single-rib buffers; and bulbous axleboxes were fitted.

CTY. H. F. WHEELLER

As late as 30th May 1937, Diagram 103 open wagon No. 4127 was photographed at Crewe Works still in LNWR livery, nearly 14½ years after the LMS took over. It must be assumed that it had been operating satisfactorily in service without needing a visit to the Works in all that time. Unfortunately, the paint date is not visible. Note the LNW number appears twice, on the curb rail and at the top of the side at the left. Double brakes both sides had been fitted and the buffers were single-rib. H. F. WHEELLER COLLECTION (55/30)

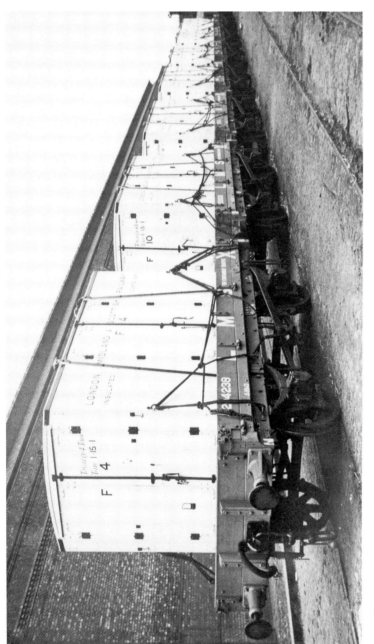

So suitable were the D103 wagons for the growing container traffic, that the LMS rebuilt many of them with drop sides and added vacuum brakes for express running. The vertical vacuum cylinder worked onto a cross-shaft which meant that the handbrake on one side had to be reversed and the lever on that side operated via a cam.

An official LMS picture of D103 No. 210401 rebuilt with drop sides, fully fitted vacuum brakes and screw couplings. All this made surprisingly little difference to the tare weight which, on this example, was 6.0.1. For some reason the LMS often shortened the LNWR brake levers and moved the rack nearer to the axleguard. One would suspect it was to bring the design in line with Midland practice. Certainly the Midland produced large numbers of wagons in exactly this configuration but there were others where the pin rack was inboard of the axleguard and the lever relatively short. Most likely the objective of the LMS was to eliminate the extension of the brake lever beyond the bufferbeam.

Other forms of container became popular in the 1930s and the numerous and modern D103 was ideally suited for the LMS traffic. Here we see a 'K' class container resplendent in full crimson lake livery and gold lettering, tied onto D103 No. 207802 on 25th July 1939. Both the axleboxes visible were of LMS design, but the wagon was otherwise as built.

No. 207503 is seen here in a variation of LMS livery, with '10T' and number at opposite extreme ends of the side plank. It had two oval works plates near the tare of 5-11-1. The thickening of the brake lever where it was mounted on the shaft was very prominent.

CTY. R. J. ESSERY (LW247)

Diagram 103 wagons were common well into LMS days and found a new lease of life when container traffic started to become popular. Here we see a 'D' class container which was in effect a modern and larger version of the old box coal wagon, particularly suited for bunkering ships. Wagon No. 212437 had a tare of 5.14.0 and we can see that the practice of unmatched axle-boxes continued into LMS days – that on the left being an LNWR bulbous type whilst that on the right was an LMS group standard. The photograph was taken on 27th June 1939.
COLLECTION R. J. ESSERY

Although seen here in 1946, No. 209531 was probably little altered from new. Two-rib buffers suggest a build of 1910 or after, but bulbous axle-boxes, double (vee) brakes both sides, and tare of 5-12 would have been normal for the time. However, the brake gear was in serious need of adjustment – the lever travel was completely used up.
CTY. R. S. CARPENTER

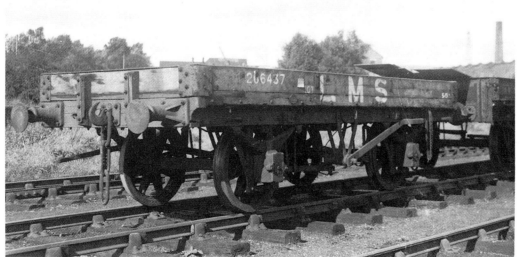

The headstock on No. 206437 was already badly split. The narrow vee of the brake safety strap can clearly be made out between the nearer wheels and is usually omitted on drawings. This time the '10T' was positioned to the left of the 'LMS'. The tare reads 5-13 and LMS flat-fronted axleboxes had been fitted.
CTY. R. S. CARPENTER

Seen here in 1946, No. 206808 had been altered by the LMS for container traffic. Fall doors with three brackets each side to shackle containers were fitted, together with new, square headstocks, vacuum brakes and screw couplings. The tare reads 5-18 and axleboxes had been renewed with LMS flat-fronted covers. There was damage to the right-hand end keeper plate and end plank. The chalked solebar dates read 5.4.45 and 22.2.46.
CTY. R. S. CARPENTER

In this view believed to have been taken in the early 1950s, No. M224594 is in BR livery. The damage of old age was apparent: the side plank was badly split and the sheet hooks had been wrenched out of line. The nearest headstock had been renewed with a square-ended plank but at the right-hand end it appears original. LMS flat-fronted axleboxes had been substituted.
ROYE ENGLAND

(906—Cattle Ticket
Book—Small)

London and North Western Railway.

CATTLE DEPARTMENT. No. 247

Wagon Numbers.	Description of Wagons.	Quantity.	Description of Stock.	Rate or Fare	Paid on.	Total Paid at	Total to Pay.
15283 17/0	4/0	110	Sheep	35/-		4/7/-	1 5 0
14118 11/0	9 c/-	30	,,	22/0			1 2 0
14025 7/0	42	20	,,	23/6			1 5 0
						3 13 0	

Sep 13th 1892

Sender Mr Morris

Consignee Wilcox

Address Whitchurch

BROOME

From Whitchurch

To Whitchurch

via Salop

Signed Leigh

— Dealers' or Drovers' Fares

Insurance on £ —

— Drovers in charge, Free.

DROVER'S PASS.

If it is desired that any Drover or Person accompanying the Live Stock shall be allowed to travel in the same Train as the Live Stock, without paying a Fare, he must travel at his own risk, and must either sign this in token that he agrees to travel at his own risk, or he must pay Fare as a Passenger.

I agree to travel at my own risk, without paying any Fare, and accept a Free Pass subject to the following Conditions, viz.:—

This Pass is issued free by the Company, and subject to the following conditions, on which it is accepted by the holder, viz.:—That it is available only for the Train by which the Stock is being conveyed.

That the holder is subject to the Bye-Laws of the Company, and he exonerates the Company from all responsibility for injury or loss to himself, howsoever occasioned, on the journey for which it is issued or used.

Witness ———— Signed ———— Drover.

Witness ———— Signed ———— Drover.

Witness ———— Signed ———— Drover.

This Pass is issued free by the Company, and subject to the following conditions, on which it is accepted by the holder, viz.:—That it is available only for the Train by which the Stock is being conveyed.

That the holder is subject to the Bye-Laws of the Company, and he exonerates the Company from all responsibility for injury or loss to himself, howsoever occasioned, on the journey for which it is issued or used.

Pass ———— in charge of above Stock.

Pass ———— To.

Pass ———— Do.

From ———— to ————

———— Agent, London & North Western Railway.

A typical Cattle Department ticket, No. 247, dated 13th September 1892 consigning 110 sheep to be transported from Broome to Whitchurch via Salop.

CHAPTER FOUR
CATTLE WAGONS

CATTLE wagons and sheep vans appear to have been amongst the first specialised vehicles to be provided by the early railway companies. In 1848 in a 'Report to the L&NWR Board, on the condition of the Rolling Stock', Capt. Mark Huish, the General Manager, recorded the existence of 495 cattle wagons and 117 sheep vans. The latter maintained a separate existence until the mid-1880s when, numbers having dwindled to 100 vehicles, they were absorbed into the cattle wagon stock. Cattle wagons were built continuously throughout the life of the company and during that time their specifications evolved in response to engineering development and legislative changes on the treatment of animals. For example, there are frequent references to the construction of cattle wagons in the official company minute books chronicling improvements to their design such as the addition of roofs, the enclosure of the end planking, the fitting of partitions and even changes to the pattern of the battens on the floor so as to give the animals a better foothold during transit.

This chapter describes the seven designs which are to be found in the 1903 Wagon Stock Diagram Book where they are listed as Diagrams 20 to 26 inclusive. The first three Diagrams – 20, 21 and 22 – are conventional designs of cattle wagon having obvious common design features amongst themselves and with the company's contemporary goods

stock. The remaining four designs, Diagrams 23 to 26 inclusive, were special vehicles for the transport of valuable prize cattle to and from agricultural shows, etc. Although officially listed as goods stock, they were more akin, in use and external appearance, to horse-boxes, although without the stalls and fittings of the latter. They were painted in a similar lined livery to combination trucks and horse-boxes and were fitted with vacuum brakes for running in passenger trains. They were a rarity compared with horse-boxes: only 43 of all four types were built over the 40 years from 1884 to 1923, and only six needed to be renewed. All passed into the hands of the LMS in 1923.

SUMMARY

Diagram	Introduced	Description
20	1876★	Small cattle wagon, to carry 7 tons
21	1868★	Medium cattle wagon, to carry 7 tons
22	1869★	Large cattle wagon, to carry 10 tons
23	1888	Special cattle wagon, to carry 6 tons
24	1884	Fowlers' cattle wagon, to carry 6 tons
25	1899	Cattle wagon with compartment, 6-tons
26	1902	Cattle wagon with compartment, 6-tons

NOTE:
★ indicates earliest date wagons were known to be in service.

DIAGRAM 20 – SMALL CATTLE WAGON

The Diagram 20 small 7-ton cattle wagon design was indeed the smallest of the three sizes of conventional LNWR cattle wagons, both physically and in the quantity built. No general arrangement drawing has survived, neither is there an official photograph in the NRM York collection. For details of their appearance and construction we are dependent on the 1903 Wagon Stock Diagram Book sketch (below, left) which shows them to be 13ft 8½in long and 7ft 11in wide externally, with an 8ft 0in wheelbase. Additionally, a 1909 sketch (below, right) and rather poor quality photograph (right), show the lower plank on each side replaced by vertical iron bars. This style of construction has been noted occasionally in photographs of other LNWR cattle wagons in traffic and on other companies' vehicles, for example, the L&Y cattle wagon in plate 14 of *British Goods Wagons* (Essery, Rowland and Steel, David & Charles, 1970). From the available evidence it is unclear whether the bars were an unsuccessful short-lived experiment or the standard design in an earlier age.

The 1902 Wagon Stock Age Book records that 324 vehicles, apparently to this small design, were still extant at that date, having been built between 1876 and 1882. An 1878 minute ordered the construction of 13ft 6in long (presumably inside length) cattle wagons for the Holyhead American livestock traffic in place of condemned ordinary goods wagons; i.e. revenue replacements. In 1882 a further 200 small cattle wagons were ordered on capital account. Subsequently, the 'medium' design seems to have been adopted as standard and the small ones were replaced as they were condemned. The design finally became extinct by 1918.

The livery of the small cattle wagons prior to 1908 would have been similar to that of the medium vehicle, a photograph of which is shown on page 117. It is difficult to see how they could have carried the post-1908 16in-high 'LNWR' letters on their small side panels. It is logical to presume that, as with single-plank vehicles, they carried a similar livery but used smaller lettering. There is documentary evidence from surviving 'Cattle Tickets', i.e. invoices, for some wagon (or register) numbers carried by small cattle wagons during the 1880s (see list below). Note that there is

This poor photograph of a small cattle wagon to Diagram 20 is the only one known. Note the vertical bars at the bottom of the sides, typically stained white by limewash.

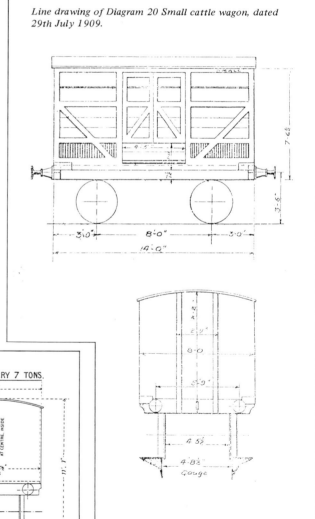

Line drawing of Diagram 20 Small cattle wagon, dated 29th July 1909.

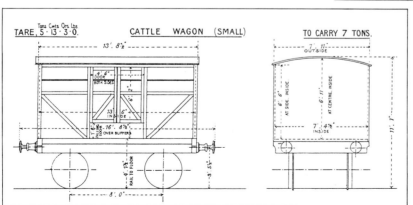

Diagram Book page of Diagram 20.

no real evidence of block numbering except perhaps the 467xx and 468xx series which may correspond to the batch of 200 small wagons ordered and built in 1882. Without further photographic evidence, the only tare weight we have is the 5ton 13cwt 3qrs given in the Diagram Book. By inference from other LNWR wagons built in the 19th century, the axleboxes would be the 7-ton grease-box type and the buffers the 3-bolt round-base style. For the design of brake blocks and couplings see the section below on medium and large wagons.

Known examples of Diagram 20:
Diagram book tare for type: 5.13.3

934	14790	15447	32667
3583	14861	15847	46757
12492	15094	15911	46786
14576	15158	15938	46794
14580	15166	16145	46840
14586	15177	21521	46896
14623	15217	22096	
14635	15301	24750	

DIAGRAMS 21 & 22 – MEDIUM & LARGE CATTLE WAGONS

Because of the similarities of their design details and historical development, these two sizes of cattle wagons will be discussed together. The earliest surviving record which distinguishes between the stock of each type is the 1863 stock valuation list. This records a total stock of 1,433 cattle wagons, of which 964 were 'medium' and 469 'large'. The meaning of the terms 'medium' and 'large' seems to have varied with time. An 1889 Goods Conference minute states

that a medium cattle wagon was 15ft 6in long internally, whilst the large one was 17ft 10in. The medium wagon shown below, which dates from 1885, has 15ft 4in and 15ft 0in painted on the cantrail. This refers respectively to the internal length between end planking and between the bottom rails at the ends, i.e. the length of the floor. The earliest surviving official drawing, Earlestown GA 12, dated 8th July 1895, and reproduced on pages 118/119, gives the external

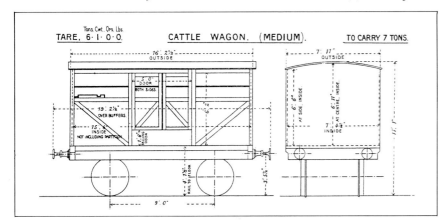

Diagram Book page of Diagram 21.

This fine photograph of a medium cattle wagon, Diagram 21, taken at Earlestown in 1885, clearly illustrates the standard constructional details of the time. The dimensions were: 15ft 6in over headstocks, 7ft 11in wide, on a 9ft wheelbase. Later the length was increased to 16ft 2½in so as to maintain an internal length of 15ft 6in as required by Railway Clearing House regulations. Note in particular, the early strapping detail, the single wooden brake block operated by a straight lever on one side only, the characteristic LNWR grease axleboxes and the screw coupling, which had been the standard fitting since 1879. The wagon was not fitted with the two-position rail for the location of the medium/small partition — it only became the standard after 1891.
CTY. EDWARD TALBOT

118

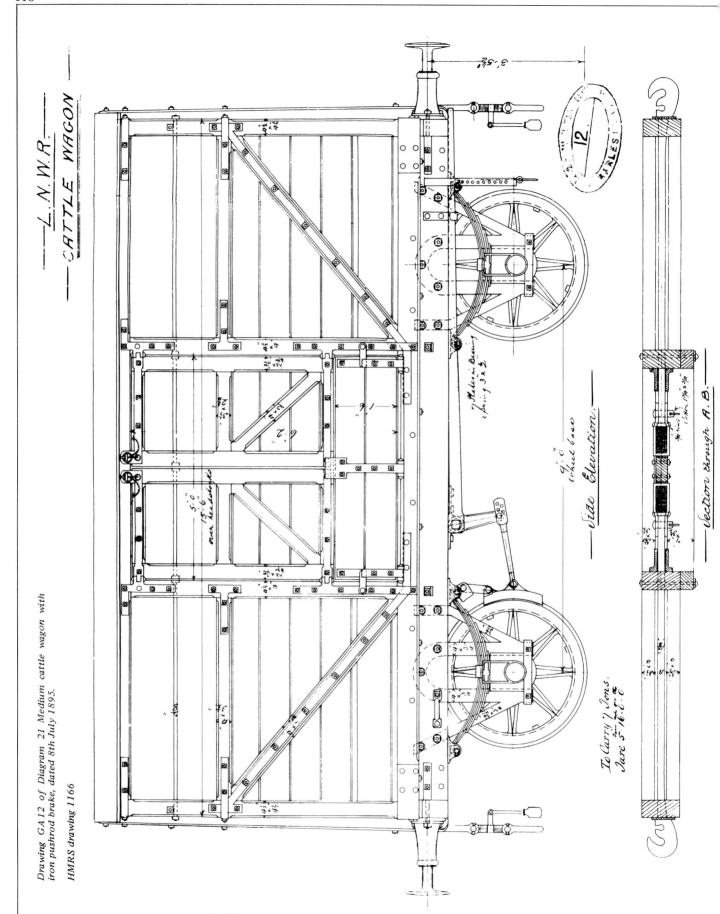

— L.N.W.R. —
— CATTLE WAGON —

Drawing GA12 of Diagram 21 Medium cattle wagon with
iron pushrod brake, dated 8th July 1895.

HMRS drawing 1166

— Side Elevation. —

— Section through A.B. —

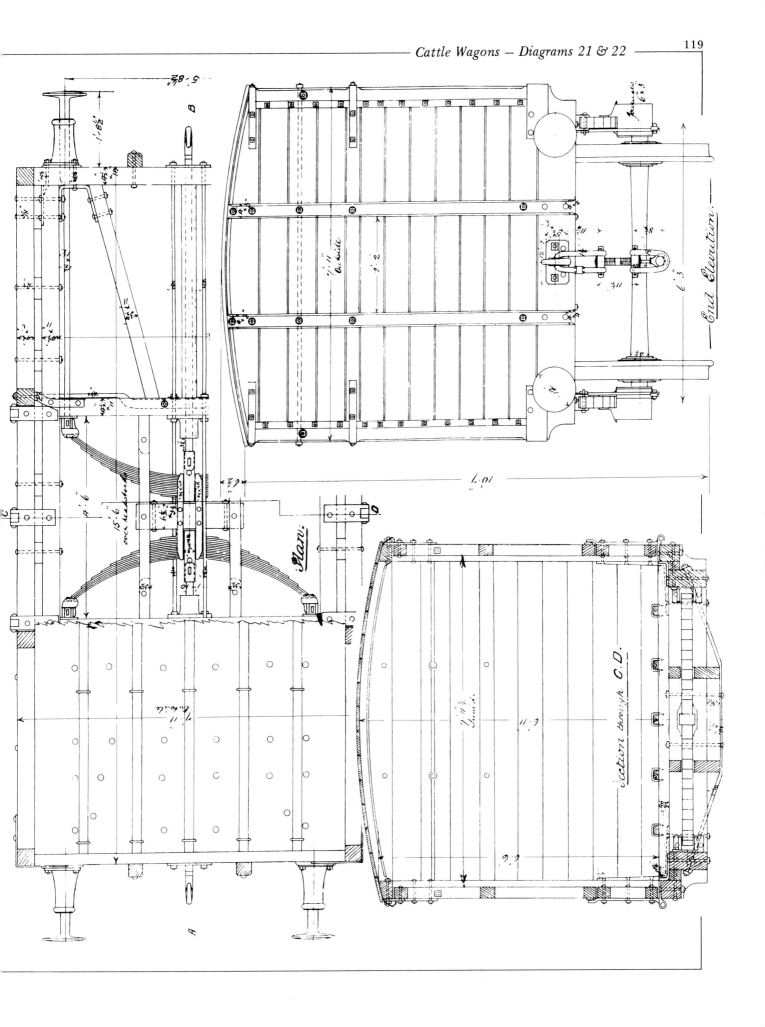

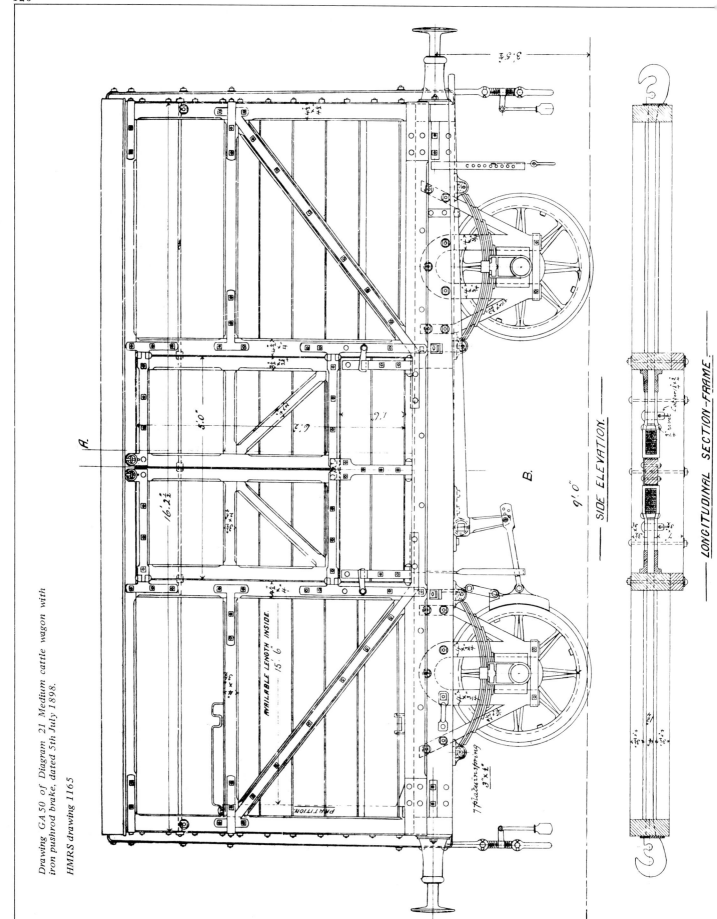

Drawing GA50 of Diagram 21 Medium cattle wagon with iron pushrod brake, dated 5th July 1898.

HMRS drawing 1165

SIDE ELEVATION.

LONGITUDINAL SECTION-FRAME.

AVAILABLE LENGTH INSIDE.
15' 6"

PARTITION.

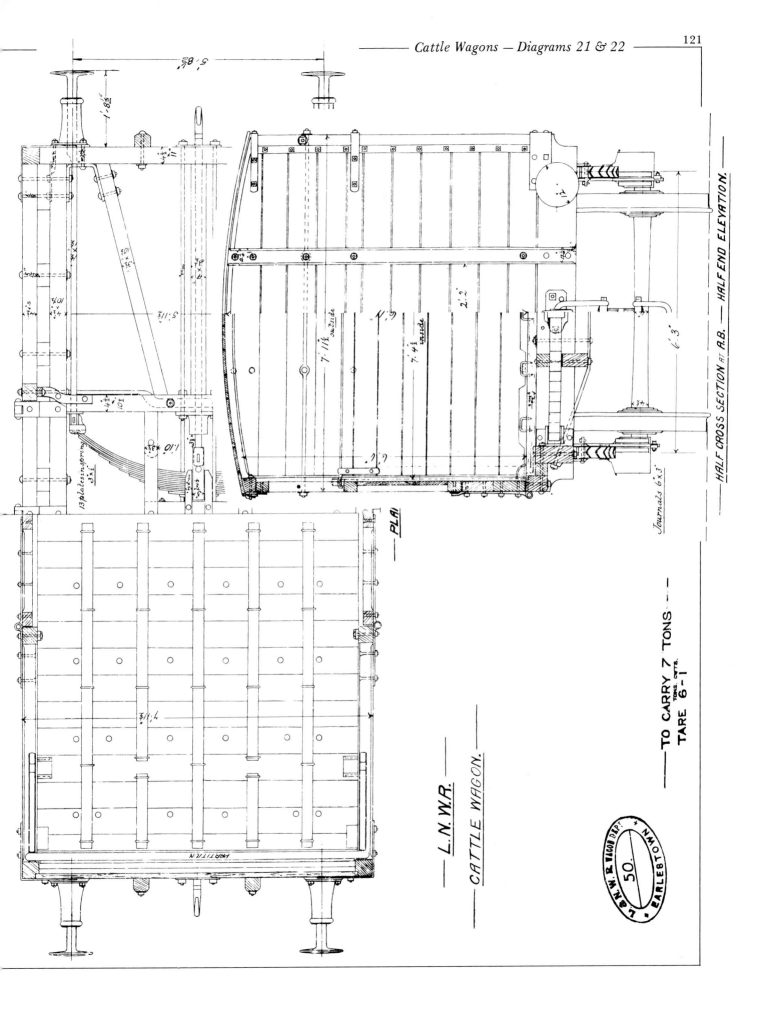

HALF CROSS SECTION *at* A.B. — HALF END ELEVATION.

— L.N.W.R. —

— CATTLE WAGON. —

— TO CARRY 7 TONS —
TARE 6 - 1

An unidentifiable medium cattle wagon, Diagram 21, in late LNWR livery. The paintwork looks very faded and the lower planks were well caked with the lime wash disinfectant. It had the later welded strapping and appears to have been fitted with brakes on all four wheels. The axleboxes were the flat-fronted first oil-filled pattern, see Fig. 2. A small 'P.F.' on the top right-hand plank reveals that it was pipe fitted and could therefore run in express goods or passenger traffic. This branding was necessary on fitted vehicles because although through pipes were first ordered in 1898, they were only fitted progressively as wagons went through the works and even by 1919 an official table shows that only 693 out of 1,433 medium cattle wagons had been converted. The photograph is undated but was probably taken in the 1920s.

CTY. DR. NIALL FERGUSON

length as 15ft 6in. Later drawings and minute book references record an increase in external length of a medium cattle wagon to 16ft 2⅛in during the early 1890s. At the same time the large cattle wagons were increased to 18ft 9in externally. There was a 17ft 10in wagon for which no drawing or photo survived. There were believed to be only a few left by 1903 and they were included with Diagram 22 and no separate diagram was issued.

The reason behind these changes appears to have been complaints from livestock dealers who in 1894 reported the company to the Board of Trade over the use of movable partitions which reduced the internal space of the wagon below that laid down in an Act of Parliament, the *Rates and Changes Order, Confirmation Act 1891*. The company replied that in the reconstruction of the present stock and in the building of new, they would make the dimensions correspond strictly to those named in the Act. The standard minimum inside dimensions laid down were: small 13ft 6in, medium 15ft 6in and large 18ft 0in. These were the distances between the wall at one end and the inside of the movable partition at the other.

The drawing shown on pages 120/121, Earlestown GA 50, dated 5th July 1898, shows the 1898 version of a medium cattle wagon. The comparable drawing for the large cattle wagon Earlestown GA 13, dated 20th May 1897, is reproduced on pages 126/127. Notice in both drawings that the frame, complete with notches, to support the movable partition is visible at the left-hand end of the body. At floor level the partition was located in a short length of channel

section which projected only a short distance into the interior so as not to injure the animals. The purpose of the partition was to ensure that the animal dealers got exactly what they paid for and no more. The effect of this system can be seen on invoices which record the vehicle usage as 'large as medium' or 'medium as small', etc.

Apparently, early cattle wagons were roofless and open at the ends above waist level as well as at the sides. During the 1860s there are several minute book references to boarding up the ends and adding a roof. An 1870 minute records that all future cattle wagons are to be fitted with sprung buffers and also comments that some small old wagons rated at 4¼ tons had sprung buffers at one end and dumb buffers at the other. No photographs of these earlier LNWR wagons survive but roofless and open-ended wagons can be seen in early GWR and later Irish photographs.

The mechanical specification of both the 'medium' and 'large' cattle wagon designs evolved in step with general changes in the company's goods stock. The photo on page 117 shows that in the mid-1880s vehicles had 3-bolt round-based buffer castings 12in long, grease axleboxes with 6in x 3in journals, a single wooden brake block and, perhaps surprisingly, screw couplings. The minute books reveal that in 1879 the ordinary three-link coupling was ordered to be replaced with a screw coupling in an effort to avoid injury to the animals through snatching. By 1898 a single cast-iron brake block had started to replace the wooden one, and vacuum pipes, but not brakes, were ordered to be fitted to all new cattle wagons.

A Diagram 21 medium cattle wagon as built from 1910 on. The two-rib buffers were introduced under A. R. Trevithick from this date. The gaps between the lower two planks usefully enabled ventilation, and effluent to flow out and, in early days, limewash.

In this close-up of No. 215219 taken in LMS days, 1937 or after, the label holder was now on the second plank to the right of the door. The brake blocks, with two attachment points so they could fit either way up, can be seen. The later spring shoes seen here had the extension which fitted up the front face of the solebar but note there was no similar extension at the back. A bolt was fitted into the wood of the solebar on the inside and its nut was the one we see clamping on the metal extension. The short two-plank fall door was secured by pins either side and the extension upwards of the central strap locked the cupboard doors above shut.

CTY. HMRS

124

Around 1910 a start was made upon uprating the 7-ton 'medium' wagons to ten tons by fitting oil-filled axleboxes (first pattern) with 9in x 4in journals and stronger springs. Those not uprated were reduced to six tons capacity to take account of the wear on their 6in x 3in journals. At about the same time hand-operated brakes were fitted to both wheels on each side. Note that even as late as 1919 only two each of

the 'medium' and 'large' cattle wagons were fitted with full vacuum brakes. A drawing, Earlestown GA 60, dated 30th August 1910, of a 'large' cattle wagon to this specification is shown on pages 128/129, and a 1909 photograph of a 'large' cattle wagon, No. 15483, in identical condition except for the later 'carriage type' axleboxes is shown opposite. The 'P.F' to the right of the number indicates it is pipe-fitted.

This medium cattle wagon in LMS livery had already had several planks replaced and the brake pin rack was already bent. No. 215861 was 'through piped' and had flat-fronted axleboxes and two-rib buffers. The racking for the movable partition, to convert to 'small' size can be seen at the right-hand end.
CTY. G. H. PLATT

At Ferme Park on 28th February 1950 in BR livery, No. M215129 had lasted well beyond the average age of cattle wagons, calculated by the LNWR at 11.5 years. By this date it had experienced few changes: the axleboxes were flat-fronted but many other features could have been unaltered since new. The two-rib buffers date the build to 1910 or after, and most likely it was 1918 or later. The tare was 6-14, in this case recorded on the bottom plank at extreme right.

Note the different widths between GA13 – 8ft o½in – and GA60 – 7ft 11in.

In addition to the more obvious changes listed above, there were small changes in strapping detail between 1895 and 1910. Even beyond that date the design continued to evolve. Buffers were changed to a 4-bolt rectangular base with firstly a single rib and later a double rib to strengthen the cast buffer housing which was lengthened to 15in. The exact dates of the introduction of these changes is unknown because they are not recorded in the minute books, but prior to approximately 1912 the 3-bolt round-base buffer would

have been normal. From 1912 to 1918 the single-rib 4-bolt rectangular-base type would have co-existed with the earlier type and it is unlikely that the double-rib type was much in evidence before about 1918. Certainly the rate of introduction of these changes would have been slow and their progress can be judged from the quantity of each type fitted with the various features discussed above by 1919. For example, 832 out of a total of 1,433 'medium' wagons still had grease axleboxes some ten years after the introduction of the oil-filled type. Progress from 'one side' to 'both side' brakes was similarly slow. By the same date 779 had been converted

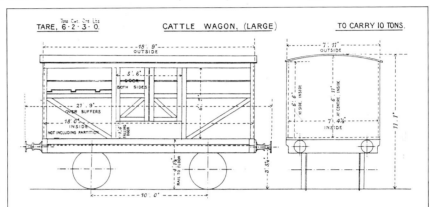

Diagram Book page of Diagram 22.

This official photograph of a large cattle wagon, Diagram 22, can be dated to October 1909 by the paint date on the left-hand end of the solebar. It was probably taken to illustrate an alternative form of wood preservative because only the metalwork shows any evidence of paint. The dimensions were 18ft 9in over headstock, 7ft 11in wide, on a 10ft wheelbase. It had the later welded strapping and was fitted with brakes on all four wheels. The axleboxes were the flat-fronted first oil-filled pattern and the screw coupling is clearly visible. The wagon was fitted with the three-position rail for the location of the large/medium/small partition. The 'P.F' on the top right-hand plank reveals that it was pipe fitted.
NATIONAL RAILWAY MUSEUM (ETN 69)

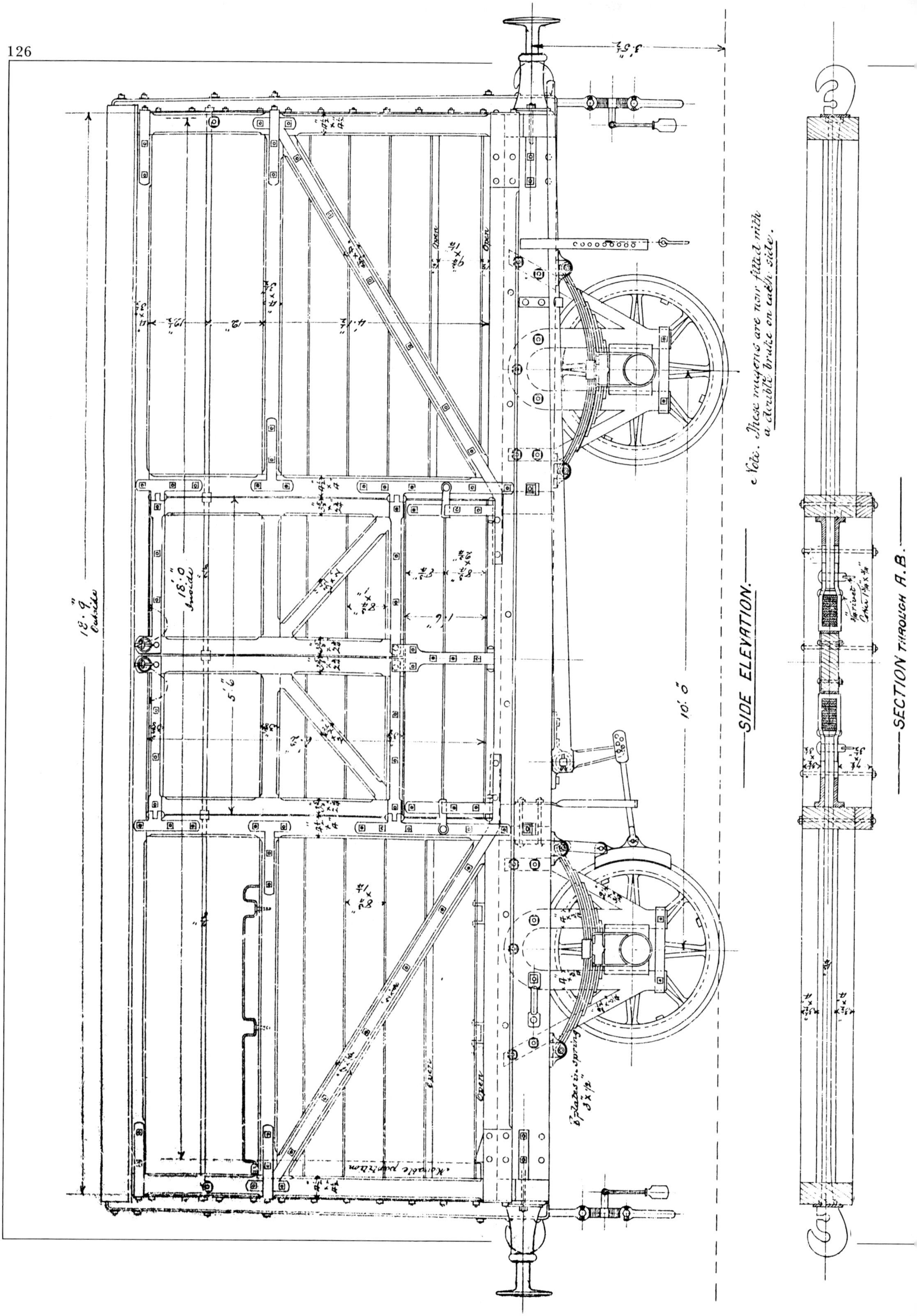

SIDE ELEVATION.
SECTION THROUGH A.B.
Note. These wagons are now fitted with a double brake on each side.
18' 9" Outside
18' 0" Inside
10' 0"
5' 6"
Movable partition
Open

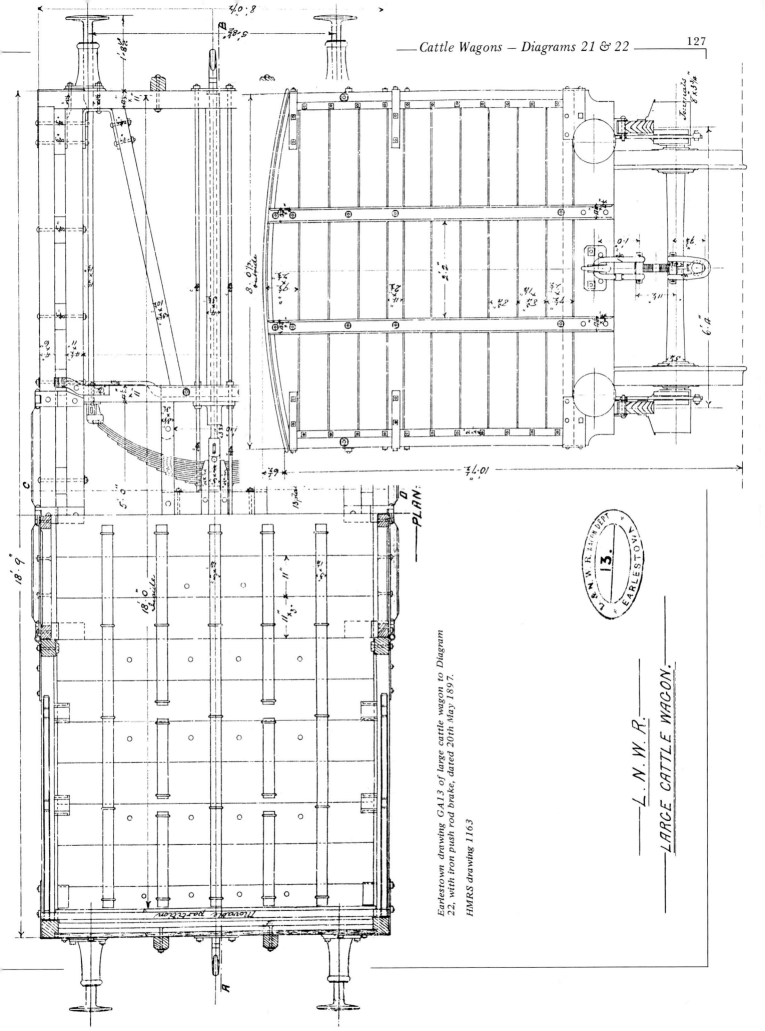

Earlestown drawing GA13 of large cattle wagon to Diagram 22, with iron push rod brake, dated 20th May 1897.

HMRS drawing 1163

L. N. W. R.

LARGE CATTLE WAGON.

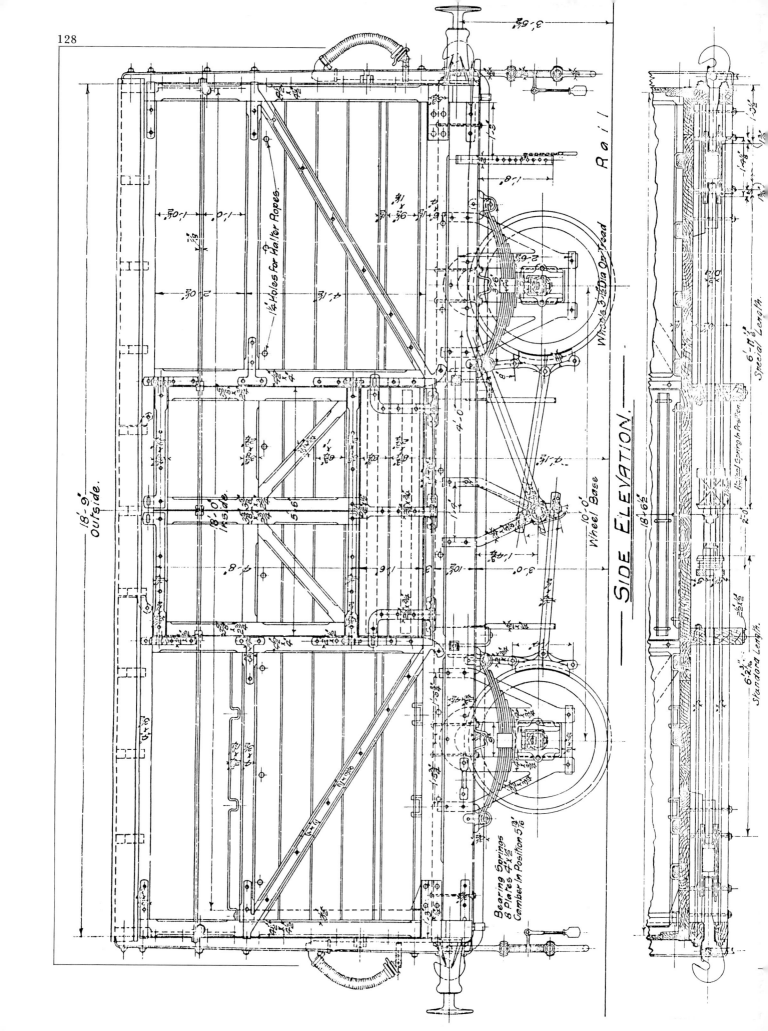

1/4 Holes for Halter Ropes.

18'-9" Outside.

Bearing Springs
8 Plates 4"x1/2"
Camber In Position 5 1/8"

Wheels 3'-8" Dia On Tread

Wheel Base

— SIDE ELEVATION. —

Rail

Special Length.

Standard Length.

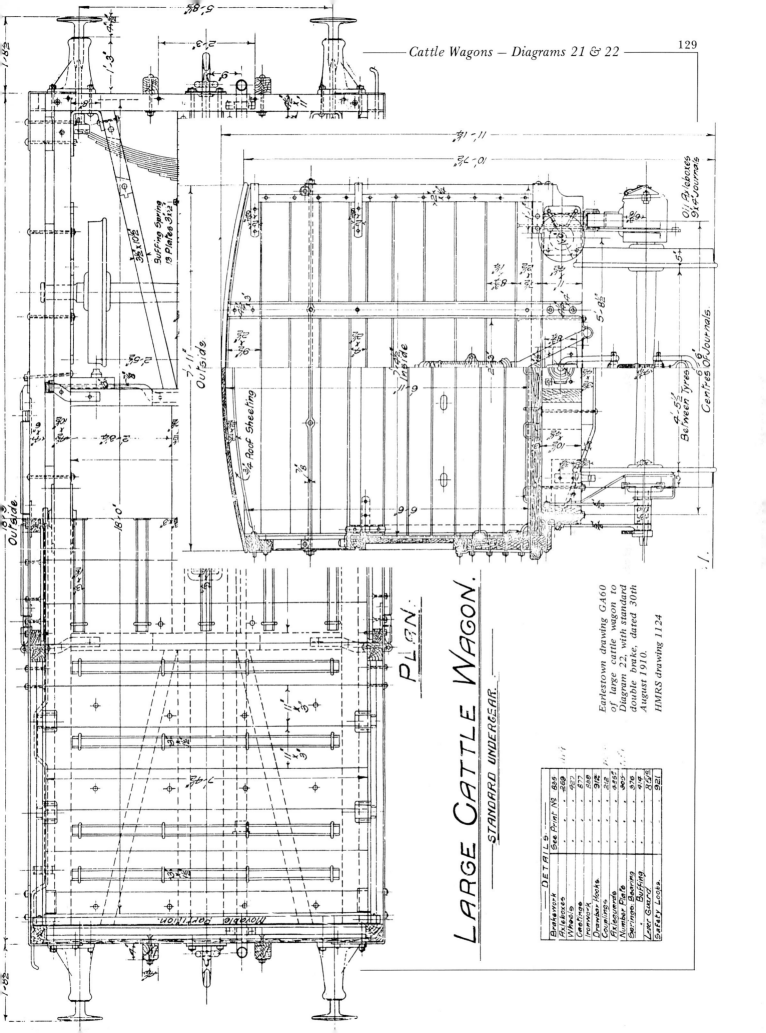

LARGE CATTLE WAGON.

— STANDARD UNDERGEAR. —

PLAN.

Earlestown drawing GA60 of large cattle wagon to Diagram 22, with standard double brake, dated 30th August 1910.

HMRS drawing 1124

DETAILS	See Print No	
Brakework	835	
Axleboxes	269	
Wheels	427	
Castings	877	
Ironwork	888	
Drawbar Hooks	912	
Couplings	212	
Axleguards	458	
Number Plate	303	
Springs, Bearing	376	
" Buffing	414	
Lever Guard	859	
Safety Loops	921	

Buffing Spring 3½ x 2
13 Plates 3 x ½

3½ x 10½

Oil Axleboxes 9 x 4 Journals

Centres Of Journals.

6' 6" Between Tyres

4' 5½"

5' 8¼"

18' 0"

¾ Roof Sheeting

Movable Partition

to both-sides brakes but 654 were still single-sided. Known examples below show the effect of these changes on the tare weight of a vehicle. In the 1880s a 'medium' wagon weighed about 5.16.0 but by 1910 the same size wagon fitted with all the above new features weighed over seven tons.

Usage and wear and tear on these vehicles was high; consequently there was a need for constant renewal of condemned vehicles. This may be judged from the fact that in 1902 the average age of the cattle wagon stock was 11.5 years compared with 20 years for the covered vans. A similar indication comes from data on the rate of replacement; for example, in a five-year period at the turn of the century, 17.3% of the cattle wagons were renewed compared with only 13.6% of the covered vans. To maintain a steady stock of about 2,300 during the thirty-eight years between 1882 and 1920, the total number of cattle wagons constructed seems to have been almost 2,700.

In general the LNWR goods stock gave the appearance of a random approach to numbering rather than that of a systematic block numbering system for each class of vehicle. At one time it was thought that only the few surviving photographs could be used as evidence of cattle wagon running numbers. However, recent research by Peter Ellis has discovered over 1,000 written records in the form of cattle tickets (invoices) or number takers book records, spread over five or six locations, and dating between 1862 to 1922. The information gathered to date is summarised in *Table 4.1*. The numbers can be seen to fall into closely defined groups which are in general agreement with the building records. Since this evidence is more circumstantial, modellers may prefer to limit themselves to photographic evidence, so the numbers listed below are for medium and large cattle wagons which can be substantiated from surviving photographs.

One of the best documentary sources of cattle wagon numbers is that held at the Public Records Office, consisting of 250 Cattle Tickets in a bound volume comprising a record of weekly shipments from the LNWR agent at Chapel en le Frith to various destinations between October 1880 and November 1885.[†] The wagons are identified as S or Small, M, Medium or 15ft, and L or Large. Various other descriptions such as 'L as Half' or 'M as S' indicate part loads, although proper partitions are not thought to have come into use until about ten years later. A similar cattle ticket from 1892 is illustrated on page 114 and a 1921 wagon label on page 115.

[†] Ref. 13, Bibliography and References.

Another LNWR large cattle wagon in LMS days. The photographer is unknown but the print is dated 22/8/1936. It appears to have had similar design features to No. 15483 on page 125, i.e. the dimensions were 18ft 9in over headstock, 7ft 11in wide, on a 10ft wheelbase. It had the later welded strapping and was fitted with brakes on all four wheels. The two major differences visible between this vehicle and No. 15483 are the fitting of the bulbous-style axleboxes, and the later style spring shoes which were extended upwards over the face of the solebar and bolted through it. Judging from photographs of other types of wagon, this style of spring shoes was in use around 1921/2. On the original print the white letter 'N' on a dark square, which signified the non-common user status of the wagon, is visible on the outside corners of the bottom planks.

CTY. PETER ELLIS

In 1923 at the Grouping 1,425 medium and 891 large LNWR cattle wagons passed to the LMS.

Known examples of Diagram 21 – Medium Cattle Wagon:
Diagram book tare for type: 6.1.0
With full vacuum brakes: 7.1.1

Number	Tare	Buffers	Brakes	Axleboxes	Notes
14784	–				15ft 6in
16055	5.17.2		Wood 1S	Grease	15ft 6in
214701★	6.15.0				
215129★	6.14.0	2-rib	DBBS	Flat-fronted	16ft 2½in
215219★	6.15.2				
215223★	6.10.0	3-bolt			
21586★	–	2-rib	DBBS	Flat-fronted	16ft 2½in
215931★	–				

Known examples of Diagram 22 – Large Cattle Wagon:
Diagram book tare for type: 6.2.3
With full vacuum brakes: 7.8.2

Number	Tare	Buffers	Brakes	Axleboxes	Notes
14625					17ft 10in
15283					17ft 10in
15483	7.14.2			flat	
30909	–				
131543★§	–	2-rib	DB?S	Bulbous	as at 1937
182212★§	7-2-2	2-rib	DBBS	Bulbous	as at 1934 or after
206329★	7.7.0				
232584★	7.5.2				
265692★	–				

★ LMS numbers.
§ Numbered by LMS in L&Y series.

Another Guy Hemmingway photograph dating from 1938, according to the oil and lifting dates on the solebar. The LMS livery appears to have been identical to No. 205692 on page 132 with a slight livery change in that the tare weight had been moved up to the fourth plank on the right-hand side. The small oval plate to the left of the cast numberplate on the solebar was a regular LMS feature. It is not legible in the photograph but no doubt said somewhat incongruously 'LMS Earlestown 1910' or whatever the appropriate year was. It is noticeable on photographs of vehicles in LMS condition that the limewash disinfectant had been discontinued. HMRS (H5010)

TABLE 4.1 – A RECONSTRUCTION OF BUILDING DATA & NUMBERS OF LNWR CATTLE WAGONS

Year	Capital build	Assigned number range	Register Numbers Recorded Examples
pre-1862	1682	14321–16002	842 records, 14520 to 16200 [1680]
1865	6	20270–22190	44 records, 22064 to 22148 [84]
1866	22	22191–25735	A few scattered records found
1867	52	25736–26733	A few scattered records found
1869	135	26994–27513	69 records, 27352 to 27549 [197]
1870	33	27514–28777	A few scattered records found
1871	8	28778–30865	A few scattered records found
1872	150	30866–34196	50 records, 32567 to 32703 [136]
1876	1	40386–40711	None recorded
1878	1	41685–42577	None recorded
1879	56	no new nos. used	Probably took nos. of scrapped other types
1882	200	45906–47006	82 records, 46754 to 46947 [193]
	2346	TOTAL	1087 records, representing a 46% sample

NOTES
1. The quantity built on Capital Account are the additions to stock which would have been issued with new register numbers at the top of the then current number range.
2. The assigned number range indicates the new register numbers issued in each succeeding year, calculated from the total stock at the beginning and end of each year after deducting the Brake vans and Ballast wagons which were numbered separately.
3. The numbers in brackets are the quantities enclosed by the upper and lower register numbers identified within each group. i.e. the maximum number of wagons in the group *if* all were cattle wagons. The data is still insufficient to support such an assertion.
4. The re-numbering in 1862 seems to have grouped together all the then existing cattle wagons. Since there were only 1,433 wagons at the time compared with the 1,680 numbers within the range, not all these numbers could have been carried by cattle wagons.
5. The above 1,000 records are part of a collection of over 10,000 records covering all types of wagon. The statistical significance of a 46% sample, taken together with the obvious agreement with the building records, leads to the conclusion that the vast majority of cattle wagons were numbered in the groups identified above, rather than widely spread throughout the entire register number range.
6. A comparison of the 'assigned number range', derived from the surviving building records, and the range of the cattle wagon numbers found in contemporary records such as invoices, etc, shows that the two sources are closely matched but not exact. In the absence of the original Earlestown records this reconstruction is probably the best that can be achieved at the present time, and certainly shows that the cattle wagon numbers were closely confined in five groups rather than randomly spread over the whole range of numbers.

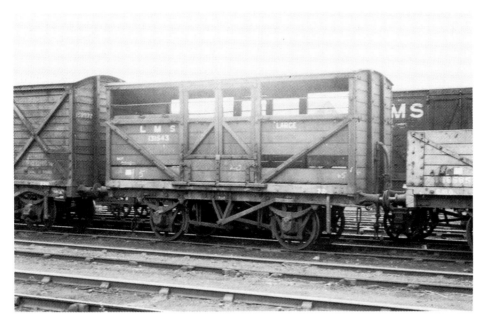

A Diagram 22 large cattle wagon in a parlous state with one plank completely missing. Seen here in LMS livery in 1937, it had been numbered in the L&Y series, originally being LNWR No. 31543 but with 100,000 added instead of 200,000. This is thought to have been due to the LNW/L&Y merger. Note the strapping at either end fixing the roof down.

CTY. G. H. PLATT

Large cattle wagon No. 182212 was seen in LMS livery, with brake gear right at the limit of its travel. The build date would be 1910 or after as 2-rib buffers were fitted, with bulbous axleboxes. The tare is 7.2.2 and the label holder was positioned at the far right on the second plank.

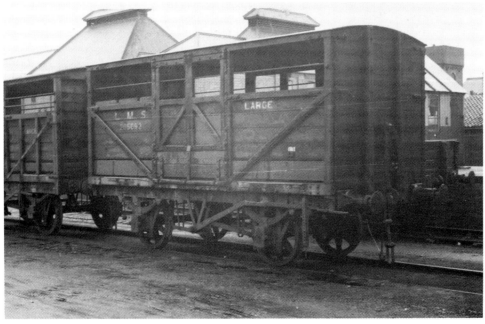

This LNWR large cattle wagon in LMS livery appears to have identical design features to the one on page 130, i.e. the dimensions were 18ft 9in over headstock, 7ft 11in wide, on a 10ft wheelbase. It had the later welded strapping and was fitted with double brakes both sides. The axleboxes were the flat-fronted LMS pattern and the through pipe and screw coupling are clearly visible on the end of the vehicle. The wagon was fitted with the three-position rail for the location of the large/medium/small partition except that a spring label clip had replaced the cast-iron LNWR label holder on the second plank on the right-hand side.

HMRS (H4009)

DIAGRAM 23 – SPECIAL CATTLE WAGONS

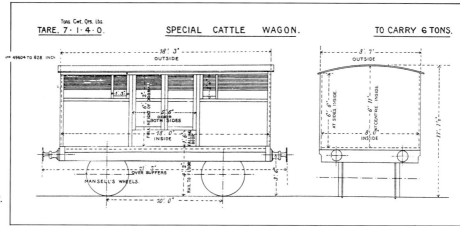

Diagram Book page of Diagram 23.

Twenty-five of these special cattle wagons were authorised to be built in 1888 at a cost of £102 each for the transport of prize beasts to and from agricultural shows. They had much in common with the standard large cattle wagon (Diagram 22) but the sides were completely enclosed and the length was only 18ft 3in and carried only six tons. Unlike contemporary horse-boxes, they were devoid of internal stalls, padding or fittings because it was feared that such fittings would be damaged by the regular use of disinfectants. Rings were fitted around the centre rail to which the animals' halter rope could be tied.

Full constructional details are visible in the official general arrangement drawing dated 30th May 1883, and reproduced on pages 134/135, and an official photograph showing a vehicle in largely the same condition as in the drawing above. Note in particular that the handbrake operates on one wheel only. In general, the running gear, couplings and buffers are similar to contemporary passenger stock so that these vehicles could travel in express passenger trains.

The 3ft 7in diameter Mansell wheels also are redolent of passenger vehicles rather than goods wagons. Although not fitted with full automatic brakes, they were equipped with through pipes for both the normal vacuum brake and the Westinghouse pattern, the latter presumably allowing them to operate through to Scotland on Caledonian trains north of Carlisle. The lined-out 'Lake' livery is an adaptation of the non-passenger carriage livery, but the large 'LNWR' letters, as shown in the photograph dated November 1909, are typical of the goods livery. Prior to February 1908 the only identification marks would have been two white diamonds.

The wagon numbers are recorded in the 1903 Wagon Diagram Book as 49604 to 49628 inclusive. Most of the twenty-five vehicles had a long and useful life. But one, No. 49626, possibly following an accident, was renewed in 1912 as a Diagram 26 vehicle. Three more were scrapped in the period 1921-23 and were also renewed as Diagram 26 wagons. The remaining twenty-one passed to the LMS in 1923

when they were almost 40 years old. This unusual longevity probably indicates that they led a much quieter life than the average ordinary cattle wagon.

Known examples of Diagram 23:
Diagram book tare for type: 7.1.4

Number	Tare	Buffers	Brakes	Axleboxes
49604–49609				
49610	7.6.2	3-bolt	Wood 1S	Grease No.2
49611–49628				

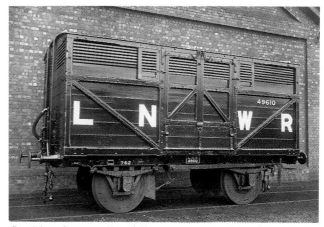

Special cattle wagon No. 49610, Diagram 23, was one of twenty-five built in 1888. It is shown here in an official photograph taken at Earlestown in November 1909, presumably after a major overhaul and repaint. It was 18ft 3in long over headstocks, 8ft 7in wide and had a 10ft wheelbase. Even at this late date it retained its coupling side chains and was fitted with only a simple handbrake consisting of a wooden brake block operated by a straight handle and pushrod. Note also the 3ft 7in Mansell wheels and screw coupling to facilitate its running in passenger traffic. These vehicles were originally fitted with vacuum pipes only but later Westinghouse pipes were added. This was to make them acceptable to the Caledonian company, north of the border. It is seen painted in the 'quick brown' colour used for horse-boxes and other non-passenger coaching stock and was lined out in yellow. Their purpose was to transport valuable prize cattle to agricultural shows quickly by passenger train. The omission of the diamonds from the livery was undoubtedly due to its passenger train status. None of the photographs of these special cattle wagons show diamonds in the livery. Note the three white-painted roof grab handles – one at each end, one centrally above the door. **NATIONAL RAILWAY MUSEUM (ETN 76A)**

134

Drawing of Diagram 23 special cattle wagon, dated
30th May 1883.
HMRS drawing 1164

SIDE ELEVATION.

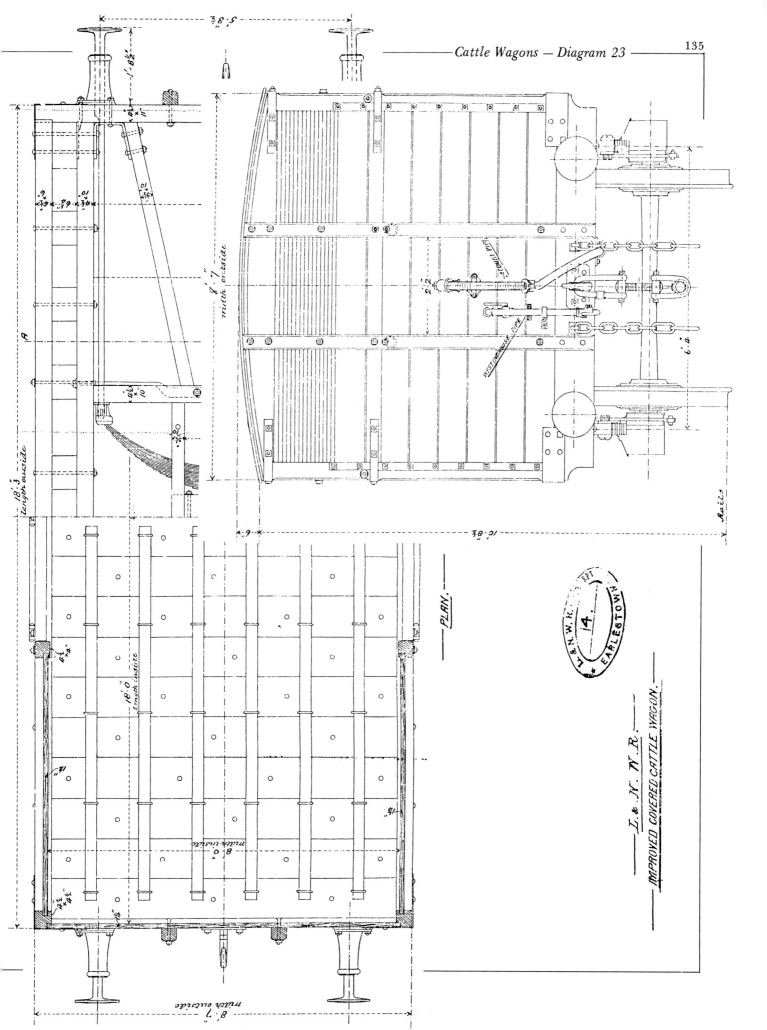

PLAN.

L. & N. W. R.

IMPROVED COVERED CATTLE WAGON.

DIAGRAM 24 – FOWLER'S CATTLE WAGON

This rather poor reproduction of a Railway Magazine original, May 1901, is the only known photograph of one of P. H. Fowler's special cattle wagons. The only drawing available is the Diagram Book sketch; so much of the construction detail of these wagons is unknown. However, the detail and extent of the lettering visible in the photograph indicates that the outside of the vehicle was solid boarded. Because the two wagons were built especially for Mr. Fowler's trade, they have unique design features such as the central footsteps and a water tank on the roof. Naturally, the mechanical features reflect the normal standards of the 1880s. Where detail is not visible, it is reasonable to assume that it would be similar to the Diagram 23 special cattle wagon shown on pages 133-5, which was designed less than four years later. Both had Mansell wheels, side chains, a single wooden brake block operated by a straight lever and normal 3-bolt buffers. The axleboxes were the wider, 10-ton, No. 2 type to accommodate the higher tare weight of these vehicles.

There seem to have been numerous examples of privately lettered combination trucks hired to the private trader and running on the LNWR. There is even evidence of a similar hiring arrangement for privately lettered Refrigerator Wagons (Diagram 46). But these two cattle wagons are the only known examples where a cattle dealer, Mr. P.H. Fowler of Watford, had special vehicles built and lettered for his own use.

G.P. Neale, in his book *Railway Reminiscences* p.281, records that Mr. Fowler had long been dissatisfied with the ordinary cattle wagons for the conveyance of his valuable livestock. The use of a horse-box was considered unsatisfactory because of possible damage to the fittings by the disinfectants. Mr. Neale tells how he had the task of scheming with Mr. Fowler the construction of 'special vehicles by which his cattle are now conveyed'.

Mr. Percival Henry Fowler was a cattle dealer and importer of valuable Jersey and Guernsey cattle, who had a cattle repository in St. Albans Road, Watford, close to Watford Junction station.

There were just two vehicles, which were built in 1884 to carry six tons. No general arrangement drawing seems to have survived neither is there a good quality photograph. The Diagram Book sketch shows the original condition of the vehicles. Most copies of the Diagram Book have hand alterations indicating that the roof water tank and the internal fittings were removed at some later stage. The only known photograph was published in the *Railway Magazine* Vol. viii. p.488 in 1901. The extent of the lettering suggests that the sides were externally planked. It is reasonable to assume that the running gear was similar to that of Diagram 23, and they were probably fitted for running in express traffic. The numbers were 49476 and 49477 and they lasted in service until 1912-13, which seems to be when Mr. Fowler retired from business. After this time 49476 became an 'ordinary' special cattle wagon, Diagram 23, whilst 49477 was broken up and renewed as a Diagram 26 Cattle Wagon with Drovers' Compartment.

Known examples of Diagram 24:
Diagram book tare for type: 8.7.0

Numbers
49476
49477

Lettering on the side of a Fowler's Diagram 24 special cattle wagon appears to be:

P.H.FOWLER

Importer of Jersey & Guernsey

COWS

WATFORD.HERTS
(crest)

BY APPOINTMENT

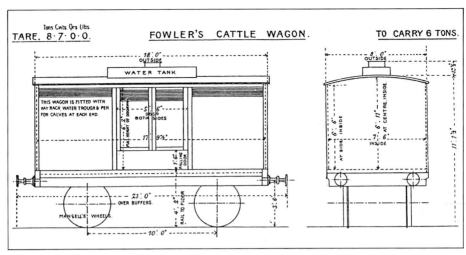

Diagram Book page of Diagram 24.

DIAGRAM 25 – 19ft 9in CATTLE WAGON WITH DROVERS COMPARTMENT

A further six wagons for prize cattle traffic were built in 1899. For the first time these incorporated a drovers compartment. There is no known photograph of this type but a general arrangement drawing, GA15, on pages 138/139, still exists. The cattle section was similar to the Diagram 23 vehicles but a careful comparison of their respective drawings shows that the lengths were shorter. The drawing indicates that these vehicles had both hand and vacuum brakes with Westinghouse through pipes for running north of the border or elsewhere. It is worth noting that the early version of the clasp brake rigging operates on the outside tyre only of all four wheels, only the single shoe handbrake working on the inside. Note also the release valve for the vacuum sack which was located in the centre of the solebar and indicated by a letter 'A', standing for 'Automatic Vacuum', also that the drawing is marked with a note 'fitted with handbrake on each side'. So, surprisingly, it seems Diagram 25 had handbrakes on both sides but the later Diagram 26 did not.

The numbers assigned to these wagons were 67397 to 67402 inclusive. In the absence of a photograph, we may reasonably assume that the livery was again the modified 'Quick Brown' with yellow lining so as to match the contemporary non-passenger carriage stock, and with lettering similar to that shown in photographs of Diagram 26 on pages 140/141. All six survived to pass into the hands of the LMS in 1923. Nos. 67397 and 67400 were withdrawn in August and November 1933 respectively. They had been renumbered 43960 and 43961 in the LMS Passenger Stock series that year but it is unlikely that the new numbers were ever carried.

Known examples of Diagram 25:
Diagram book tare for type: 8.10.0

Number	Tare	Buffers	Brakes	Axleboxes
67397–67402			Clasp BS	

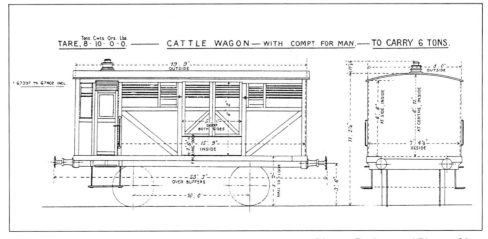

Diagram Book page of Diagram 25.

Drawing GA15 of Diagram 25 19ft 9in special cattle wagon with drover's compartment.
HMRS drawing 1159

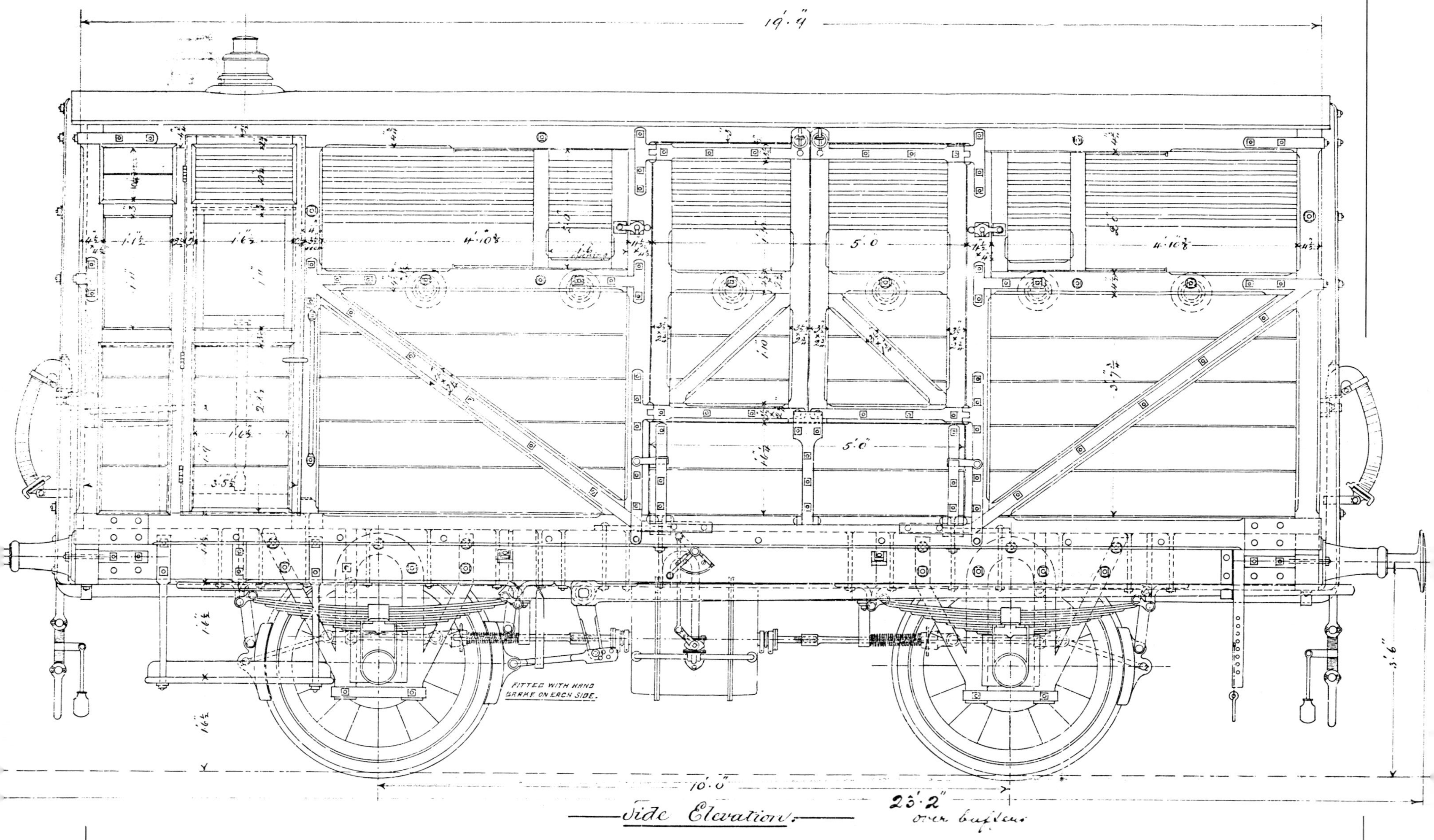

Side Elevation.

23'2" over buffers

19'4"

10'0"

9'5"

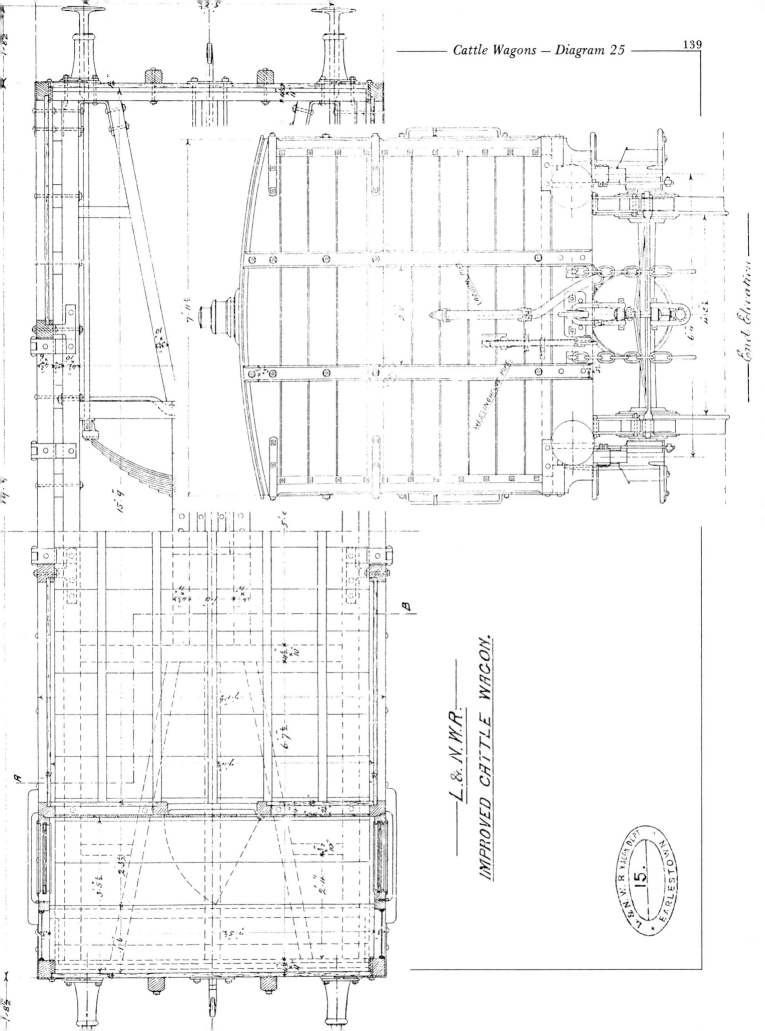

—*End Elevation*—

—*L. & . N. W. R.*—

IMPROVED CATTLE WAGON.

DIAGRAM 26 – 22ft 0in CATTLE WAGON WITH DROVERS COMPARTMENT

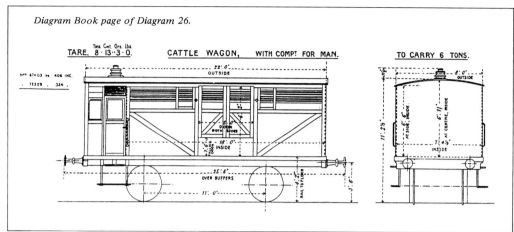

Diagram Book page of Diagram 26.

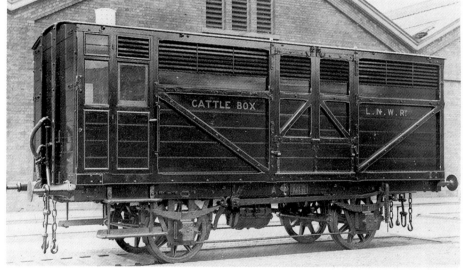

This photograph of a special cattle wagon (Cattle Box) with compartment for a man, Diagram 26, No. 72331, is not dated but seems to show a vehicle in original condition, i.e. about 1902. It was 22ft 0in long over headstocks and 7ft 11½in wide with an 11ft wheelbase. Notice that it was fitted with 'vacuum pipes and blocks', the correct LNW term, and Westinghouse pipes. The horizontal vacuum cylinder can be seen centrally below the solebar and there was additionally a hand brake operating on one wheel only. The vacuum release valve is visible to the left of the number-plate in the centre of the solebar marked by a letter 'A'. The wagon is seen painted in the 'quick brown' colour and lined out in yellow. Compare the livery with the similar vehicle of the same type shown opposite. This is the only photograph showing this type of livery and indicates the company ownership as L.N.W.Ry. There are no diamonds in evidence which perhaps indicates its close associ-ation with passenger operations, despite being numbered in the goods stock.
LNW SOCIETY (9581)

In 1902 a final batch of ten special cattle wagons was built by the LNWR at Earlestown. Like those to Diagram 25 they incorporated a drovers compartment, but in comparison, the cattle section was enlarged so that the overall length was increased to 22 feet. A surviving official general arrangement drawing, Earlestown GA 64, dated 23rd October 1901, is reproduced on page 142. This records the details of the mechanical specification. Note that full vacuum brakes were fitted with a cast-iron block on each side of each wheel, being commonly termed 'clasp brakes'. The hand-brake operated a single block on one wheel on one side only. A Westinghouse through pipe was also fitted.

The wagon/register numbers fall into two separate batch-es: Firstly, 67403 to 67406 inclusive which, perhaps surpris-ingly, follow directly on to the numbers assigned to the batch of Diagram 25 special cattle wagons which were built sever-al years earlier in 1899. Since there is absolutely no evidence that these Diagram 26 cattle wagons were built until 1902, we must conclude that this batch of numbers was reserved

against future construction. It seems likely that all ten were ordered in 1899 but that the change to the Diagram 26 design was agreed before the last four were started. Consequently, the numbers were held in abeyance until building to the new design commenced in 1902. The remaining six were allocated 72329 to 72334 inclusive which are numbers clearly associated with a 1902 building date.

No. 49626 was built in 1912 as replacement for a Diagram 23 vehicle, presumably following an accident.

Known examples of Diagram 26:
Diagram book tare for type: 8.13.3

Number	Tare	Buffers	Brakes	Axleboxes	Notes
67403–67406			Clasp BS		
72329–72331			Clasp BS		
72332	8.11.1		Clasp BS		
72333–72334			Clasp BS		
49626	8.16.2	1-rib square base	Clasp BS	Pointed-front oil	After 1912

This photograph of a special cattle wagon (Cattle Box) with compartment for a man, Diagram 26, No. 72332, is dated March 1909 and shows a vehicle in later livery compared with that of vehicle No. 72331 opposite. All the other constructional and mechanical features appear identical. As with all the other special cattle wagons, it was painted in the 'quick brown' colour and lined out in yellow. The photograph below shows No. 49626, a 1912 replacement for a former Diagram 23 wagon. In line with company policy, it was not a reproduction of the scrapped vehicle but rather a new vehicle 'of the type now building', i.e. a Diagram 26 type vehicle. Being built later than 72332, No. 49626 had later brake gear and its axleboxes were of the second oil-filled pattern.
NATIONAL RAILWAY MUSEUM

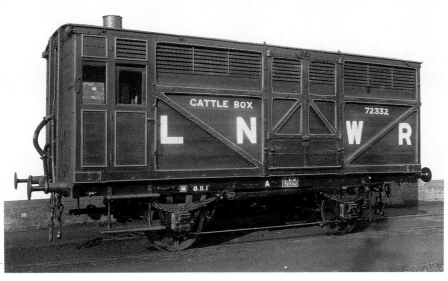

An official photograph of 22ft 0in D26 Special Cattle Wagon with Drover's Compartment No. 49626 taken no doubt shortly after its paint date of March 1912. Lined out in the 'Lake/Quick Brown' livery, it had the running gear and fittings below the solebars painted in photographic grey. This enables the steam heating through pipe running from end to end to be clearly seen. Note the panel edging above and below the drover's compartment windows were lined out. The roof ventilator above the compartment was white, hinting at the roof colour, which cannot otherwise be confirmed. The tare reads 8.16.2 and the picture shows pointed-front axleboxes, clasp brakes, single-rib buffers and screw couplings. The wagon was dual-fitted and had a cam-action handbrake. Note the lower step support went through the step and that the train alarm indicator at the top right-hand corner showed its red face to the guard, being in the 'on' position.
NATIONAL RAILWAY MUSEUM (ETN 88)

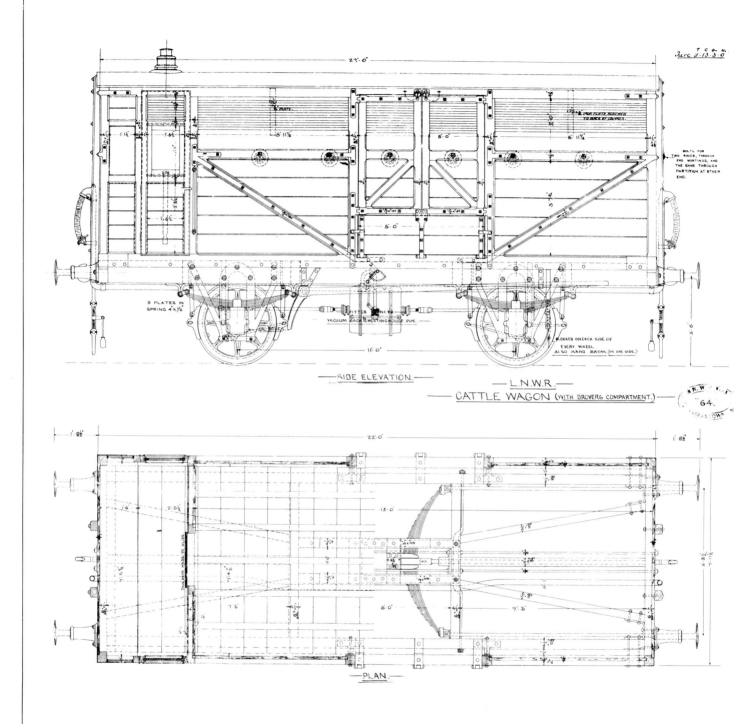

— SIDE ELEVATION. —

— L.N.W.R. —
CATTLE WAGON (WITH DROVERS COMPARTMENT.)

— PLAN. —

Earlestown drawing GA64 of Diagram 26, 22ft cattle wagon with compartment for man, dated 23rd October 1901. The tare is 8-13-3.

HMRS drawing 1158

This Diagram 26 prize cattle wagon was photographed in LMS livery with the 'LMS' legend in the lower left main panel and 'CATTLE BOX' on the top side plank to the right of the cattle door. Two-rib buffers and bulbous axleboxes confirm a build date after 1910, so it cannot have been one of the first two. The oil light pot can be seen on the roof of the drover's compartment. Alarm gear had been added by the LMS. When activated, the red signal flap projecting beyond the sides, normally horizontal, rotated to the vertical, presenting the red face to the guard, so identifying where the chain had been pulled.
CTY. J. P. RICHARDS

In BR days, M43968 was photographed parked unused in a wintry siding. It was labelled 'XP' at the lower right-hand side, but little identified it for cattle — the 'CATTLE BOX' designation had gone. The handbrake had been replaced by a short LMS version with a Morton clutch, and the axleboxes were flat-fronted.

M43966 also carried alarm gear for the drover when photographed in BR livery, but 'CATTLE BOX' can be seen below the number. The 'XP' indicating its suitability for express traffic, was at the right-hand end, a conventional LMS vertical vacuum brake cylinder, piping and screw couplings having been fitted. Note the iron step hangers passing through the wooden steps and the right-hand wheels were 3-hole disc steel. The pin rack was again stoved in.
CTY. G. B. ELLIS (11825)

A typical large timber load being loaded by crane onto at least three Diagram 12 timber wagons. The wagon most easily seen was D12 No. 28904, carrying post 1908 livery but still with dumb buffers, single wooden brake block and a tare of 4.10.1. The wagon to the right appears to have been identical, but too filthy to make out any lettering. Two of the young men can be seen holding a tape measure between them, probably for measuring the girth of the tree, from which the charge for carriage could be calculated. The picture is full of interesting features, such as the standard yard crane with long octagonal jib, a two-handed saw lying in the foreground and the grab used to lift the log. The unusual signal box is thought to have been on the GNR Stafford line.
COLLECTION A. G. ELLIS (5879)

CHAPTER FIVE
TIMBER WAGONS

IN this chapter we will look at vehicles officially classified as timber wagons, i.e, those listed in the summary table. First, it is important to separate out the Diagrams which could carry timber but which really belong in other categories. Although from 1909 Diagram 97 wagons were fitted with detachable bolsters able to carry timber and rail, etc., and Diagram 110 Warflats and some Diagram 109 Rectanks also had bolsters fitted in later years, all three were described as 'Trolleys' and will therefore be included in that category when covered in a later volume. Timber wagons could, of course, carry a wide range of other loads such as rails, rolled steel sections, pipes and fabrications of considerable size (see *Appendix 3*). In fact the official description for such wagons, following from the Railway Accounts Act, was 'Rail & Timber Wagons'.

Whishaw in 1842 (Bibliography & References Ref: 10) describes the wagons used on many railways but only the Liverpool and Manchester descriptions include what we would now refer to as a timber or bolster wagon:

'When timber is to be conveyed on the railway, it is placed on two trucks properly built for the purpose. Above the ordinary truck-platform are fixed cross pieces of timber, curved towards the middle, which is higher than the sides by about 2 inches, above these are cross-timbers 12 inches by 8 inches, and curved upwards as to their ends, which are 4 inches above the fixed cross-pieces. Each of these pieces turns on a swivel fixed in the middle of the cross-timber. This arrangement allows the wagons to have proper play in going round curves. Chains are used to secure the logs to the carriages. We observed one log of timber placed on two trucks, which was upwards of 50 feet in length.'

SUMMARY

Diagram	Introduced	Description
12	1870	Timber wagon (ordinary), 10 tons
13	1875	Twin timber wagons, each 10 tons
14	1877	Timber wagon 24ft long, 10 tons
[14a	1910	Timber wagon 24ft long, fast sides & drop ends, 10 tons]
107	1911	Timber trolley, 30 tons

The length of the description suggests that the Liverpool and Manchester was unusual, perhaps unique in this respect. One must also question the accuracy of a log 50 feet in length being carried on only two short wagons. It is possible that the wagons were not coupled, and were joined only by the load, since no mention is made of runner wagons.

The next reference point we have is the Huish report of 1848 (Bibliography & References Ref: 11), only six years after Whishaw but after the amalgamation of 1846. Curiously, this shows that the Southern Division was alone in having timber wagons − twelve of them. Neither the Northern Division nor the Manchester and Birmingham Division had any. D.K. Clarke's *Railway Machinery* of 1855 (Bibliography & References Ref: 9) includes a drawing of a Southern Division bolster wagon which looks remarkably modern and little different from wagons built almost 50 years later. They appear to have been rated at 6 tons and all twelve were withdrawn in 1892.

DIAGRAM 12 − TIMBER WAGON

The next timber wagons appeared in 1870 and seem to have been of two types, 7-ton and 10−ton. In the 1903 diagram book they were all classed as Diagram 12. In 1870 a total of 163 of the 7-ton wagons were built followed by forty-three of the 10-ton version, although in 1877 forty-nine of the later 10-ton wagons were downgraded to 7-tons.

Building continued steadily until 1880, by which time they totalled 1,358. Wagons built as 7-tons normally had journals 6in x 3in whereas wagons built as 10-tons had journals of 8in x 3¾in. It is possible that the two types were identical in all other respects. All 212 7-ton wagons lasted until 1892 when they began to be renewed by 10-ton versions, the last three going in 1914. A few replacements for accident victims were built in 1881−2 and more batches from 1890−1911, when it was decided to replace ninety of them with a new Diagram 107 bogie design and from then on numbers began to decline. A total of 1,467 remained to pass into LMS ownership in 1923.

The design and construction of Diagram 12 followed the standards in most respects. The external length was 12ft with dumb buffers protruding a further 15½in beyond the head-

stocks each end. The external width was 7ft 7½in. The floor was of 7in x 2½in planks, the sides and ends 5in x 3in. The effective height of the sides was thus 2½in above the floor. The main feature was, of course, the bolster which was 10in x 11in and fixed by a 2¼in diameter pivot which passed right through the wagon and was secured by a key beneath to prevent the bolster being lifted out. By removing this key, the bolster could be removed and bolsters were therefore all numbered in a separate sequence from the wagons themselves.

Curved wooden guides faced with steel were provided on top of the floor at either end of the central transom to ensure that the bolster would swivel smoothly through about 15 degrees. Wooden stops were fitted at the end of these guides to ensure that this travel was not exceeded, which would have allowed the bolster to tilt to one side, making the load unstable.

At the ends of the bolster, steel stanchions 2ft 0in high and 6ft 6in apart were fitted. They were removable to facilitate loading and unloading, so that cranes did not have to lift the load so high. It also meant that with the aid of improvised

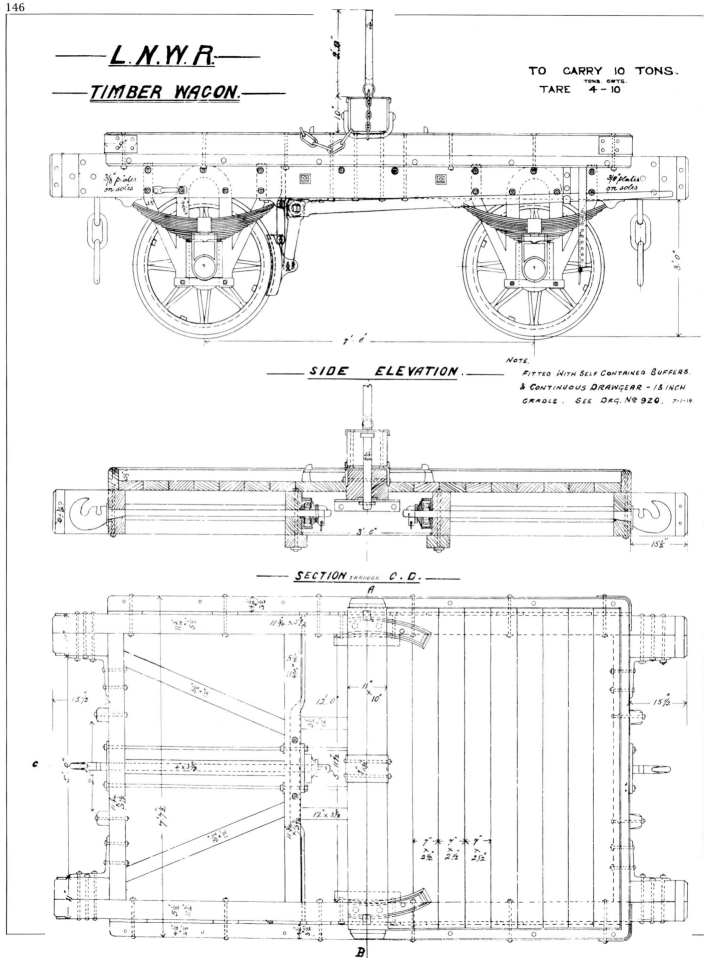

L.N.W.R.
TIMBER WAGON.

TO CARRY 10 TONS.
TONS. CWTS.
TARE 4 - 10

3/8" plates on soles

3/8" plates on soles

SIDE ELEVATION.

NOTE.
FITTED WITH SELF CONTAINED BUFFERS
& CONTINUOUS DRAWGEAR - 18 INCH
CRADLE. SEE DRG. Nº 920. 7-1-14.

SECTION THROUGH C. D.

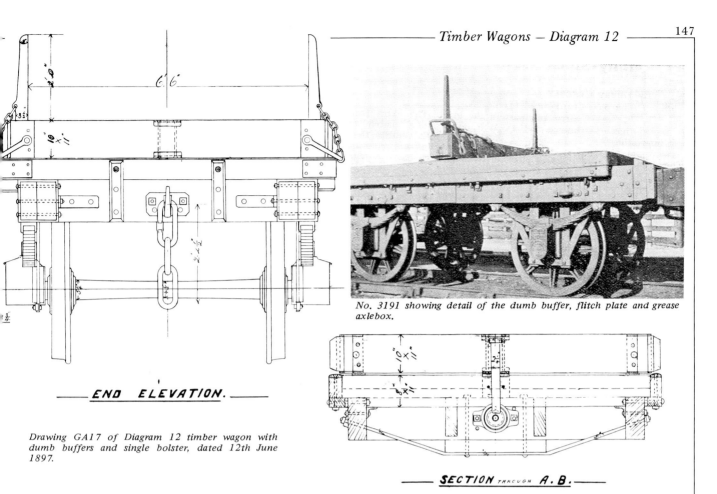

END ELEVATION.

Drawing GA17 of Diagram 12 timber wagon with dumb buffers and single bolster, dated 12th June 1897.

No. 3191 showing detail of the dumb buffer, flitch plate and grease axlebox.

SECTION THROUGH A.B.

Diagram 12 No. 28821, taken by the official Earlestown photographer in August 1909 to record the new livery. The date on the right-hand axlebox reads 1896 which may have been correct. The steel flitch plate is very obvious in this view as it clearly stopped short of the buffers. Note also the steel band or 'hoop' around the buffer to help prevent splitting on impact. The bolster had '185 LNW' incised into the side and '185' stamped on the end.

NATIONAL RAILWAY MUSEUM (55A)

wooden ramps and restraining ropes, it was possible to unload many items such as rails or pipes without a crane at all. This would not have been possible had the stanchions been fixed. Later examples had stanchions 2ft 6in high. A set of chains and adjusting screws was attached to each bolster.

The rating of a wagon usually assumed an even distribution of the load, but in the case of a bolster wagon all the weight was concentrated in the centre, and a large 8in x 11in transom was therefore fitted. It rested on the 'central' longitudinals of the frame and was rebated for the 5½in x 12in solebars which took some of the weight. In spite of the short 7ft 6in wheelbase, a further attempt was made to strengthen the frame of 10-ton versions by fitting ⅜in flitch plates to the solebars.

From the start they were built with dumb buffers and rubber sprung drawgear which transferred the load to the strong 'central' crossmembers. The buffing strains were taken direct by the solebars which were extended to form the buffers. Both buffer beams were 12in deep, as were the solebars, unlike many LNWR wagons which had deeper buffer beams than solebars.

All 1,653 Diagram 12 wagons still had dumb buffers as late as 1913 when it was decided to modernise 1,583 of them and scrap the remaining 70. This exercise began the following year and entailed cutting the solebars and flitch plates back flush with the buffer beam. A separate ½in steel plate was then bent up and planted over the flitch plate and buffer beam end, masking the joint. Self-contained RCH standard

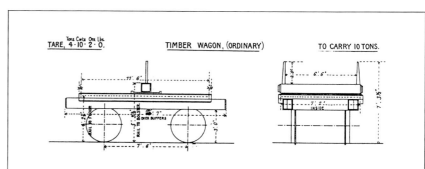

Diagram Book page of Diagram 12.

Although similar to the lower picture opposite, this view of D12 No. 37767 shows several differences. This time the date was perhaps six or seven years earlier; the paint date records 11/22 and the lifting date 14.11.22. The standard LNWR iron brake blocks were fitted (both sides) which, having a lug for the brake hanger at one end only, were handed. The corner plate rivets had been replaced by small bolts with square nuts and the label holder appears to have been mounted on a wooden plinth which had then been fixed to the solebar.

CTY. J. P. RICHARDS

buffers were bolted and screwed on and continuous drawgear fitted with a central 18in box and helical spring. The magnitude of the work involved had been the main complaint by the LNWR about the introduction of legislation requiring abolition of dumb buffers and the fitting of either-side brakes. The company obtained an extension of time because of the large numbers of dumb-buffered timber wagons still in use.

Brakes were originally of the single wooden block type, followed by single iron block with direct action, and later with pushrods. Some of those with pushrods had them on both sides. After 1914, some had double brakes fitted but these were always comparatively rare. Indeed, these wagons seem to have been very slow to acquire modern fittings, and only a few ever received oil axleboxes.

Known examples of Diagram 12:
Diagram book tare for type: 4.10.2

Number	Tare	Buffers	Brakes	Axleboxes	Notes
28818	4.18.0	Self cont.	Pushrod 1S	Grease	as at 1924
28821	4.11.0	Dumb	SB1S	Grease	as at Aug.1909
28904	4.10.1	Dumb	Wood 1S	Grease	after 1908
28951	4.16.2	Self cont.	Pushrod 1S	Grease	as at 1931
35320	4.17.2	RCH	SBBS	Grease	
37767	4.17.2	Self cont.	SBBS	Grease	after 1922, LNW No. retained

No. 28818 was photographed at Earlestown in 1924, by which time the number appeared on the side plank, and self-contained buffers had been fitted. There is no sign of company markings apart from the numberplate. The label holder was again mounted on a wooden plinth fixed to the solebar and the lifting date was on a black-painted patch above the right-hand axleguard. The brake was pushrod one side only.
HMRS (AAG 924)

Diagram 12 No. 28951, as rebuilt with self-contained buffers, raising the tare weight to 4.16.2. The solebars were simply cut off flush with the headstocks and a separate steel plate wrapped around the corner, bolted on and covered by the buffers. Amazingly, the photograph was taken in 1931, yet the LNWR livery was still clearly visible. The single iron pushrod brake had received a later, double-ended block and some of the nuts, particularly on the solebar, had been replaced by hexagonal ones, but otherwise the picture could have been taken ten years earlier.
CTY. GORDON COLTAS

This interesting photograph appeared in the LNWR Gazette for November 1922. It shows three D12 timber wagons carrying rail being unloaded by a steam crane. Second from left was a D12 converted from dumb buffers. The headstock had been cut off square and the flitch plate wrapped round the ends, thereby removing the recessed headstock end. Note the hook hanging from the shackle on some of the bolsters, also the rectangular section of the stanchion and how it tapered outwards.

An unusual oblique view of timber wagons, taken at Stafford to show how the load had been inadequately secured, as a result of which it had slipped and was out of gauge. The load itself was chained to a pair of Cambrian Railways bolster wagons, the LNWR vehicle acting as a runner due to the overhanging load. Nearest the camera can be seen the corner plate, which had small rivets through the end plank, but replacement bolts with nuts through the side plank. Such piecemeal modifications seem to have been very common, with parts only being replaced when strictly necessary. The wagon, No. 35320, had a tare of 4.17.2, so it probably had a single iron brake on each side. On the curb rail, the bolt nearest the camera had, unusually, a large washer beneath its head and lower down can be seen the later, improved tarpaulin cleat and the steel plate bent around the corner of the solebar and beneath the buffer. The buffers were to an RCH design used by the LNWR specifically for conversion of dumb buffered wagons, but obviously made by the LNWR itself as this one had the letters 'LNWR' cast into the base!

CTY. EDWARD TALBOT

DIAGRAM 13 – TWIN TIMBER WAGON

An official view of 12ft 9in twin timber wagons Nos. 40386 and 40356, to Diagram 13. The bolster of No. 40386 was lettered 'LNW 1728', whilst that on No. 40356 reads 'LNW 2169'. The 3-bolt buffers were of the longer type, as usual for the diagram, although why this should have been so is uncertain. The photograph probably dates from around 1900-02 and even at this early date the eye-bolts at the outer ends of the solebars and the lack of washers behind the W-iron nuts suggest that the solebars had steel flitch plates. The lack of a curb rail seems to have been usual on D13 and left little room on the side for lettering and diamonds which, together with the end numbers, had to be smaller than standard (refer to Liveries, Introduction). A. G. ELLIS COLLECTION (23325)

Twin timber wagons were first introduced in 1875 and 1876 when 136 were built. The next examples appeared in 1894 and further batches were constructed at intervals until 1902 by which time there were 1,436 (i.e. 718 pairs). However, in 1920/1 an additional 122 wagons (61 pairs) were built and these subsequently lasted in BR service until the mid-1950s. In the final years of the LNWR's existence some twin timber wagons were scrapped without replacement so that eventually 1,538 wagons (769 pairs) passed to the LMS in 1923.

The external length was 12ft 9in, i.e. 27ft over headstocks of the pair including the central buffer. New wagons built in 1899 and after were to an increased length of 14ft 10½in, giving a new overall length of 31ft 3in over headstocks. However, sometimes it was necessary to construct a single wagon perhaps as a replacement for an accident victim and it is thought that in this case, the new vehicle would have been built to the old dimensions in order to match with its twin.

Construction was very similar to Diagram 12 and included the dumb buffers and rubber-sprung drawgear bearing on the 'central' crossmembers. The buffer beams and solebars were all 12in deep. Bolsters were exactly as Diagram 12, dimensioned 10in x 11in and pivoted in the same way. Between each member of the pair was a central buffer/coupling which consisted of blocks of timber radiused in plan and faced with iron rubbing plates. An unsprung flat iron drawbar coupled these blocks. As a consequence of adopting centre buffers, the diagonal timbers behind the inner buffer

beams of each pair were angled the opposite way to normal so as to transfer buffing forces towards the point of contact.

For such small wagons with simple brake gear, the tare weights, at 5.10.0 and 5.9.1 respectively, seem surprisingly high, but the reason lies in the need on single bolster wagons for the bolster to swivel about the vertical centre line of the vehicle. If the bolster simply revolved on the planked floor it would wear it rapidly. The answer was to provide iron rubbing plates. A plate covering the arc of swing of the bolster was fitted to the floor and the underside of the bolster had matching rubbing plates. Together with the chains

Coupling of LNWR timber trucks.

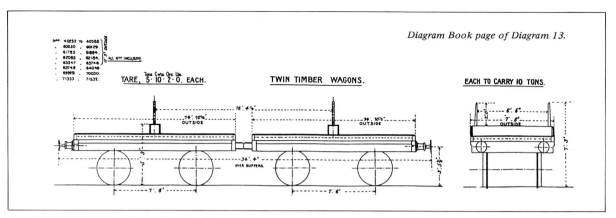

Diagram Book page of Diagram 13.

TWIN TIMBER WAGONS.

TARE, 5·10·2·0. EACH.

EACH TO CARRY 10 TONS.

Another official view of D13 timber wagons, this time a pair of 14ft 10½in wagons numbered 64011 and 64012, both with tares of 5.6.0. Both bolsters had no lettering at all, at least not on the side facing the camera. Both had paint dates of 8/09 and all readable axleboxes were dated 1904, so this could have been the date of building. The presence of a flitch plate on the solebar is not only suggested by the usual features, but proved by the steel-maker's mark rolled into the face!
NATIONAL RAILWAY MUSEUM (56A)

Although not quite in focus, this c.1904 picture of a D13 loaded with timber shows just how much could be carried by a pair of bolster wagons. The LNWR published an instruction booklet on how to load timber, showing when runner wagons were necessary and how they should be positioned and loaded (see Appendix 3).
CTY. ROGER CARPENTER (S/308)

and links on the bolster, the weight of extra metal explains the high tare figure.

At a glance, although it is easy to confuse Diagram 13 timber wagons with the very similar Diagram 48 rail wagons, the latter were 15ft 6in long and had stanchions in the bolsters only 12in tall. Diagram 48 wagons had separate curb rails whereas most Diagram 13 did not.

By 1899 the design had been modernised including the replacement of rubber drawgear by a helical spring in a fixed box. Standard 3-bolt buffers were in use by then. The brakes were handed at this period, each wagon having brakes on one side only and the levers were sited at the right-hand corner of the pair. Later still the drawgear became continuous but the coupling between members of a pair was, of course, unsprung and rigid. As with Diagram 12, it was decided in 1913 to convert all dumb-buffered twins to self-contained buffers. At that time about half the stock still had dumb buffers and 352 pairs were to be modified. After about 1910 oil boxes and double brakes were fitted but they still remained comparatively rare in LNWR days. By 1919 only twenty-five of the 710 pairs had been fitted with oil axle-boxes. As with Diagram 12, the stanchions were detachable and were later increased in height from 2ft 0in to 2ft 6in.

Known examples of Diagram 13:

Diagram book tare for type: 5.10.2 each

Numbers	Tare	Buffers	Brakes	Axleboxes
40386 +	5.10.0	3-bolt	SB1S	Grease
40356	5.9.1			
64011 +	5.6.0	3-bolt	SB1S	Grease
64012	5.6.0			

Number range from 1903 Wagon Diagram Book:

40253 to 40388	
60030 to 60129	
61785 to 61884	– 12ft 9in outside
62085 to 62184	
63347 to 63746	
63749 to 64046	
69929 to 70030	– 14ft 10½in outside
71333 to 71532	
78987 to 79108	built in 1920/1

'Pointed-front' or 'carriage' axleboxes had been fitted to Diagram 13 No. 40375 when photographed, possibly in LMS days. The date is difficult to establish. There were no diamonds, no 'LNWR' marking on the body and the only date is difficult to make out but may read 31st May 1923. The wagon in the background was in post-1908 LNWR livery. Note the chains were stowed very neatly and the floor looks very clear apart from one rag. The tare of 5.18.0 was very prominent on the curb rail.

A very interesting photograph of a pair of ex-LNWR bolster wagons at Ferme Park on the GNR just north of King's Cross on 11th November 1950, carrying steel bars. These wagons appear to have been from the batch built in 1920. The livery was pure late-LMS and the wagons, carrying consecutive ex-LNWR numbers 279102 and 279103 had presumably been kept together all their lives. They lasted another three to four years in revenue service, for No. 279102 was scrapped in 1953 and 279103 a year later. The bars at the ends of the bolsters were almost semi-circular whereas LNWR bars were normally rectangular in section, so it is likely the bolsters were LMS replacements. All other known photographs of D13, however, show wagons without curb rails. Note the axleboxes were LMS group standard replacements. Amazingly for this late date, brakes were provided on only one side of each wagon which, as each wagon of the pair was numbered separately, seems to have been stretching the RCH 'brakes either side' ruling somewhat.

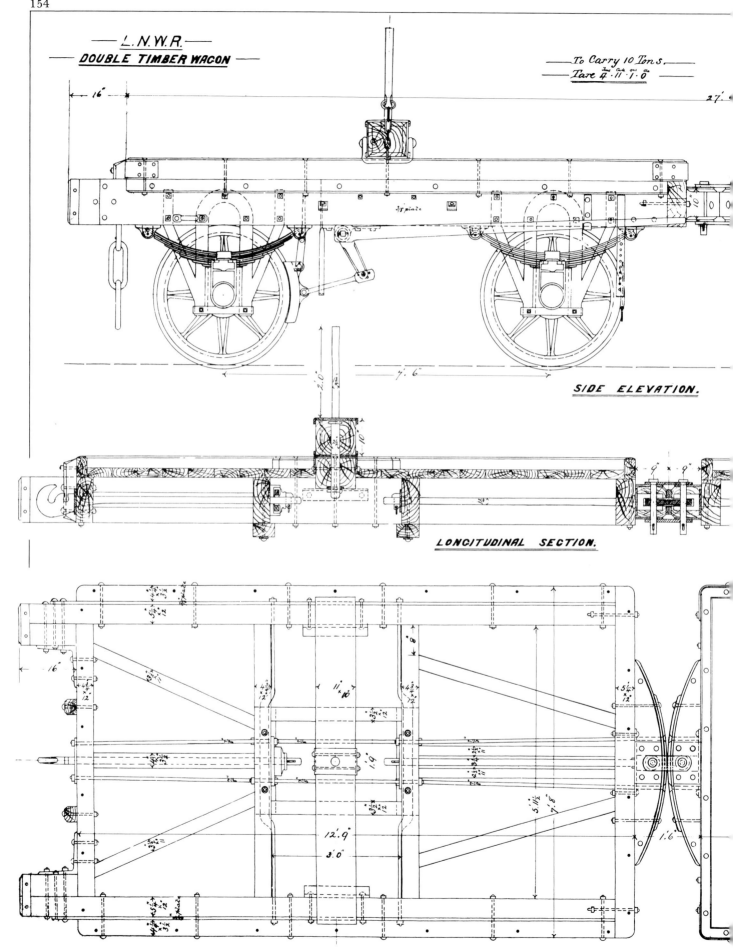

L. N. W. R.
DOUBLE TIMBER WAGON

To Carry 10 Tons.
Tare 4 . 11 . 1 . 0

SIDE ELEVATION.

LONGITUDINAL SECTION.

PLAN.

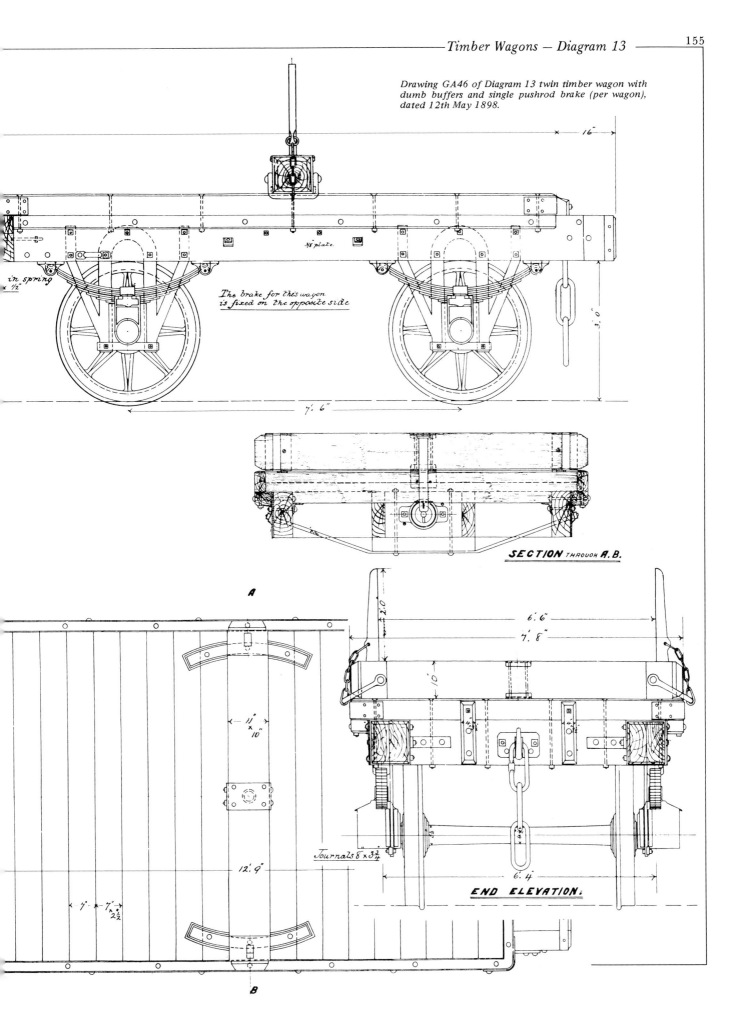

Drawing GA46 of Diagram 13 twin timber wagon with dumb buffers and single pushrod brake (per wagon), dated 12th May 1898.

The brake for this wagon is fixed on the opposite side

SECTION THROUGH A.B.

END ELEVATION.

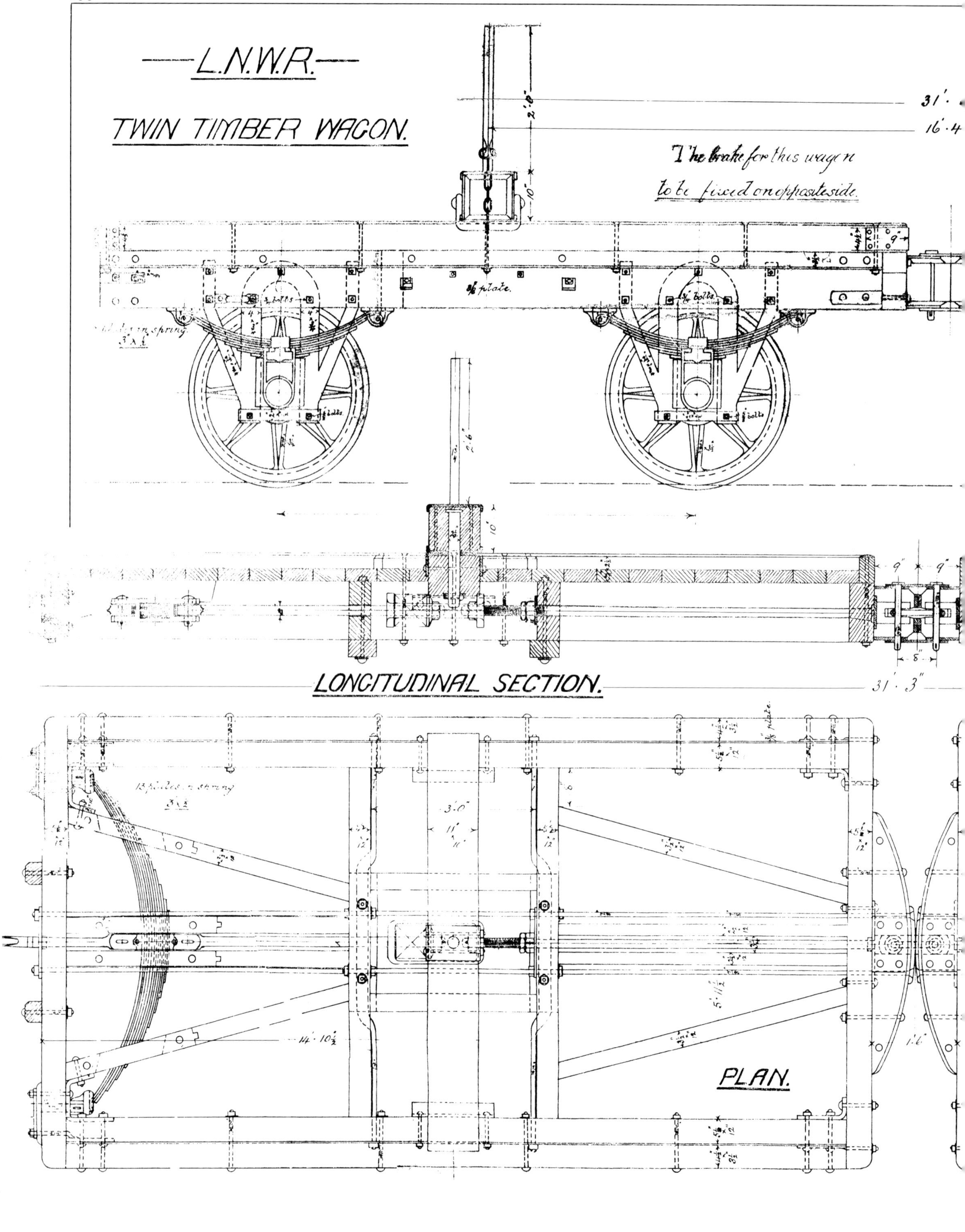

L.N.W.R.
TWIN TIMBER WAGON.
The brake for this wagon to be fixed on opposite side.
31'
16'·4
2'·0"
10"
3/8 plate.
3/4 bolts
2'·6"
10"
9"
9"
8"
LONGITUDINAL SECTION.
31'·3"
3'·0"
11"
10"
14'·10½
5'·11½
1'·6
PLAN.

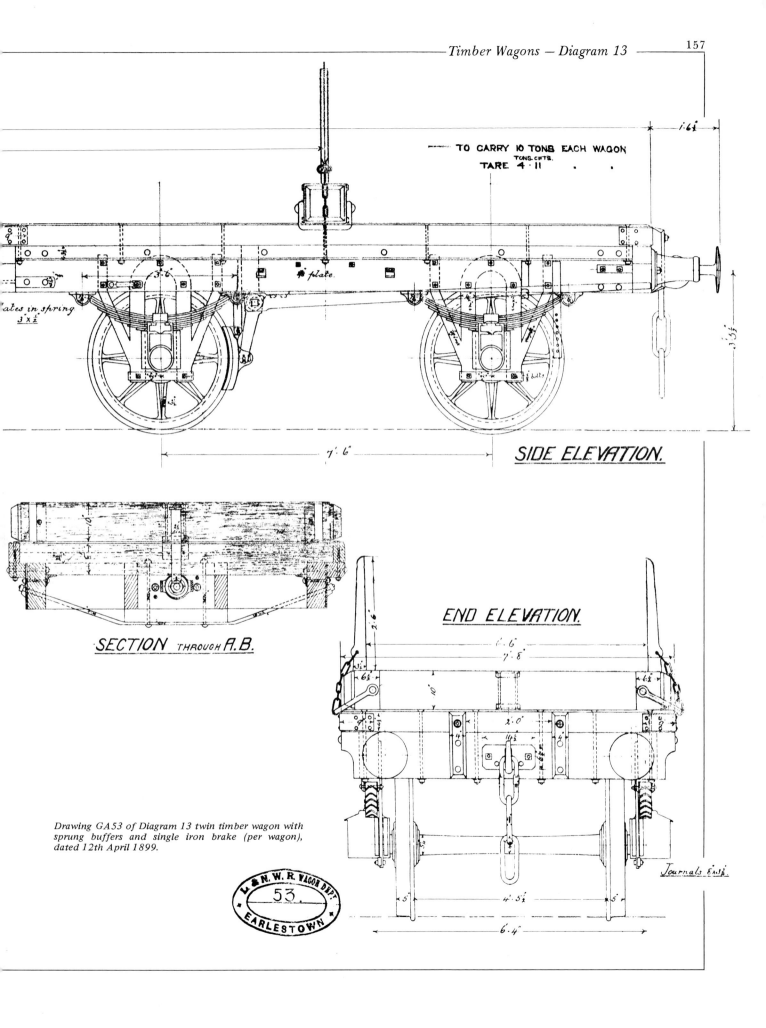

TO CARRY 10 TONS EACH WAGON
TONS. CWTS.
TARE 4 · 11

SIDE ELEVATION.

SECTION THROUGH A.B.

END ELEVATION.

Drawing GA53 of Diagram 13 twin timber wagon with sprung buffers and single iron brake (per wagon), dated 12th April 1899.

L. & N. W. R. WAGON DEPT.
53.
EARLESTOWN

DIAGRAM 14 – TIMBER WAGON, 24 ft LONG

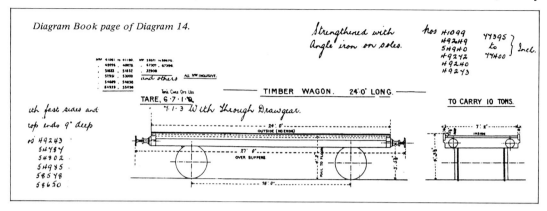

Diagram Book page of Diagram 14.

An official photograph of D14 No. 41082, taken to show the new LNWR livery applied, in this case in 8/09. It can be seen that the wagons had no ends at all, and even the smaller than standard end numbers would not fit on the edge of the floor planking without encroaching onto the bufferbeam as well. The side capping, which was common to all open wagons, had been finished off by bending down the end and bolting through the face of the bufferbeam. Additional safety hoops had been fitted to the inner ends of the brake pushrods. There were washers beneath the W-iron bolts, but the surface-mounted eye bolts show that one cannot be too precise about such things and in fact this example did not have a steel flitch plate on the solebars.
NATIONAL RAILWAY MUSEUM (ETN 57A)

The 24ft timber wagon to Diagram 14 was introduced in 1877 when a batch of 100 were built. In 1883 a further fifty were added and between 1889 and 1921 more examples were built until by 1923 there was a total of 819. Although officially described as a timber wagon, Diagram 14 was designed to carry sawn planks rather than rough logs, although the latter could be carried. They were sometimes called deal wagons. The load was therefore usually evenly distributed and, being rated at 10 tons, flitch plates were not fitted to the solebars until probably the 1890s on new wagons. Otherwise, construction followed conventional LNWR standards. To allow very long loads to be carried, no ends were fitted and the 7in x 2½in planking of the floor extended over the buffer beams, the end planks being bolted down through the beam. The sides and curb rails were combined in one 7in x 3in plank which protruded just 1in above the floor. At either end of the wagon, holes were cut in the floor and steel plates fixed to the frame to provide pockets in which to keep the chains and adjusters used for fixing down the loads.

A poor but rare photograph of one of the six D14 timber or deal wagons rebuilt in 1910 with 9in fixed sides and fall-down ends. These were unofficially designated D14A. As with the normal D14, they were primarily designed to carry finished planks rather than rough logs. No. 54787 was photographed in 1923 in the Vulcan Foundry yard.
CTY. J. P. RICHARDS

From about 1910 to 1915, many LNWR wagons were redesigned to accommodate oil axleboxes and larger bearings. The Diagram 14 design was included and from that time new wagons had the distance between the inner faces of the solebars increased from 5ft 11½in to the new standard of 6ft 1in. This enabled 9in x 4in bearings to be fitted. Probably at the same time the buffing and drawgear designs were uprated to provide a continuous drawgear. This used standard parts including spring boxes and helical springs but, due to the length of the wagon, two boxes were fitted joined by a 6ft length of 2in rod. Pushrod brakes were fitted perhaps from 1877, and to both sides from at least 1897. Grease axleboxes were replaced by oil on most examples by 1919.

In 1910, six wagons were rebuilt with 9in fixed (in LNW parlance 'fast') sides and fall-down ends. They were experimental and no more appear to have been built. The idea was not new, however, as the LNWR had built a batch of 30 low-sided open wagons with drop-down ends in 1876. We

Diagram 14 No. 54744, photographed soon after the Grouping by Jim Richards, at the Vulcan Foundry where he worked. The livery was late LNWR and the lifting date 4.1.23, but basically the wagon was as built with grease axleboxes, single pushrod brakes (with double-ended blocks) on both sides. The tare weight is 5.17.0.
CTY. J. P. RICHARDS

Another view showing the unusual end of the Diagram 14 timber wagon design, this time LMS No. 258579. This wagon had the final type of axleboxes and final 2-rib buffer stocks, but the buffer nearest the camera was clearly a replacement because it had the letters 'LMS' cast into its base. This is most likely to have been necessary because of a rough shunt. The tare reads '6.11.0' and the date is believed to have been 1939.

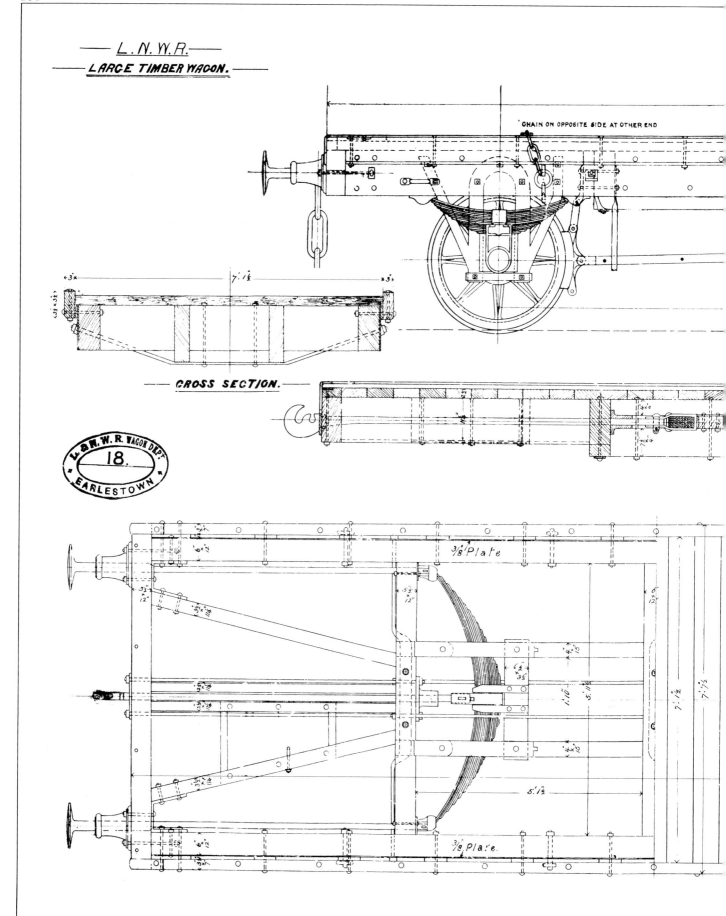

L. N. W. R.
LARGE TIMBER WAGON.

CHAIN ON OPPOSITE SIDE AT OTHER END

CROSS SECTION.

L.&N.W.R. WAGON DEPT
18.
EARLESTOWN

3/8 Plate

3/8 Plate.

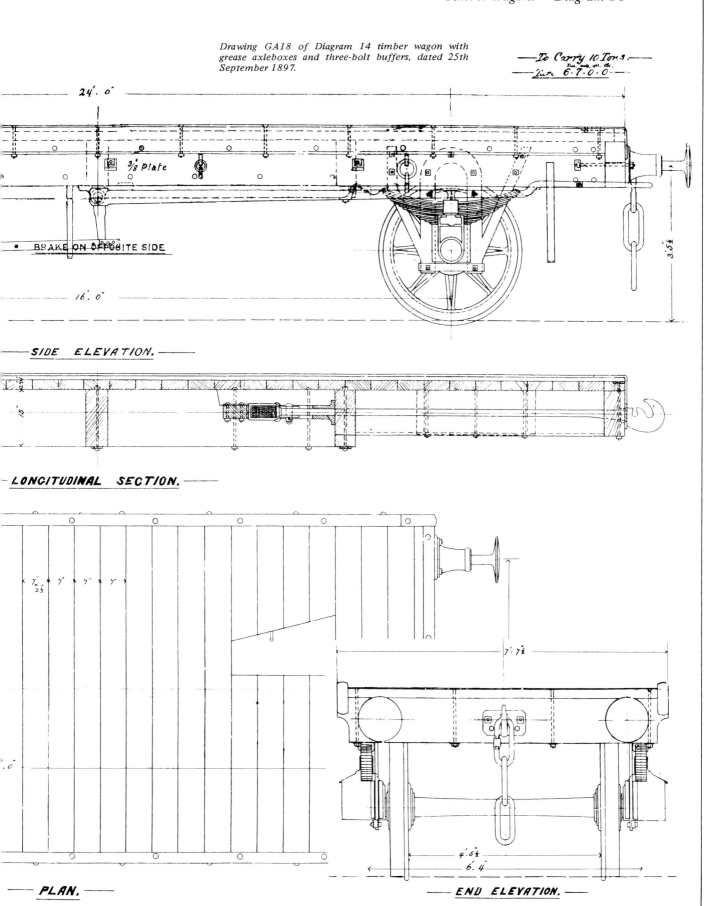

Drawing GA18 of Diagram 14 timber wagon with grease axleboxes and three-bolt buffers, dated 25th September 1897.

— To Carry 10 Tons. —
Tare 6·7·0·0

24′. 0″

3/8 Plate

BRAKE ON OPPOSITE SIDE

3′.5½″

16′. 0″

— SIDE ELEVATION. —

15″

— LONGITUDINAL SECTION. —

7″ 7″ 7″ 7″
2½

7′. 7¼″

4′.5½″
6′. 4″

— PLAN. —

— END ELEVATION. —

LARGE TIMBER WAGON.

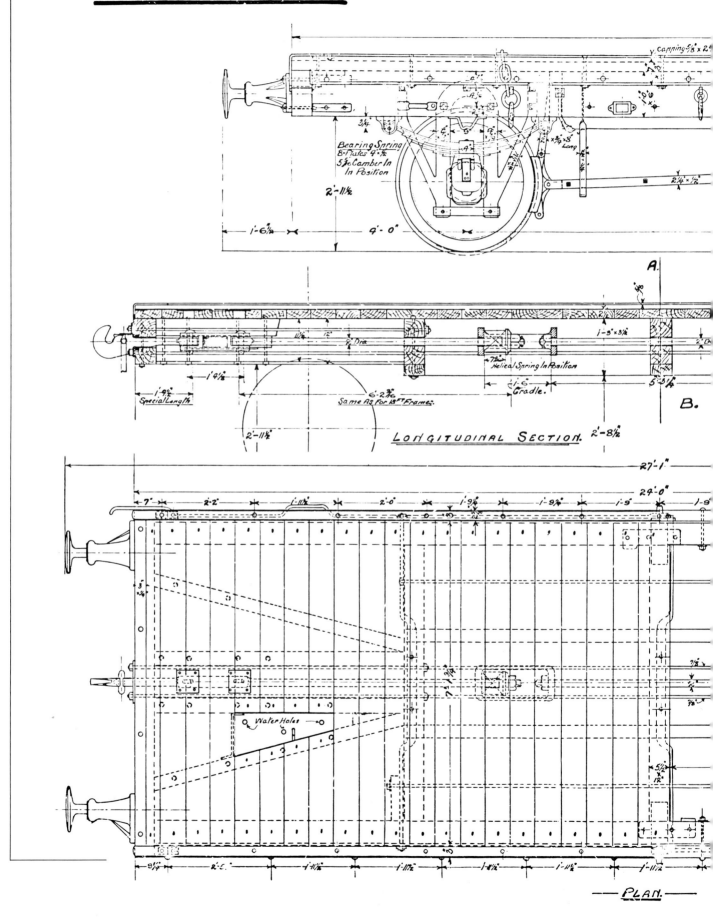

LONGITUDINAL SECTION.

PLAN.

Drawing GA36A of Diagram 14 timber wagon with bulbous No. 16 axleboxes (Fig. 21) and 2-rib buffers, dated 11th October 1915.

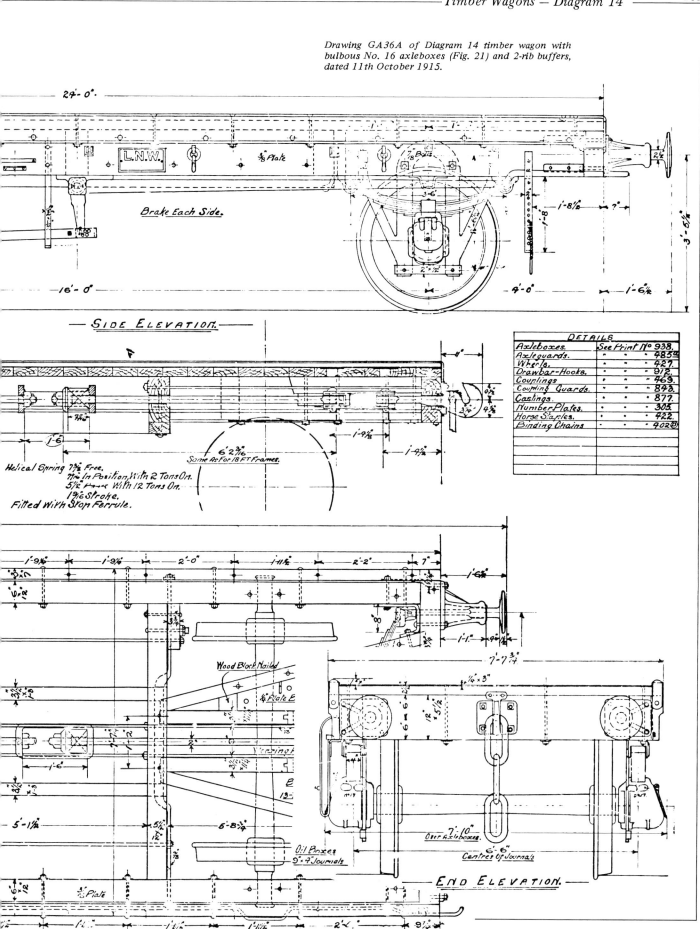

DETAILS		
Axleboxes.	See Print Nº 938.
Axleguards.	" "	485ᴬ
Wheels.	" "	427.
Drawbar-Hooks.	" "	912.
Couplings	" "	469.
Coupling Guards.	" "	848.
Castings.	" "	877.
Number Plates.	" "	305.
Horse Staples.	" "	422.
Binding Chains	" "	902⑦

refer to Diagram 14 wagons with drop-down ends as Diagram 14A but this does not appear to have been an official designation.

Diagram 14 wagons without flitch plates seem to have lasted a long time. The 1903 diagram book notes that twelve were strengthened with angle-iron on the solebars and perhaps they were so fitted as an experiment instead of the usual flat flitch plates. The size or position of the angles is not known, but is likely to have been similar to that used on the Furniture Van wagon (Diagram 38a), page 187.

A number of Diagram 14 wagons were modified to carry steam wagons (or lorries) manufactured by Fodens of Sandbach. These bore the legend 'STEAM WAGON TRUCK' and were to be returned to Sandbach when empty. Some copies of the Diagram Book list the wagons involved, and these may be the twelve wagons with solebars strengthened by angle-iron referred to above.

Known examples of Diagram 14:
Diagram book tare for type: 6.7.1
With through drawgear: 7.1.3

Number	Tare	Buffers	Brakes	Axleboxes	Notes
41082	6.10.1	3-bolt 12in	Pushrod BS	grease	
54744	5.17.0	3-bolt	Pushrod BS	grease	
58603		3-bolt	Pushrod BS	grease	
67381		3-bolt	Pushrod BS	grease	
77397	7.6.2				
258579	6.11.0	2-rib	Pushrod BS	bulbous	LMS No.
277366		2-rib	DBBS	bulbous	LMS No.

Number range:
41061 to 41160   52951 to 53000   58571 to 58670
49226 to 49275   54689 to 54838   67307 to 67396
51833 to 51852   54939 to 55038   32909
Fixed (9in) sides and drop ends:
49243, 54787, 54802, 54985, 58578, 58650
Strengthened with angle-iron solebars:
41099, 49240, 49249, 49272, 49273, 54940, 77395–77400

A side view of Diagram 14 No. 258579 in LMS livery showing the version of the iron flap and pushrod brake lengthened to suit the 16ft wheelbase of these longer wagons. Two-rib buffers indicate a build date of 1910 or later.

A most useful picture of Diagram 14 No. 277366 at Renfrew in June 1946. Although it was built in 1913, surprisingly few changes had been made in the intervening 33 years! Axleboxes, buffers and brakegear were all of the final LNWR type, with which it was probably built. However, the main interest in the picture is that it shows the housings in the floor, in which chains and shackles were stored.
A. G. ELLIS (11777)

DIAGRAM 107 – TIMBER TROLLEY

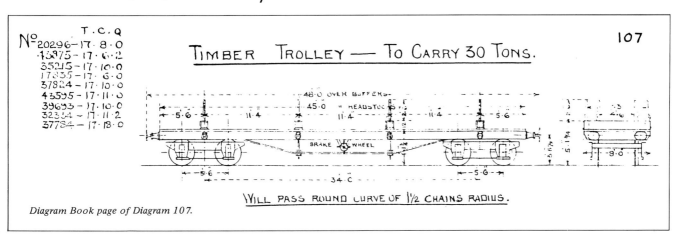

Diagram Book page of Diagram 107.

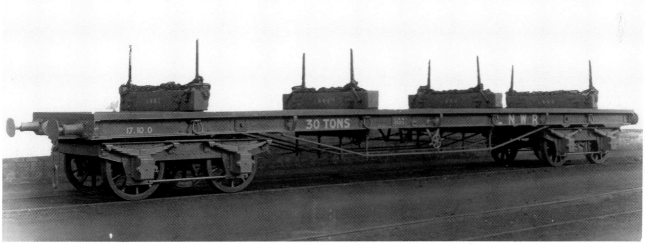

An official photograph of an early D107 30-ton timber wagon taken when new. The paint date on No. 35215 reads October 1911 and so the livery was LNWR-only without diamonds. The increased depth of the bolsters shows clearly in comparison with the smaller designs of D12 or D13. Note the movable stanchions and the brake wheel in the centre.   CTY. NATIONAL RAILWAY MUSEUM (ETN 85A)

Early in 1911 it was decided to replace ninety Diagram 12 timber wagons with fifty of a new 45ft bogie design to Diagram 107. Some records show fifty-one examples, so it is possible that a single experimental vehicle had already been built by then. The Diagram Books also suggest that the batch was built over a long period, perhaps ten years or so. No more appear to have been built after this batch. All survived until 1923 and beyond, with the exception of one which was rebuilt into a loco tool van.

The frame was made largely from 10in x 3½in rolled steel channels. The floor was of 11in x 3in planks edged with a 3in x 3in angle, giving a flush top. Four truss rods of 2in x 1in flat were bolted to the queen posts, twisted through 90 degrees just below the solebars and bolted to them also. They could carry 30 tons distributed or 15 tons over the centre bolsters. Curves of only 1¼ chains could be negotiated and the buffer stocks were of the 4-bolt type without rib and fitted with 17in x 12in oval heads. The bogies were similar to those used on the earlier Diagram 99 glass trolley (see chapter 6) but the wheelbase was lengthened to 5ft 6in and end stretchers fitted to add strength.

Double brakes were fitted to one side of each bogie, connected to a cross shaft at the centre of the wagon. A brake wheel with extended spokes as handles was fitted each end of the cross shaft. The wheel therefore had to be turned left or right to put the brakes on, depending which side of the wagon you were. Arrows painted on the solebars indicated which way to turn the wheel. As was usual with heavy vehicles, 10-spoke wheels with solid spokes and 10in x 5in journals were used, running in flat-fronted oil axleboxes.

Unlike Diagram 12 and Diagram 13, the bogie trolleys were not designed to run in multiples and therefore there was no need for the bolsters to swivel. This, together with the steel frame, enabled the massive transoms to be dispensed with. Bolsters were 11in wide as on Diagram 12 and Diagram 13, but increased in depth from 10in to 12in. They rested on the floor, secured by straps fastened to the planking. Stanchions were 2ft 6in long from the start and alternative locations were provided either 7ft 3in apart or 4ft 6in apart. The bolsters themselves were also detachable, reputedly to enable a crane to remove the load and bolsters as one, although whether any time was thus saved is doubtful.

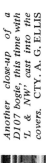

D107 timber trolley No. 253253 photographed at Renfrew in September 1946. The construction of the wagon is clear – the solebar was channel and the side was angle, bolted to it. The floor planks rested inside the angle so that their top surfaces were flush. The axlebox covers had been replaced by the LMS.

Another close-up of a D107 bogie, this time with 'L & NW' cast into the covers. CTY. A. G. ELLIS

A Diagram 107 timber trolley showing one stanchion moved to the end of the wagon, as noted below, but the one adjacent is clearly closer than recorded. Note the stanchions were rectangular in section, tapering outwards towards the top and incorporating a bulge near the base to which the chain is attached.
CTY. A. G. ELLIS

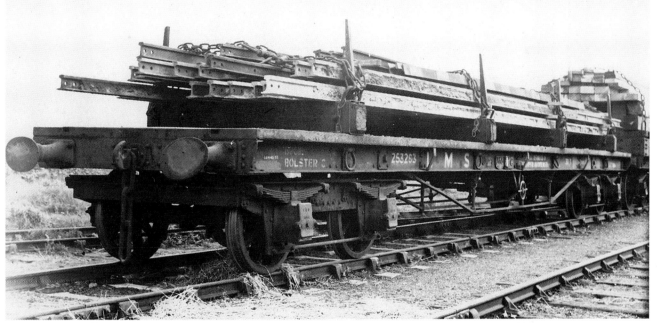

Another photo of No. 253253 on the same occasion, and showing the end detail well. The wagon was built in 1917 and yet appears to have been identical to the photo of No. 35215 on page 165, except for the bogie end stretchers which were angle rather than flat. The guide to hold the nearest oval buffer head from turning had presumably failed or worn in some way.
CTY. A. G. ELLIS

Some examples had their outer bolsters moved in later years to be right on the end of the wagon. As built the distances between them were evenly spaced 11ft 4in apart. When modified they became 16ft 4in + 11ft 4in + 16ft 4in.

Additional examples:
4365, 4368, 17695, 18438, 31434, 32311, 32326, 32444, 33973, 33984, 34008, 35200, 35223, 37319, 37443, 37763, 37819, 39673, 41579, 41679, 42339, 43564, 43585, 43842, 43851, 43879, 44141, 46501, 52740, 52830, 53201, 53293, 53364, 53683, 53694, 55078, 55251, 55308, 55312, 57468, 59616, 59341, 59616, 59626, 59707, 60143

Known examples of Diagram 107:

Number	Tare	Buffers	Brakes	Axleboxes
17835	17.6.0			
20296	17.8.0			
32334	17.11.2			
35215	17.10.0	4-bolt, no rib, oval head	Double, with handwheel	Oil, flat front
37784	17.18.0			
37824	17.10.0			
39693	17.10.0			
43875	17.6.2			
43595	17.11.0			

British Glass

for

British Homes

&

The 4 o'clock Glass Train
leaving Cowley Hill.

This rather attractive picture is taken from a publicity brochure for Pilkingtons and shows a line of D39 wagons being hauled out of the works by an industrial saddle tank. The St. Helens area, and Pilkingtons in particular, dominated the plate glass-making industry and the LNWR was ideally placed to provide the transport required. Photographs of glass wagons are, however, very rare.
CTY. PILKINGTONS

CHAPTER SIX

GLASS WAGONS

THE earliest record of glass wagons on the LNWR is in 1867 when two appeared in the annual stock list. The following year they had disappeared and no more are shown until 1877. We know little of these early examples but it is possible that they came from the South Staffordshire Railway which was absorbed in 1867. They may have been scrapped or converted for other use.

Before 1870 the largest plate glass regularly produced in Britain was 16ft 8in x 9ft 0in. Most of it came from the St. Helens area (Thos. Pilkington & Co.) and the LNWR was ideally placed to win the business with its extensive network and private sidings in the area. At that time glass was nor-

mally packed into wooden cases with the sheets standing on edge. The cases were loaded by crane onto ordinary open wagons and chained or roped down and sheeted over.

SUMMARY

Diagram	Introduced	Description
39	1892	Small glass wagon, 7-ton
40	1877	Medium glass wagon (Double door at one end), 10-ton
41	1883	Large glass wagon (Double door at each end), 10-ton
42	1897	Large glass wagon with 9in sides, to carry 10 tons
42a	1911	Large glass wagon with 9in sides and steel well, to carry 10 tons
99	1909	Glass trolley, to carry 10 tons

DIAGRAM 40 – MEDIUM GLASS WAGON

During the late 1860s and 1870s there was a tendency for the height between floors of buildings to increase. This made the larger plate glass more popular, particularly for public houses, large shops and department stores, and the need arose for special wagons (often called 'floats') to carry the largest sheets in safety. This was achieved by an 18ft long design with a well 17ft 3in x 3ft 8in wide, extending down 1ft 11in, almost to the axles. The sides were 5ft 8in high, with rounded ends 6ft 6in high at the centre, so that an 8ft high case could be packed out with wood, chained down and sheeted over. Double doors were provided at one end only so that the case could be lifted in or out by a standard yard crane, which usually had a height limit of about 15ft above rail level and could not lift the load over the sides.

Self-contained buffers were fitted to avoid obstructing the well and the drawgear was rubber-sprung, presumably for the same reason. Grease axleboxes would doubtless have been used throughout their lives and the payload was always 10 tons. With little or no diagonal bracing of the underframe

and with one end including opening doors, they must have been a flimsy design.

Four wagons were built to this design in 1877 and a further two in 1880, but with the side height reduced to 4ft 3in and ends reduced to match. One further wagon was built to this diagram in 1883 to replace one of the 1877 wagons, presumably an accident victim. In 1895, following the success of Diagram 39, iron stanchions with securing screw clamps were fitted. The sides were then reduced in height to 2ft 0in and the ends to 2ft 8in at the centre.

All wagons to Diagram 40 were scrapped between 1911 and 1916 except one which survived into LMS ownership.

Known examples of Diagram 40:
Diagram book tare for type: 6.1.1. (with stanchions)

19600 19650 40958 40959	originally built with 5ft 8in sides, later cut down to 2ft 0in.
43299 43300	originally built with 4ft 3in sides, later cut down to 2ft 0in.

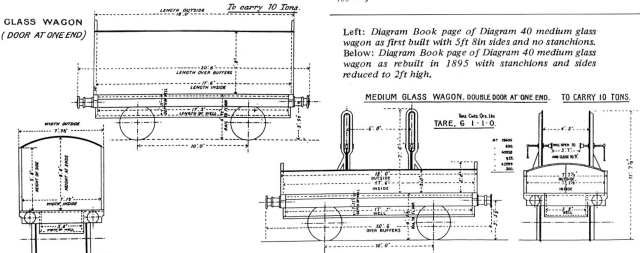

Left: *Diagram Book page of Diagram 40 medium glass wagon as first built with 5ft 8in sides and no stanchions.*
Below: *Diagram Book page of Diagram 40 medium glass wagon as rebuilt in 1895 with stanchions and sides reduced to 2ft high.*

DIAGRAM 41 – LARGE GLASS WAGON

This design first appeared in 1883 and showed a number of improvements over Diagram 40. The well was a much more satisfactory 2ft 11in deep but it still had to be at least 16ft long and the minimum wheelbase possible was therefore a lengthy 17ft 2in. Because the load was lower, the sides and ends could be reduced in height and, probably more importantly, the 4ft 1in overhang at each end enabled standard buffing and drawgear to be used whilst diagonal bracing (rakers) greatly stiffened the structure.

It appears that the first example built may have been 24ft long by 7ft 7½in wide (nominally 7ft 8in), with 4ft 10½in sides, and the rounded ends, 5ft 7in high at the centre, again included double doors at one end only. Two more examples were built to similar specifications but 25ft 4in long and this became the standard length for Diagram 41 from then on. A further five followed but with double doors at both ends, and a final batch of four was built in 1891–2 with sides only 3ft 0in high and ends 3ft 8in.

As with Diagram 40, iron stanchions were fitted from 1895, which enabled the sides to be reduced to 2ft high and the ends to 2ft 8in at the centre. The payload remained at 10 tons. Very little more is known about Diagram 41, but many details of their design were probably similar to Diagram 42 which superseded them.

From 1911, Diagram 41 wagons began to be scrapped and replaced by new stock to Diagram 42A and Diagram 99. Only two remained in 1923.

Known examples of Diagram 41:
Diagram book tare for type: 7.3.2 (with stanchions)

460
2405   } double doors at one end only
9674

49678
49679
49680   } originally built with 4ft 10½in sides and double doors at both ends
52599
52600

55397
55398   } originally built with 3ft 0in sides and double doors both ends
55399
55400

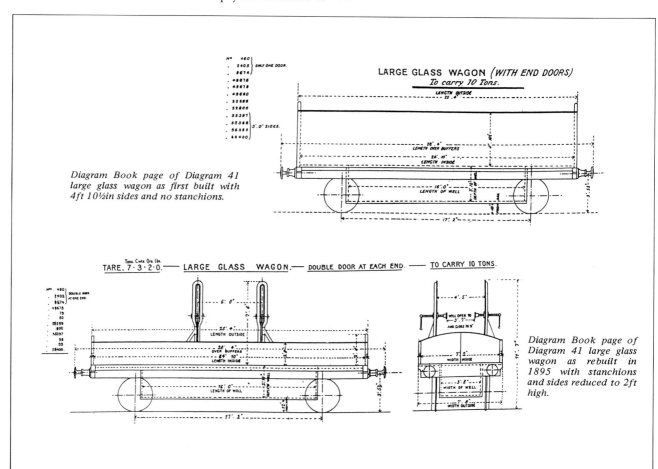

Diagram Book page of Diagram 41 large glass wagon as first built with 4ft 10½in sides and no stanchions.

Diagram Book page of Diagram 41 large glass wagon as rebuilt in 1895 with stanchions and sides reduced to 2ft high.

DIAGRAM 39 – SMALL GLASS WAGON

In the early 1890s improved techniques of glass manufacture made large sheets cheaper and traffic in this commodity increased rapidly. Steel frames or stanchions were designed to support large cases of glass, one on either side, and were fitted with adjustable screw clamps. A pair of these stanchions were fitted experimentally to an old Diagram 1 open wagon in 1892. When loaded with a standard case 8ft 0in high by up to 3ft 6in wide, however, the loading gauge was just reached, so when new wagons of this type were ordered, the standard 2¼ in thick floorboards were replaced by 1½ in boards, giving a rail to floor height of 4ft 0in. This brought an 8ft 0in x 3ft 6in case safely within the loading gauge. Whereas in the case of well wagons, the whole weight of the case was carried by the floor, in these new wagons the case itself spread the load over the longitudinal frame; hence the thinner floor did not matter.

The case of glass was held from moving sideways by four adjustable screw clamps and endways by four chains, each with two screw coupling adjusters and one end fixed to the top of the clamp guides. The clamp guides were drilled so that a pin could be inserted to hold the clamps at ten different heights.

The experimental stanchions on the converted wagon proved to be a success and so more of these wagons were built in 1893 to the new standard length of 16ft 0in. The old conversion had been a 15ft 6in wagon but it is thought that it was replaced by a new 16ft 0in vehicle in the late 1890s. Further batches followed: twenty in 1894-5 and twelve in

Diagram 39 small glass wagon No. 7960, carrying a paint date of 8/09. Both the new and the older style of label holder can be seen mounted together on the solebar, both confirming that the payload was 7 tons. The brake lever was riveted to its shaft which is unusual, although the single pushrod brakes were otherwise quite standard. One might have thought that a wagon newly overhauled and painted would have been sent out from Earlestown with a brake block not quite so worn out! The wheel tyres do not look much better. The design and working of the stanchions is self-evident, but it should be noted that this was a later type with the horizontal members being made from steel angle. Earlier wagons had these made from flat bar. The entire ironwork of the stanchions looks in such good condition that it could well have been new, begging the question whether the wagon had been newly converted from a D1. NATIONAL RAILWAY MUSEUM (58A)

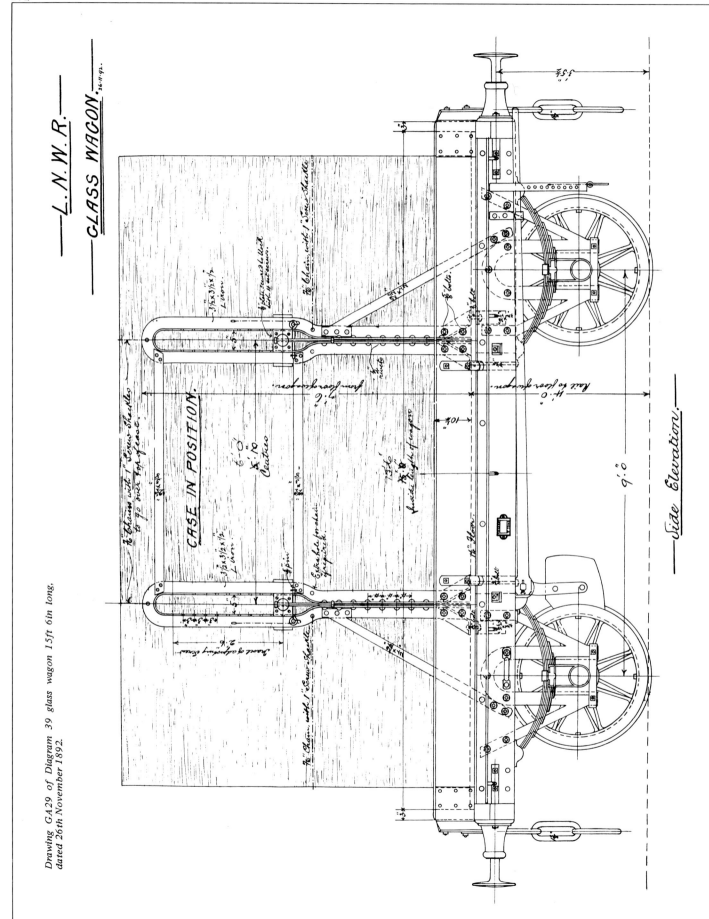

Drawing GA29 of Diagram 39 glass wagon 15ft 6in long, dated 26th November 1892.

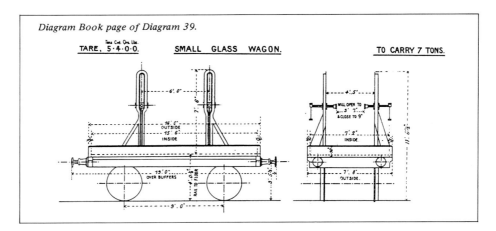

Diagram Book page of Diagram 39.

1897-8. According to the minute books, more were then added by fitting stanchions to ordinary Diagram 1 wagons: fifteen in 1897-8 and twenty in 1900. If this is so, they would probably have been 15ft 6in wagons, but it is very likely that these were accounting rebuilds and were in fact new 16ft 0in wagons which replaced old Diagram 1 wagons scrapped at that time.

All Diagram 39 wagons were probably built with 6in x 3in journals running in grease axleboxes, 3-bolt buffers and pushrod brakes one side only. Later a second set of brakes was fitted to a few (only ten by 1919). None appear to have received oil axleboxes during LNWR ownership. As was usual LNWR practice, towards the end of their lives some were downgraded from 7 tons to 6 tons. All 118 survived to 1919 and 114 passed into LMS ownership in 1923.

Known examples of Diagram 39:
Diagram book tare for type: 5.4.0

Number	Tare	Buffers	Brakes	Axleboxes	Notes
7960	4.18.2	3-bolt	Pushrod 1S	Grease	as at 1909

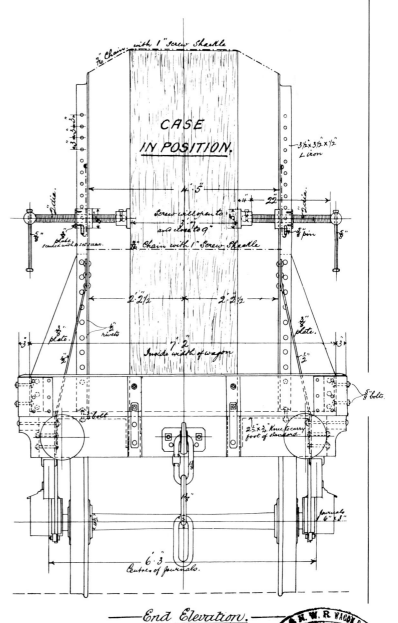

End Elevation.

FOR GLASS TRAFFIC

To be returned to St.Helens

L.N.W.
65909

909

Diagram 42 No. 65909, photographed in Earlestown Works. The date would most likely have been 1915 and it was probably taken as a record of the last wooden-welled glass wagon before being scrapped and replaced by a D42A. The ends of the planks forming the well can be seen along its base. The three supporting brackets (rather than four) were probably also typical of a wooden well, and a means of identifying these from the later D42A, which had a steel well. The horizontal steel members joining each pair of stanchions were flat, rather than the later angle type. Although the lettering varied, it seems that the entire LNWR fleet of glass wagons may have been allocated to the St. Helens area. The script form of lettering shown here was typical of the approximately pre-1908 period, after which it was generally rendered in block letters. It appears that some attempt had been made to obliterate the tare weight, which probably reads 6.13.2, its final weight at scrapping. Some official Earlestown photographs of wagons in pristine condition show no tare weight at all and it is assumed that the photographs had been taken before weighing. It is perhaps not clear, but the brake pushrod passed between the bracket supporting the well and the well itself.

A. G. ELLIS COLLECTION (23336)

DIAGRAM 42 – LARGE GLASS WAGON WITH 9in SIDES

Glass traffic continued to increase and in May 1897 the General Committee authorised the construction on Capital Account of ten glass wagons with a full-length well 17ft 3in long by 1ft 11in deep. Had the minute been carried out exactly, these wagons would have conformed to the old Diagram 40, but they were actually made to a new design drawn up in August that year and completed in early 1898.

41 design was probably also along these lines, but we have no information. They were all rated at 10 tons.

Three-bolt buffers with 10in stocks and grease axleboxes were used and probably retained throughout their lives. The brakes, however, were non-standard. Due to the long 17ft 2in wheelbase, the brake was reversed and acted on the wheel nearest the lever. Because of this there was an addi-

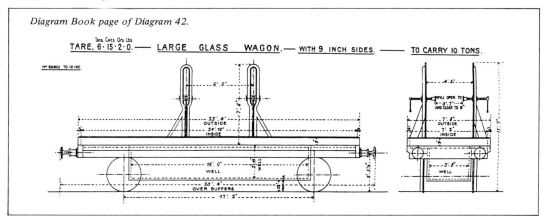

Diagram Book page of Diagram 42.

The new design later became Diagram 42 and was simply a modernised version of Diagram 41. The size of the cases of glass had not changed so the dimensions of the wagon remained the same but they were designed with stanchions from new, so had no need of high sides or end doors. A single 9in board was used for the side, simply to stop chains and blocks falling off in transit. Like an ordinary open goods wagon, the end plank was wider, 11½in, to mask the end of the 2¼in thick floor. Solebars and buffer beams were all 12in deep.

The main feature of the design was a large wooden well, 3ft 8in wide and 16ft 0in long (inside dimensions), in the centre of the wagon. The floor, what there was of it, was of 2¼in thick planking, unlike Diagram 39. The well was 2ft 11in deep and enabled much larger cases to be carried than Diagram 39.

The normal construction of the underframe, with two central transoms and splayed rakers at either end, had to be altered to a design with transoms only 2ft 0in behind the buffer beams, just clear of the well. The rakers were thus very short and the central section virtually made of four parallel solebars braced together. This enabled the well to be as wide as possible whilst still clearing the wheels, and as long as possible without obstructing the axles. The load was carried on the floor of the well, which was attached by bolts through the side and end planking to the inner solebars and inner end transoms. In order to spread the load further, steel straps ran from inside one of the outer solebars down under the floor and up to inside the other outer solebar. Because of this distribution of load, flitch plates outside the solebars were unnecessary. The construction of the earlier Diagram

tional stay on the inner V-hanger to take the reaction. This stay can be seen parallel to the large, lower end of the brake lever. They were probably fitted to both sides from new. At some time before the grouping, the well was replaced by a steel version. When Diagram 42A was introduced in 1911, it had a steel well from new and it seems likely that experience with that design led to Diagram 42 being modified. Not only was a steel well stronger, but, being ¼in plate instead of 2in timber, it increased the internal dimensions. Modified Diagram 42 wagons then technically conformed to Diagram 42A and were transferred to that Diagram. Apart from the well, their features remained as Diagram 42 and they retained the original grease axleboxes, 3-bolt buffers etc., even after modification. It appears that eight were modified in this way, the remaining two being scrapped and replaced by new Diagram 42A wagons in 1912 and 1915. All survived into LMS days.

At a glance the easiest way to tell whether a particular wagon has a wooden or steel well is by the flat steel supporting straps which are angled from the base of the well to the inside of the solebars. A wooden well had three supports, each 3in wide, whereas a steel well had four supports 5in wide.

Known examples of Diagram 42:
Diagram book tare for type: 6.15.2

Number	Tare	Buffers	Brakes	Axleboxes	Notes
65901–65905	–	3-bolt	Reversed 1S	Grease	Wooden well
65906	7.10.0	3-bolt	Reversed 1S	Grease	Wooden well
65907–65910	–	3-bolt	Reversed 1S	Grease	Wooden well

Drawing GA30 of Diagram 42 large glass wagon, 25ft 4in
long with wooden well, dated 8th April 1897.

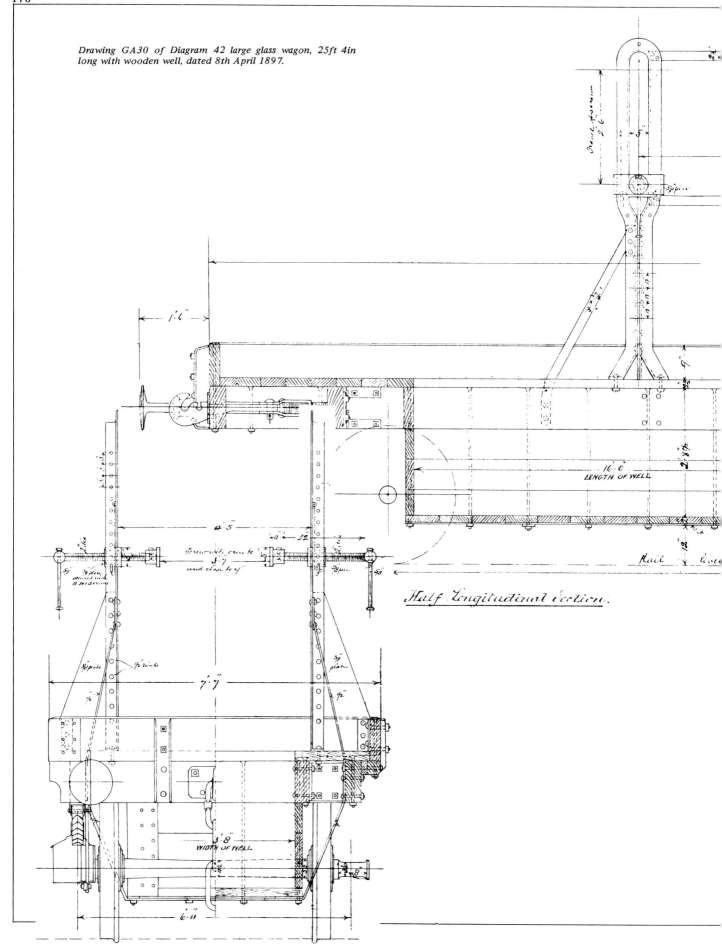

Half Longitudinal Section.

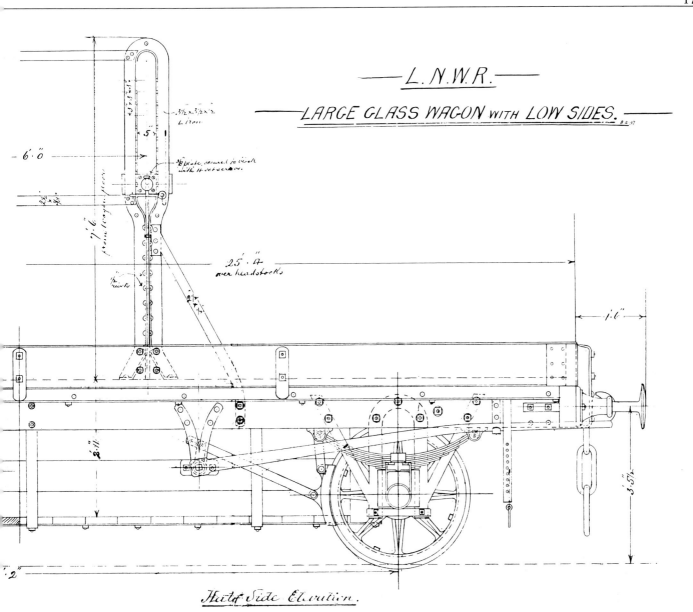

—L. N. W. R.—

LARGE GLASS WAGON WITH LOW SIDES.

Half Side Elevation.

DIAGRAM 42A – LARGE GLASS WAGON WITH 9in SIDES AND STEEL WELL

The design for Diagram 42A was drawn up in 1910 and the first examples built the following year. Although outwardly similar to Diagram 42, it was, in fact, a completely new design incorporating the latest features and became the standard LNWR glass wagon from that date.

Modern fittings included a 6ft 1in frame (the distance between the inner faces of the solebars), which allowed 9in x 4in bearings in oil axleboxes, an outside width of 7ft 10in and single-rib 13in buffer stocks. Axleboxes were flat-fronted at first, bulbous later. The sides were 9in planks, giving an internal height also of 9in and the 7in x 2½in floor planking was masked by the 11½in end plank. Solebars and buffer beams were 11in deep and ⅜in flitch plates were fitted. They were rated at 10 tons. Most of these features became standard between 1910 and 1915 for all LNWR wagons. The well, of

course, prevented the use of continuous drawgear and a large leaf spring was fitted behind the headstocks for both buffing and drawgear.

Many other small features were changed and these enable us to readily identify the two diagrams. Diagram 42 wagons had 6-bolt corner plates, whereas Diagram 42A had 5. The body knees were outside on Diagram 42 but inside on the latter, in line with the practice of the time (Ref: Diagram 103), so the ironwork could be seen extending down over the curb rail on Diagram 42 whereas on Diagram 42A it was kept short at 7in. Additional strapping was provided to strengthen the sides where the stanchions were bolted through and these were later fitted to Diagram 42 also. Stanchions were as Diagram 42 except that the distance apart increased from 4ft 5in to 4ft 8in in line with the increased

Glass wagon No. 40959, built new to D42a, shows the three-quarter elevation. It did not have the external body knees along the side of ex-D42 rebuilds. Single-rib buffers, bulbous axleboxes, five corner-plate nuts on each side and end, and, of course, a steel well supported by four brackets, not three, complete the picture.

overall width of the wagon. Also the longitudinal supports – two each side – were strong 2½ in x 2⅜ in angles instead of flat. These angles were fitted to Diagram 42 later and also some to Diagram 39. Brakes were of similar design to Diagram 42 and fitted to both sides. Compared to Diagram 42, the length over headstocks was actually reduced to 25ft and the wheelbase to 17ft, but this did not affect the size of

the well, which was of all-steel construction using ¼ in plate and 3in x 3in x ⅜ in angles. Sixteen holes were provided for drainage. The steel was thinner than the timber used for Diagram 42 and it was possible to increase the internal size of the well to 16ft 4in long, 3ft 8in wide and 3ft 1½ in deep.

From 1911 many of the earlier glass wagon diagrams began to be withdrawn and replaced by new Diagram 42A stock.

A late example of D42A, probably photographed in about 1923-4. Bulbous axleboxes and single-rib buffers, assuming they were the originals, probably date construction to about 1912-14. The number is illegible, but was fortunately recorded by the photographer as No. 40929. The lettering on the side reads: 'FOR GLASS TRAFFIC / EMPTY TO ST HELENS' and to the right of 'LNWR' it reads '10 TONS'. The tare weight is 9.6.3. In the shadows two vertical straps can be made out on the side of the well to cover joints in the steel plates, confirming again that this was a wagon with a steel well.
CTY. J. P. RICHARDS

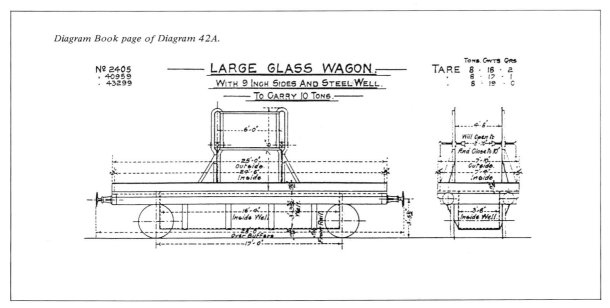

Diagram Book page of Diagram 42A.

This Diagram 42 large glass wagon, almost certainly No. 65906, had been rebuilt with a steel well to conform to Diagram 42A. The four iron straps supporting the well and the rivets visible on the skyline beneath the wagon identify this as a steel well although in other respects it conforms to D42, retaining grease axleboxes and 10in 3-bolt buffer stocks, both of which were obsolete before the first new D42A wagons were built. Other modifications carried out since it was built include the dropped keeper plates, replacement corner plate bolts and angle horizontal supports to the stanchions. Brakegear had been strengthened with deeper vee hangers and a diagonal stay. The pushrod now passed in front of the well bracket instead of behind it. Notice also the additional strapping on the side. The wagons behind are worthy of note, the three on the left being drop-sided Diagrams 3 or 5 (they are unlikely to be D62 ballast wagons because of their varied load which includes barrels, and also because most ballast wagons had extended end stanchions to support rails in transit). The hopper wagon could be one of a number of similar diagrams, but amazingly still carried pre-1908 livery of diamonds without 'LNWR', even though the photograph was probably taken about 15 years later.

CTY. J. P. RICHARDS

The distribution of construction was:

Year	Qty
1911	4
1912	5
1913	–
1914	2
1915	2
1916	2
1917	–
1918	–
1919	–
1920	2
	——
	17

In addition to these, eight Diagram 42 were modified with steel wells and transferred to this diagram – see Diagram 42.

Known examples of wagons built new as Diagram 42A:

Number	Tare
2405	8.18.2
9674	
19650	
40959	8.17.1
43299	8.19.0
43300	
49679	
49680	8.16.0
52599	8.14.2
55397	8.12.2
55398	
55400	8.16.2
55399	8.13.2
65909	8.16.0

A further three were built, one of which was 65907, but no further details are known.

DIAGRAM 99 – GLASS TROLLEY

Plans were drawn up for a 21ft steel glass wagon with a 1ft 9½in deep well 17ft 6in long. It was to have a fixed angle-iron framework 4ft 5in above normal floor level. None appear to have been built and the tried and proven wooden designs were perpetuated until 1909 when a radical new type of glass wagon did appear. This was a 40ft 6in x 8ft bogie trolley wagon designated Diagram 99. A second was built in 1911 as replacement for an elderly Diagram 41.

Construction was entirely of steel rolled sections and flat plate. Buffers were of the 4-bolt type without ribs and, unusually for a bogie wagon, had round heads, albeit 15in diameter. The bogies were a new design with 5ft wheelbase

and flat-fronted oil axleboxes. The wagon weighed about 14¼ tons (considerably more than its 10 tons payload!), for which standard split eight-spoke wheels were adequate. Double brakes were fitted to one side of each bogie but the brake wheel was mounted on the bogie frame and worked the brakes on that bogie only. The bogies were very conventional compared to earlier LNWR goods stock and had outside frames of steel angle with conventional leaf springs and hangers. Tie rods were fitted and the whole kept together by the central stretcher on which it was pivoted, no end stretchers being considered necessary. The wagon could pass round curves down to 1½ chains radius.

The first Diagram 99 glass trolley built, No. 39851, probably photographed when new in 1909. It can be seen that the end platforms, which served only to support the bogie, were open and had no floor, allowing daylight to shine through onto the bogie below. The bogie was also of light construction and had no end stretchers. Brakes were operated by the hand wheel on both wheels on one side of the bogie, those on the other bogie being entirely independent. LNWR bogie and heavy wagons were almost as standardised as the more numerous four-wheeled wagons so bogies, axleboxes and buffers, for example, were to be seen on many other diagrams of the period. The frames for holding glass sheets could be angled by use of the pins and chains at either end, the photograph showing them in the central position. CTY. R. J. ESSERY

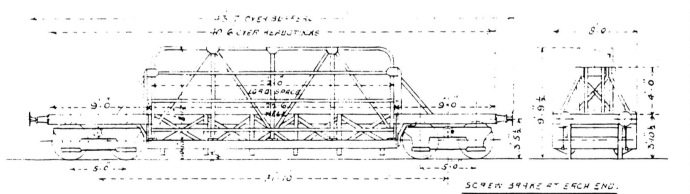

Diagram Book page of Diagram 99.

The well had no floor, and so a framework of flats and angles to support the sheets was provided at each side. These were hinged along their lower edges and enabled glass sheets to be carried on both sides, or, by standing one frame upright and lowering the other, sheets could be carried on one side only at an angle to allow the largest size possible to fit within the loading gauge. The load space was 22ft long. Both continued into LMS days.

Known examples of Diagram 99:
Diagram book tare for type: 14.13.0

39851 built 1909
  460 built 1911

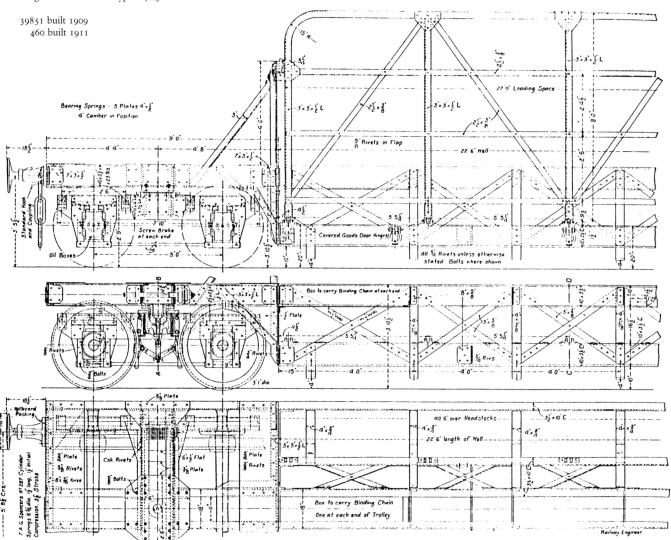

Figs. 3 and 4. 10-Ton Glass Trolley : London & North Western Railway.

Drawing as printed in The Railway Engineer, *October 1909 of Diagram 99 10-ton glass trolley.*

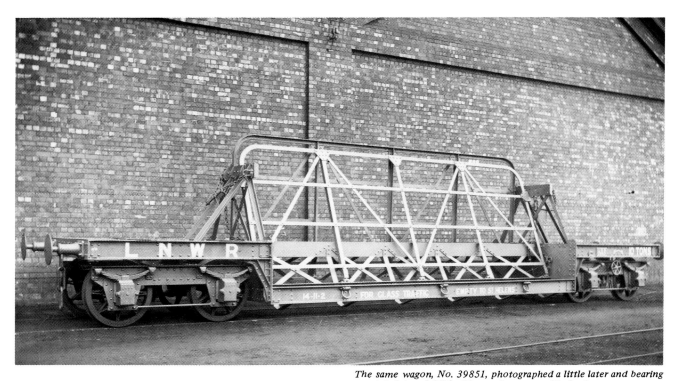

The same wagon, No. 39851, photographed a little later and bearing a paint date of 2/12. Diamonds were omitted when wagons were repainted after 1910 so they would not have been included when it was repainted. The frame for holding glass sheets had been tilted in this view, which shows how the whole frame was hinged at its base. In service this would have been done to give the maximum possible width, which was diagonally across the loading gauge.

NATIONAL RAILWAY MUSEUM (ETN 86A)

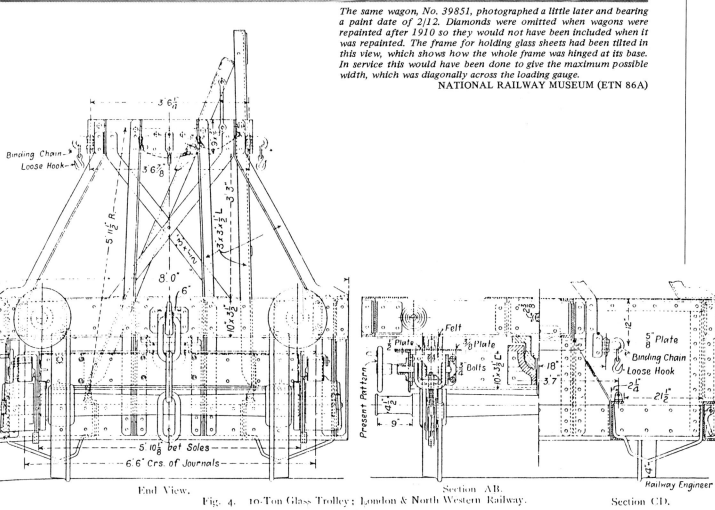

Fig. 4. 10-Ton Glass Trolley; London & North Western Railway.

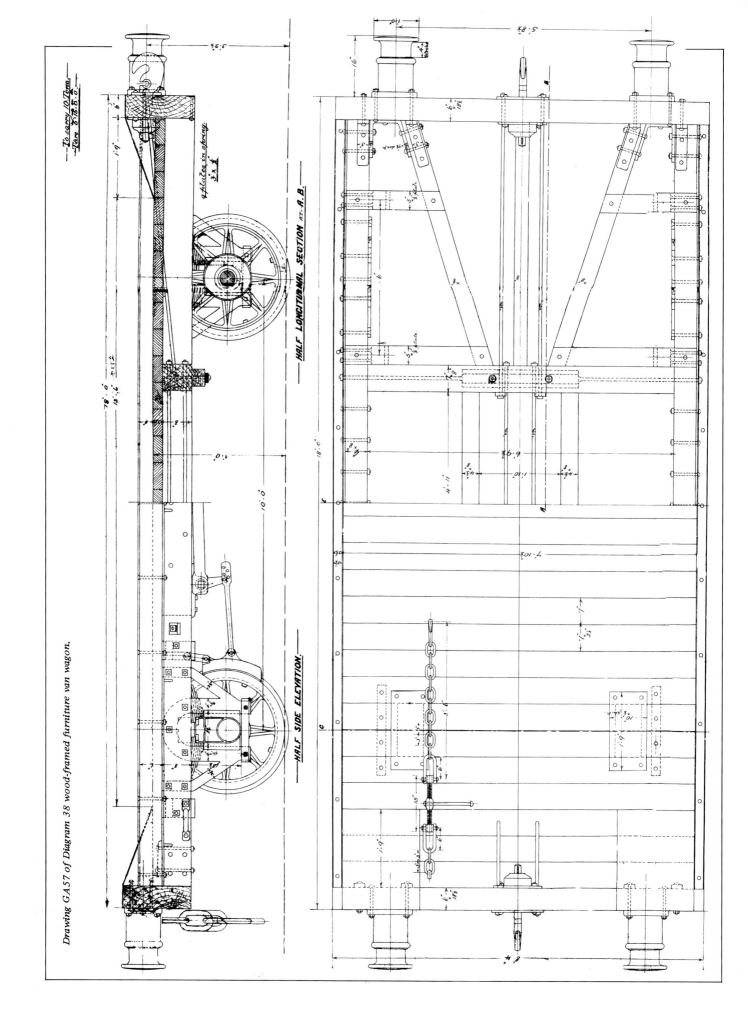

Drawing GA57 of Diagram 38 wood-framed furniture van wagon.

CHAPTER SEVEN

FURNITURE VAN WAGONS

THE term 'furniture wagon' was used by the LNWR to refer to wagons designed to carry furniture vans. Throughout the LNWR period a change of house involved hiring a horse-drawn pantechnicon and, if relocation was for any distance, then this vehicle would be taken to the local station where it would be man-handled from an end-loading dock onto a furniture van wagon.

They are first mentioned in official records in May 1862 when a minute read '50 lowest sided long wagons to be altered so that their ends may drop and enable large furniture vans to be carried. Such wagons to be apportioned among different stations and painted "to be returned to depot".' Presumably they were long compared with the 15ft 6in standard adopted for open wagons in 1859. Whether the conversions ever took place is unclear (see also chapter 5, Diagram 14 – Timber Wagon, 24ft long). The reference to 'large' furniture vans infers that a smaller standard was also in use. These were probably carried in standard open wagons.

SUMMARY

Diagram	Introduced	Description
38	1869*	Furniture wagon, to carry 10 tons
38a	1916	Furniture wagon, to carry 10 tons

NOTE:
*indicates earliest date wagons were known to be in service.

The title 'furniture wagon' does not appear in the annual stock valuation lists until 1877 when there was a general increase in the sub-division and detail of the vehicle stock presented. At that time there were 109 furniture wagons. The 1902 Wagon Stock Age Book shows that building had begun by at least 1869. Numbers slowly increased to 158 in 1888. The stock was maintained at this number by replacement building until about 1920. At the Grouping, 154 remained to be passed to the LMS, of which 134 were to Diagram 38 and twenty to Diagram 38A.

DIAGRAM 38 – FURNITURE WAGON

It would appear that all the furniture wagons described above conformed to this diagram, with the exception of those described in the 1862 minute. They were 18ft long over headstocks by 8ft 4in wide externally with a wheelbase of 10ft. They were rated at 10 tons. A pair of short ramps were fitted at either end to enable horse-drawn wagons to be wheeled on and off. They were plated in iron, later steel, to reduce wear. The flat platform floor was 13ft 6in long by 7ft 10in wide and just 3ft above rail level. Everything was done to keep the floor as low as possible. Although the split-spoke wheels were only 2ft 8in diameter, even then the wooden floor was so low that four 19in x 7in holes had to be left for clearance. These were covered by ½in steel plates, 21in x 10½in, rebated into the planks to present a flush-top face.

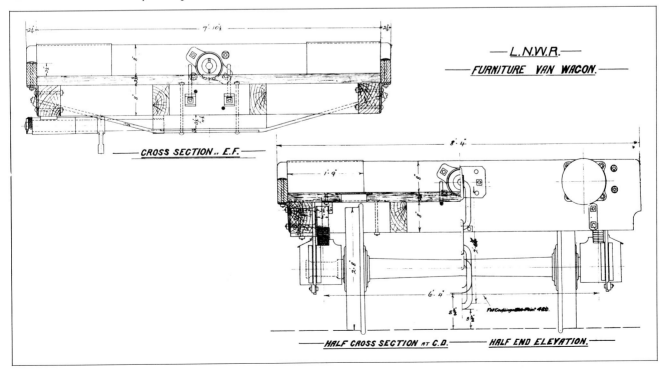

— L.N.W.R. —
— FURNITURE VAN WAGON. —

CROSS SECTION at E.F.

HALF CROSS SECTION at C.D. — HALF END ELEVATION. —

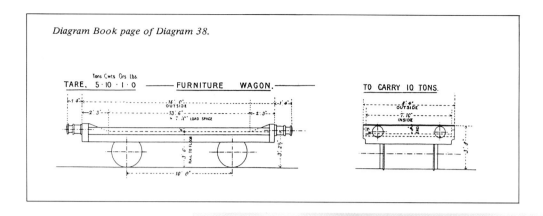

Diagram Book page of Diagram 38.

TARE. 5·10·1·0 ——— FURNITURE WAGON. ——— TO CARRY 10 TONS.

This Diagram 38 wagon, believed to be No. 19886, was photographed around 1923. The filthy condition makes identification of the livery difficult, but it appears to have had 'LNWR' closely spaced in the centre of the side. The self-contained buffers were of the design used extensively by the LNWR, both for new construction and conversion of old dumb-buffered wagons until the early 1900s.
CTY. J. P. RICHARDS

Even the buffer height was reduced by 3in to 3ft 2½in. The buffer beams themselves were a massive 6in x 18½in.

The lowered floor and short ramps precluded the normal sprung buffer arrangement, so self-contained buffers were used with a total length over head of 1ft 4in. The buffers were an LNWR standard for conversions from dumb buffers and also where clearances behind the headstock were tight, as in this case, and on some bogie wagons. A special short coupling was provided to match and was sprung by means of an india-rubber washer visible above the floor. Also visible at this point were the ⅞in tie-rods normally hidden beneath the floor of most wagons. Chains with turnbuckles were fitted to eye bolts through the end planks at each corner of the wagon to secure the wheels of the pantechnicon.

The low floor level led to all sorts of problems with axle-boxes and wheels. Firstly, the 8in x 6in solebars (usually 10in x 4½in, as in Diagram 1) were set at 6ft 9½in apart instead of the standard 5ft 11½in, in order to accommodate springs behind the 'W' iron. To allow the springs to lie inside the solebars instead of underneath them, special forged cradles were made to bear on the underside of the solebars. They were bolted to it on the inside, and at the top fitted against steel plates 5in x ½in bolted on top of the solebars and rakers. This brought the spring hangers to be almost flush with the underside of the floor, rather than the underside of the sole-

bar as on a standard wagon. Even with the small 2ft 8in diameter wheels the grease axleboxes would have fouled the solebars when the springs were compressed, so long cut-outs had to be made in the bottom of the solebars, further weakening them. To counter this, the normal flitch plate and curb rail were replaced by a heavy 8in x 3in angle which covered the face of the solebars.

At first, brakes were of the single iron block, pushrod type on one side only, then on both sides for new construction from the early 1890s. It appears that during the 1914–18 war some wagons were downgraded to 6 tons.

Known examples of Diagram 38:
Diagram book tare for type: 5.10.1

Number	Buffers	Brakes
19886	self cont.	Pushrod BS

Further examples of running numbers:
NOTE: Almost all of these numbers come from a list marked up on Mr. Emmett's own copy of the Diagram Book. Page 38 bears a hand-written note which says: 'Up to and including 18887 these wagons have a single brake on one side only. From 10050 to 10137 inclusive = 38 wagons, they have a single brake on both sides. From 10192 onwards they have a single brake on one side only.' This appears to say that *all* Diagram 38 wagons have a single brake one side only except for 10050 to 10137. The reason why the original statement was not worded more precisely, without an overlap, is not known.

99	1999	3553	5283	7166	8258	10137	11345	18905	25678	45738
128	2076	3600	5300	7173	8382	10191	11554	19042	26577	45740
185	2200	4138	5824	7248	8421	10192	11624	19393	26838	46093
283	2328	4313	5950	7514	8523	10196	11755	19886	27827	46094
367	2512	4322	6056	7639	8700	10327	11843	20188	27828	
842	2686	4487	6171	7701	9043	10335	12153	20214	27830	
899	2961	4537	6401	7742	9359	10345	12252	20723	45731	
1355	2981	4557	6593	7887	9623	10536	12427	21144	45732	
1445	2997	4669	6754	7953	9672	11061	12473	21399	45733	
1571	3002	4741	6880	8126	9689	11107	17992	21519	45734	
1627	3143	4815	6896	8223	9821	11140	18361	22448	45735	
1710	3184	4824	7115	8226	10050	11267	18762	22610	45736	
1844	3292	4951	7153	8247	10112	11332	18887	23841	45737	

DIAGRAM 38A – FURNITURE WAGON

These appear to have been introduced in 1916 and were simply an updated version of Diagram 38. In spite of its recent date, no detailed drawing is known to the authors, and there are a number of details on which we are uncertain. The wagon sides were made of steel, instead of wood and, as a wider load space was not needed, the overall width was reduced to 8ft 1in. The additional strength thus provided enabled the 8in x 3in angle on the solebars to be dispensed with and a conventional flitch plate used instead. A separate steel angle was used for the curb rail, the sides being bolted vertically to it, as normal. The LNWR had stopped using its own self-contained buffers by this time, preferring the RCH standard pattern similar to dumb-buffered conversions of timber wagons, which were 1ft 6in long over the head. The

An official Earlestown photograph of D38A No. 7248. The oil date had not yet been painted on, nor can we see a paint date, but the lifting date beneath the brake lever reads 16/9/21. Much of the wagon looks new, although some of the underframe could have been re-used. The sides of these wagons were made from a single steel channel, with holes for fixing ropes and chains. Most unusually for an LNWR wagon, and maybe uniquely, disc wheels had been used. The axleboxes were of the standard late bulbous type with sloping covers, but a modified design because the leaf springs were inboard of the solebars. The steel-maker's name, rolled into the angle between the side and the flitch plate covering the solebar, reads 'Dorman Long & Co Ltd'. Because Crewe Works had a steelmaking plant, it is commonly assumed that all steel used by the company was manufactured there, but this is quite untrue, the majority having to be bought in. Although clearly a special wagon for a particular purpose, the basic design was still very similar to other LNWR types. Notice, for example, the cross tie-rods protruding through the solebar at an angle and the equivalent longitudinal rods just visible behind the bufferbeam through which they protruded, with nuts on the drawplate. It was not possible to have a continuous drawbar, due to the floor being lower than the drawbar, so rubber springs were used instead, held in place by the heavy steel disc and securing pin visible behind the bufferbeam.
NATIONAL RAILWAY MUSEUM (ETN 128)

When horse-drawn furniture vans became a thing of the past, furniture wagons, with their convenient wheel ramps, were used for carrying all types of lightweight wheeled vehicles. No. 204824 was photographed on 12th March 1940 and carrying an RAF trailer loaded with what are believed to have been cylinders containing gas for filling barrage balloons. The tare was 6.0 and again we can see both the non-common user letter 'N' and the 'TRH' plate on the sole bar. This wagon also had wheels with eight solid spokes.

CTY. R. J. ESSERY

buffer beam itself was made even deeper which necessitated its being in two pieces rather than one, but gave a buffer height of a more reasonable 3ft 4in.

Detail differences apparent in photographs include No.16 bulbous-type oil axleboxes with sloping lids; holding-down chains now fixed by an eye bolt through each buffer beam rather than the floor; disc wheels (but still 2ft 8in); standard coupling chains; holes in the steel sides through which ropes could be tied; and double brakes both sides. All twenty wagons to Diagram 38A were built as replacements for Diagram 38, as follows: 6 in 1916, 6 in 1917, 6 in 1918 and 2 in 1921.

As mentioned, the sides were made of steel angle, looking inwards, the bottom flange being bolted to the steel angle

curb rail. There was a variant which had sides made of steel channel looking inwards. We are uncertain of the overall width of this type but believe that it conformed to Diagram 38A and are included in the above figures.

Known examples of Diagram 38A:
Diagram book tare for type: 6.10.3

Number	Tare	Buffers	Brakes	Axleboxes	Notes
7248	6.6.0	self cont.	DBBS	No.16 bulbous	disc wheels
204824	6.0	self cont.	DBBS		LMS No., as at 3/40
217992	5.18	self cont.	DBBS	No.16 bulbous	LMS No., solid spoke wheels

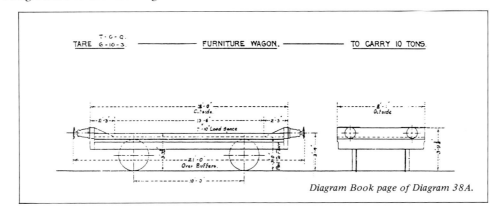

Diagram Book page of Diagram 38A.

A similar D38A in LMS days, No. 217992, showing that chains and shackles were provided, fixed to eye bolts behind the bufferbeams, either side of the drawbar. The LMS plate 'TRH', fitted just to the left of the numberplate, was the LMS designation for what they called a Traction Truck (TR) of 10-ton capacity (H). The letter 'N' to the left of the LMS lettering and number denoted it was not a 'common user' wagon. The wheels appear to have had eight solid spokes. This type of self-contained buffer (actually an RCH standard design) became the LNWR standard, superseding those with parallel-sided stocks. What appears to have been a 'generally repaired' plate near the end of the bufferbeam on the side of the wheel ramp, is, alas, unreadable.

A. G. ELLIS COLLECTION (11804)

APPENDIX I
LNWR WAGON DIAGRAM NUMBERS

Sorted in numerical order.
[Notes in square brackets are not part of the official description]

1	Open goods wagon – 9in sides, to carry 7 tons
2	Open goods wagon – 20in sides, to carry 7 tons
3	Open goods wagon – 20in sides, fall doors, to carry 7 tons
4	Open goods wagon – 36in sides, door on each side, 7 tons
5	Open goods wagon – 20in sides, fall doors, to carry 10 tons
6	Open goods wagon – 20in sides, to carry 10 tons
7	Slate truck wagon (fall doors), to carry 10 tons
8	Open goods wagon – 22in sides (West Cumberland), to carry 10 tons [door one side only]
9	Open goods wagon – 36in sides, door each side, 10 tons
10	Open goods wagon – 42in sides, door each side, 20 tons
11	High-sided open goods wagon, to carry 10 tons
12	Timber wagon (ordinary), to carry 10 tons
13	Twin timber wagons, each to carry 10 tons
14	Timber wagon 24ft 0in long, to carry 10 tons
[14a	Timber wagon 24ft 0in long, fast sides & drop ends, to carry 10 tons]
15	Beer van, to carry 10 tons
16	Goods brake van [10 tons]
17	Goods brake van [20 tons, 6-wheeled]
17a	Goods brake van [20 tons, 4-wheeled]
17b	Goods brake van [20 tons, 4-wheeled, 'Crystal Palace']
18	Goods brake van [double ended]
19	Butter van, to carry 7 tons
20	Cattle wagon (small), to carry 7 tons
21	Cattle wagon (medium), to carry 7 tons
22	Cattle wagon (large), to carry 10 tons
23	Special cattle wagon, to carry 6 tons
24	Fowlers' cattle wagon, to carry 6 tons
25	Cattle wagon with compartment for man, to carry 6 tons
26	Cattle wagon with compartment for man, to carry 6 tons
27	Coal wagon, S.& C., end door only, to carry 10 tons
28	Hopper iron ore wagon (West Cumberland), to carry 10 tons
29	Hoppered coke wagon (West Cumberland), to carry 10 tons
30	Hopper wagon, railed for coke (West Cumberland), 10 tons
30a	Coke wagon, Hoppered (West Cumberland), 10 tons
31	Coke wagon, to carry 10 tons [16ft]
31a	Coke wagon, to carry 10 tons [18ft]
32	Covered goods van, 7 tons [door one side only, 15ft 6in]
33	Covered goods van, to carry 7 tons [door both sides, 16ft]
34	Covered goods van, to carry 10 tons
35	Covered goods van, to carry 10 tons
36	Covered goods van, to carry 10 tons
37	Covered goods van, to carry 15 tons [27ft]
38	Furniture wagon, to carry 10 tons
38a	Furniture wagon, to carry 10 tons
39	Small glass wagon, to carry 7 tons
40	Medium glass wagon (Double door at one end), 10 tons
41	Large glass wagon (Double door at each end), 10 tons
42	Large glass wagon with 9in sides, to carry 10 tons
42a	Large glass wagon with 9in sides and steel well, 10 tons
43	Gunpowder van, to carry 5 tons
43a	Gunpowder van, to carry 7 tons
44	Hopper wagon, to carry 10 tons
44a	Hopper wagon, to carry 10 tons
45	Meat van, to carry 6 tons [16ft]
45a	Meat van (insulated), to carry 6 tons [18ft]
45b	Meat van (insulated), to carry 6 tons [18ft]
46	Refrigerator van, to carry 6 tons [16ft]
46a	Refrigerator van, to carry 6 tons [18ft]
47	Propeller wagon, to carry 10 tons
48	Rail wagons, each to carry 10 tons
49	Rail wagons, each pair to carry 50 tons [each 6 wheeled]
50	Rail wagons, each pair to carry 60 tons [each 6 wheeled]
51	Shunting wagon
52	Pooley's tool van, to carry 7 tons and 10 tons [15ft 6in and 18ft]
53	Traffic coal wagon, to carry 8 tons
54	Traffic coal wagon (converted from 8 to 10 tons)
55	Traffic coal wagon, Private Owner's standard specification, to carry 15 tons
56	Traffic coal wagon, 19ft long, to carry 15 tons
57	Traffic coal wagon, 20ft long, to carry 15 tons
58	Traffic coal wagon, 20ft long, to carry 15 tons
59	Traffic coal wagon, to carry 20 tons
60	Tranship van, to carry 7 tons
61	Chemical pan trolley, to carry 12 tons
62	Ballast wagon, to carry 10 tons [16ft]
62a	Ballast wagon, to carry 10 tons [18ft]
63	Coal wagon, Carr. dept, to carry 10 tons [curved ends, side doors, 16ft]
64	Loco coal wagon, 10 tons [curved ends, no doors, 16ft]
64a	Loco hopper wagon, to carry 10 tons [16ft]
64b	Loco hopper wagon, to carry 15 tons [18ft]
64c	Loco coal wagon, to carry 10 tons [no doors, 18ft]
64d	Loco coal wagon with end door, to carry 10 tons [18ft]
65	Loco coal wagon – steel body and frame, to carry 20 tons
66	Steamboat coal wagon, to carry 10 tons
67	Agricultural engine trolley, to carry 10 tons
68	Tram car trolley, to carry 10 tons
69	Boiler trolley, to carry 10 tons
70	Tram car trolley, to carry 15 tons
70a	Trolley, to carry 20 tons
71	Tram car trolley, to carry 15 tons
72	Tram car trolley, to carry 15 tons
73	Trolley, to carry 20 tons
74	Platform trolley, to carry 20 tons [6 wheeled]
75	Tram car trolley, to carry 20 tons
76	Boiler trolley, to carry 20 tons
77	Boiler trolley, to carry 25 tons
77a	Trolley, to carry 25 tons
78	Agricultural engine trolley, to carry 20 tons
79	Boiler trolley, coupled, to carry 30 tons
80	Platform trolley, to carry 30 tons [6 wheeled]
81	Boiler trolley, to carry 35 tons
82	Boiler trolley, to carry 36 tons
83	Boiler trolley, to carry 50 tons [12 wheeled]
84	Open goods wagon, to carry 10 tons [36in sides, 18ft]
84a	Open goods wagon, to carry 10 tons [36in sides, 18ft – may be LMS]
85	Covered goods van, to carry 10 tons [16ft]
85a	Covered goods van, to carry 10 tons [13ft 9½in]
86	Banana van, to carry 7 tons [16ft]
87	Covered goods van for express traffic, to carry 10 tons [16ft]
88	Covered goods van, to carry 10 tons [18ft]
88a	Covered goods van (insulated), to carry 10 tons [18ft]
89	Banana van – with sliding doors, to carry 10 tons [16ft]
90	Traffic coal wagon, to carry 10 tons [18ft]
91	Iron Ore hopper wagon, to carry 20 tons [steel]
92	Fruit van, to carry 10 tons [18ft]
93	Goods brake van, hand & vacuum [15 tons, double ended]
93a	Goods brake van, hand & vacuum [15 tons]
94	Goods brake van – ogee seats, hand & vacuum [15 tons]
95	Fruit van with sliding doors – steam heated – hand & vacuum, 10 tons [18ft]
95a	Fruit van insulated with sliding doors – steam heated – hand & vacuum, 10 tons [18ft]
96	Trolley, to carry 40 tons
97	Platform trolley, to carry 40 tons
98	Wire rope trolley, to carry 38 tons
99	Glass trolley, to carry 10 tons
100	Trolley, to carry 40 tons
101	Trolley, to carry 40 tons
102	Trolley, to carry 40 tons
103	Open goods wagon – 9in sides, to carry 10 tons [18ft]
104	Ingot trolley, to carry 25 tons
105	Trolley, to carry 20 tons
106	Chemical Pan trolley, to carry 15 tons
107	Timber trolley, to carry 30 tons
108	Trolley, to carry 25 tons
109	Rectank trolleys, to carry 35 tons
110	W.D. bogie trolley, to carry 40 tons [ex. Warflat]

APPENDIX 2
LNWR WAGON DIAGRAMS, LISTED BY USE
[Notes in square brackets are not part of the official description]

OPEN GOODS WAGONS

1   Open goods wagon – 9in sides, to carry 7 tons
2   Open goods wagon – 20in sides, to carry 7 tons
3   Open goods wagon – 20in sides, fall doors, to carry 7 tons
4   Open goods wagon – 36in sides, door each side, to carry 7 tons
5   Open goods wagon – 20in sides, fall doors, to carry 10 tons
6   Open goods wagon – 20in sides, to carry 10 tons
7   Slate truck wagon (fall doors), to carry 10 tons
8   Open goods wagon – 22in sides (West Cumberland), to carry 10 tons [door one side only]
9   Open goods wagon – 36in sides, door each side, 10 tons
10   Open goods wagon – 42in sides, door each side, 20 tons
11   High sided open goods wagon, to carry 10 tons
84   Open goods wagon, to carry 10 tons [36in sides, 18ft]
84a   Open goods wagon, to carry 10 tons [36in sides,18ft – may be LMS]
103   Open goods wagon – 9in sides, to carry 10 tons [18ft]

COAL, COKE AND HOPPERED WAGONS

28   Hopper iron ore wagon (West Cumberland), to carry 10 tons
29   Hoppered coke wagon (West Cumberland), to carry 10 tons
30   Hopper wagon, railed for coke(West Cumberland), 10 tons
30a   Coke wagon, hoppered(West Cumberland), to carry 10 tons
31   Coke wagon, to carry 10 tons [16ft]
31a   Coke wagon, to carry 10 tons [18ft]
44   Hopper wagon, to carry 10 tons
44a   Hopper wagon, to carry 10 tons
53   Traffic coal wagon, to carry 8 tons
54   Traffic coal wagon (converted from 8 to 10 tons)
55   Traffic coal wagon, Private Owner's standard specification, to carry 15 tons
56   Traffic coal wagon, 19ft long, to carry 15 tons
57   Traffic coal wagon, 20ft long, to carry 15 tons
58   Traffic coal wagon, 20ft long, to carry 15 tons
59   Traffic coal wagon, to carry 20 tons
90   Traffic coal wagon, to carry 10 tons [18ft]
91   Iron Ore hopper wagon, to carry 20 tons (steel)

DEPARTMENTAL COAL WAGONS

27   Coal wagon, S.&C., end door only, to carry 10 tons
63   Coal wagon, Carr. dept, to carry 10 tons – [curved ends, side doors, 16ft]
64   Loco coal wagon, to carry 10 tons [curved ends, no doors, 16ft]
64a   Loco hopper wagon, to carry 10 tons [16ft]
64b   Loco hopper wagon, to carry 15 tons [18ft]
64c   Loco coal wagon, to carry 10 tons [no doors, 18ft]
64d   Loco coal wagon with end door, to carry 10 tons [18ft]
65   Loco coal wagon – steel body and frame, to carry 20 tons
66   Steamboat coal wagon, to carry 10 tons

BALLAST WAGONS

48   Rail wagons, each to carry 10 tons
49   Rail wagons, each pair to carry 50 tons [each 6 wheeled]
50   Rail wagons, each pair to carry 60 tons [each 6 wheeled]
62   Ballast wagon, to carry 10 tons [16ft]
62a   Ballast wagon, to carry 10 tons [18ft]

TIMBER WAGONS

12   Timber wagon (ordinary), to carry 10 tons
13   Twin timber wagons, each to carry 10 tons
14   Timber wagon 24ft 0in long, to carry 10 tons
[14a   Timber wagon 24ft 0in long, – fast sides & drop ends, to carry 10 tons]
107   Timber trolley, to carry 30 tons

CATTLE WAGONS

20   Cattle wagon (small), to carry 7 tons
21   Cattle wagon (medium), to carry 7 tons
22   Cattle wagon (large), to carry 10 tons
23   Special cattle wagon, to carry 6 tons
24   Fowlers' cattle wagon, to carry 6 tons
25   Cattle wagon with compartment for man, to carry 6 tons
26   Cattle wagon with compartment for man, to carry 6 tons

COVERED GOODS VANS

32   Covered goods van, to carry 7 tons [door one side, 15ft 6in]
33   Covered goods van, to carry 7 tons [door both sides, 16ft]
34   Covered goods van, to carry 10 tons
35   Covered goods van, to carry 10 tons
36   Covered goods van, to carry 10 tons
37   Covered goods van, to carry 15 tons [27ft]
85   Covered goods van, to carry 10 tons [16ft]
85a   Covered goods van, to carry 10 tons [13ft 9½in]
87   Covered goods van for express traffic, to carry 10 tons [16ft]
88   Covered goods van, to carry 10 tons [18ft]

VANS FOR PERISHABLE TRAFFIC

19   Butter van, to carry 7 tons
45   Meat van, to carry 6 tons [16ft]
45a   Meat van (insulated), to carry 6 tons [18ft]
45b   Meat van (insulated), to carry 6 tons [18ft]
46   Refrigerator van, to carry 6 tons [16ft]
46a   Refrigerator van, to carry 6 tons [18ft]
86   Banana van, to carry 7 tons [16ft]
88a   Covered goods van (insulated), to carry 10 tons [18ft]
89   Banana van – with sliding doors, to carry 10 tons [16ft]
92   Fruit van, to carry 10 tons [18ft]
95   Fruit van with sliding doors – steam heated – hand & vacuum, 10 tons [18ft]
95a   Fruit van insulated with sliding doors – steam heated – hand & vacuum, 10 tons [18ft]

MISCELLANEOUS VANS

15   Beer van, to carry 10 tons
43   Gunpowder van, to carry 5 tons
43a   Gunpowder van, to carry 7 tons
52   Pooley's tool van, to carry 7 tons and 10 tons [15ft 6in & 18ft]

FURNITURE WAGONS

38   Furniture wagon, to carry 10 tons
38a   Furniture wagon, to carry 10 tons

GLASS WAGONS

39   Small glass wagon, to carry 7 tons
40   Medium glass wagon (Double door at one end), 10 tons
41   Large glass wagon (Double door at each end), to carry 10 tons
42   Large glass wagon with 9in sides, to carry 10 tons
42a   Large glass wagon with 9in sides and steel well, 10 tons
99   Glass trolley, to carry 10 tons

BRAKE VANS

16   Goods brake van [10 tons]
17   Goods brake van [20 tons, 6-wheeled]
17a   Goods brake van [20 tons, 4-wheeled]
17b   Goods brake van [20 tons, 4-wheeled, 'Crystal Palace']
18   Goods brake van [double ended]
93   Goods brake van, hand & vacuum [15 tons, double ended]
93a   Goods brake van, hand & vacuum [15 tons]
94   Goods brake van – ogee seats, hand & vacuum [15 tons]

BOILER TROLLEYS
69 Boiler trolley, to carry 10 tons
76 Boiler trolley, to carry 20 tons
77 Boiler trolley, to carry 25 tons
79 Boiler trolley, coupled, to carry 30 tons
81 Boiler trolley, to carry 35 tons
82 Boiler trolley, to carry 36 tons
83 Boiler trolley, to carry 50 tons [12-wheeled]

TRAM CAR TROLLEYS
68 Tram car trolley, to carry 10 tons
70 Tram car trolley, to carry 15 tons
71 Tram car trolley, to carry 15 tons
72 Tram car trolley, to carry 15 tons
75 Tram car trolley, to carry 20 tons

GENERAL BOGIE TROLLEYS
70a Trolley, to carry 20 tons
73   Trolley, to carry 20 tons
77a Trolley, to carry 25 tons
96   Trolley, to carry 40 tons

97   Platform trolley, to carry 40 tons
98   Wire rope trolley, to carry 38 tons
100 Trolley, to carry 40 tons
101 Trolley, to carry 40 tons
102 Trolley, to carry 40 tons
108 Trolley, to carry 25 tons
109 Rectank trolleys, to carry 35 tons
110 W.D. bogie trolley, to carry 40 tons [ex. Warflat]

MISCELLANEOUS WAGONS
47   Propeller wagon, to carry 10 tons
51   Shunting wagon
61   Chemical pan trolley, to carry 12 tons
67   Agricultural engine trolley, to carry 10 tons
74   Platform trolley, to carry 20 tons [6 wheeled]
78   Agricultural engine trolley, to carry 20 tons
80   Platform trolley, to carry 30 tons [6 wheeled]
104 Ingot trolley, to carry 25 tons
105 Trolley, to carry 20 tons
106 Chemical Pan trolley, to carry 15 tons

APPENDIX 3
HOW TO LOAD TIMBER – AN LNWR INSTRUCTION NOTICE

The LNWR published an instruction booklet detailing the correct procedure to follow when loading long and projecting traffic. It is reproduced here in its entirety, particularly as it is very relevant to the loading of timber on timber wagons. Note that procedures are included to carry rigid loads requiring up to five wagons; perhaps the surprising omission is guidance on the minimum radius curve such a set could traverse, especially for rails, rolled sections and plates which were to be shackled to every bolster.

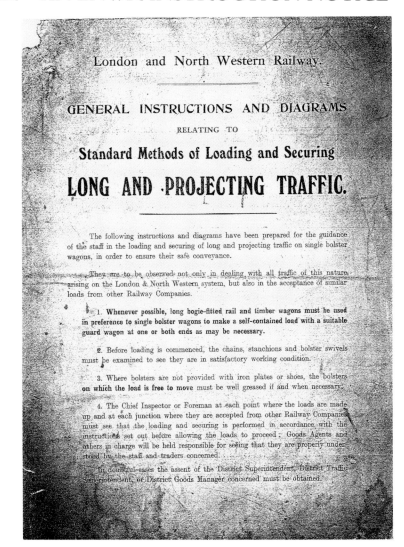

London and North Western Railway.

GENERAL INSTRUCTIONS AND DIAGRAMS

RELATING TO

Standard Methods of Loading and Securing

LONG AND PROJECTING TRAFFIC.

The following instructions and diagrams have been prepared for the guidance of the staff in the loading and securing of long and projecting traffic on single bolster wagons, in order to ensure their safe conveyance.

They are to be observed not only in dealing with all traffic of this nature arising on the London & North Western system, but also in the acceptance of similar loads from other Railway Companies.

1. Whenever possible, long bogie-fitted rail and timber wagons must be used in preference to single bolster wagons to make a self-contained load with a suitable guard wagon at one or both ends as may be necessary.

2. Before loading is commenced, the chains, stanchions and bolster swivels must be examined to see they are in satisfactory working condition.

3. Where bolsters are not provided with iron plates or shoes, the bolsters on which the load is free to move must be well greased if and when necessary.

4. The Chief Inspector or Foreman at each point where the loads are made up and at each junction where they are accepted from other Railway Companies must see that the loading and securing is performed in accordance with the instructions set out before allowing the loads to proceed; Goods Agents and others in charge will be held responsible for seeing that they are properly understood by the staff and traders concerned.

In doubtful cases the assent of the District Superintendent, District Traffic Superintendent, or District Goods Manager concerned must be obtained.

Diagram No. 1

METHODS OF CARRYING RIGID ROUND TIMBER.

2 Wagon set.

A. A. B.

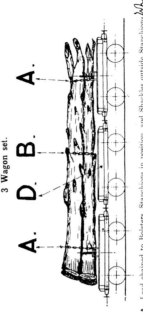

A Load chained to Bolsters, Stanchions in position, and Shackles outside Stanchions.
B Load chained free of wagon.

16. **Two-Wagon Set** (Diagram No. 1).—Loads requiring two wagons must be bound tightly to the bolsters of the wagons and stanchions used. If the load exceeds the length of two wagons, a guard wagon must be used.

Diagram No. 2

3 Wagon set.

A. D. B. A.

A Load chained to Bolsters, Stanchions in position, and Shackles outside Stanchions. *[handwritten: When owing to the full width of Bolster the pins cannot be connected to properly the pins]*
B Load chained free of wagon. *[handwritten: are marked to D numbers 1, 2, 3, 4, 5, 6, 7, 8 & 9.]*
D Bolsters to be removed. *[handwritten: This applies to D. 9-1-30.]*

17. **Three-Wagon Set** (Diagram No. 2).—Loads requiring three wagons, exclusive of guard wagon, must only be bound to the bolsters of the first and third wagons and stanchions used. In the event of the centre wagon being a bolster wagon, the bolster must be removed and the load tightly chained free of wagon.

In certain cases where timber is of awkward shape, it may be undesirable to remove the bolster of the second wagon. It would then be better to bind the load on the bolsters of the butt-end and second wagons, the stanchions remaining on both these wagons; the bolster and chain on the third wagon to be used, but stanchions removed, and the width of the load on this wagon not to exceed five feet.

---

5. Care should be taken that the carrying wagons are not loaded in excess of their registered carrying capacity.

6. Loads exceeding sixty feet in length must not be forwarded until the assent of the General Superintendent has been obtained.

7. It is desirable that all loads should overlap the bolsters on which they are carried by **at least 2 feet 6 inches.**

8. Vehicles in all cases should be so coupled as to limit the **maximum** possible movement between any two vehicles to 1 foot 4 inches.

9. Bolsters removed from their normal position in under-running wagons should be disconnected and, when possible, laid in a safe place in the wagon. Care must be taken to see that the pivot pins accompany the bolsters.

GENERAL INSTRUCTIONS RELATING TO TIMBER.

10. In loading timber of unequal lengths, the longer pieces should, as far as possible, be placed at the bottom and in the centre of the load, and the shorter pieces on the top, and all be firmly bound together.

11. Whenever practicable, straight trees should be loaded at the bottom and crooked ones on the top, as the latter are liable to bind on the wagon ends and so prevent the swivel bolsters moving freely when rounding curves.

12. In all cases, the loaders must see that the timber is clear of the bodies of wagons.

As far as possible, wagons with bolsters of equal height should be used in each set.

13. When timber is loaded on three, four, or five wagon-sets, the butts to be loaded at one end, as shown in diagrams Nos. 2, 3, and 4.

14. All loads must be tightly bound to the wagons at the butt-end, but loose enough at the other bearing to permit of longitudinal movement.

15. It is undesirable to use ropes for binding loads of poles and tapering timber free of wagons at the tapering end, but where difficulty is experienced in obtaining chains for the purpose ropes may be used in cases of emergency.

METHOD OF CARRYING RIGID ROUND TIMBER.

5 Wagon set.

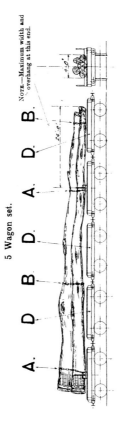

Note.—Maximum width and overhang at this end.

A Load chained to Bolsters, Stanchions in position, and Shackles outside Stanchions.
B Load chained free of wagon.
D Bolsters to be removed.

19. **Five-Wagon Set** (Diagram No. 4).—Loads requiring five wagons must be chained to the bolsters of first and fourth wagons from the butt-end and stanchions used: The load to be chained free of wagons midway between the bearing points and also at the narrow end. In the event of the intermediate and guard wagons being bolster wagons, the bolsters to be removed. The width of the load at the tapering end must not exceed 4 feet, at a maximum overhang of 24 feet.

Long loads of this description can be loaded as shown in Diagram No. 3, a long flat wagon being substituted for the second and third wagons shown in Diagram No. 4.

METHOD OF CARRYING RIGID ROUND TIMBER.

4 Wagon set.

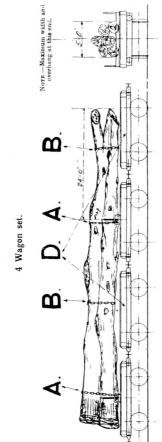

Note.—Maximum width and overhang at this end.

A Load chained to Bolsters, Stanchions in position, and Shackles outside Stanchions.
B Load chained free of wagon.
D Bolsters to be removed.

18. **Four-Wagon Set** (Diagram No. 3).—Loads requiring four wagons only can be bound to the bolsters of first and third wagons from the butt-end and stanchions used. The bolsters of the second and fourth wagons to be removed. The load to be chained free of wagons midway between the bearing points and also at the narrow end, and the width of the load at the tapering end must not exceed five feet at a maximum overhang of 24 feet.

METHOD OF CARRYING FLEXIBLE LOADS, SUCH AS RAILS,
ROLLED SECTIONS, POLES, PLATES, &c.

3 Wagon set.

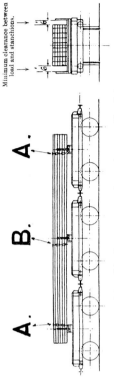

Minimum clearance between load and stanchions.

Total weight of load not to exceed carrying capacity of two wagons.

A Load chained to Bolsters, Stanchions in position, and Shackles outside Stanchions.

B Load chained free of wagon.

22. **Three-Wagon Set** (Diagram No. 6).—Loads requiring three wagons must be chained to the bolsters of first and third wagons and stanchions used. The load to be also chained free of wagons about the centre and the outer stanchions of centre bolster to be left in position. The clearance between the load and stanchions on centre wagon must not be less than 6 inches at each side. The total weight of the load not to exceed the carrying capacity of two wagons.

In the case of poles and tapering timber, the butt-end wagon to be loaded to the full width of the bolster, stanchions to be used on butt-end and second wagons and load chained to these wagons. The stanchions must be removed from the third wagon and load chained free of wagons.

METHOD OF CARRYING FLEXIBLE LOADS, SUCH AS RAILS,
ROLLED SECTIONS, POLES, PLATES, &c.

2 Wagon set.

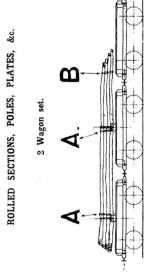

A Load chained to Bolsters, Stanchions in position, and Shackles outside Stanchions.

B Load chained free of wagon.

20. **Precaution to be observed with all flexible loads.**—Wagons with bolsters of equal height should be used, as far as possible, in each set.

21. **Two-Wagon Set** (Diagram No. 5).—Loads requiring two wagons must be bound tightly to the bolsters of the wagons and stanchions used. If the load exceeds the length of two wagons, a guard wagon must be used. Neither wagon must be loaded beyond its registered carrying capacity.

Diagram No. 8

METHODS OF CARRYING FLEXIBLE LOADS, SUCH AS RAILS, ROLLED SECTIONS. POLES, PLATES, &c.

4 Wagon set.

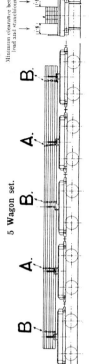

Note.—Maximum width of load at this end.

Note.—Load to be full width between stanchions at this end.

Total weight of load not to exceed two-thirds of the carrying capacity of the four wagons.

A Load chained to Bolsters, Stanchions in position, and Shackles outside Stanchions.
B Load chained free of wagon.
C Bolsters to be retained.

24. **Four-wagon Set** (Diagram No. 8).—Poles and tapering timber may be loaded to the full width of bolster on the butt-end wagon, but the width should not exceed 4 feet 6 inches on fourth wagon. Stanchions to be removed from second and fourth wagons and load chained free of wagons.

Diagram No. 9

5 Wagon set.

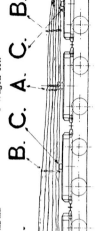

Minimum clearance between load and stanchions.

Total weight of load not to exceed two-thirds of the carrying capacity of the five wagons.

A Load chained to Bolsters, Stanchions in position, and Shackles outside Stanchions.
B Load chained free of wagon.

25. **Five-wagon Set** (Diagram No. 9).—Loads requiring five wagons must be carried on all bolsters and chained to the bolsters of second and fourth wagons. The load must also be chained, free of wagon, at first, third and fifth wagons and all outside stanchions left in position. The load to be centrally placed and the clearance between load and the stanchions must not be less than 1 foot 8 inches on each side, and the total weight of the load not to exceed two-thirds of the carrying capacity of the five wagons.

Diagram No. 7

METHOD OF CARRYING FLEXIBLE LOADS, SUCH AS RAILS, ROLLED SECTIONS. POLES, PLATES, &c.

4 Wagon set.

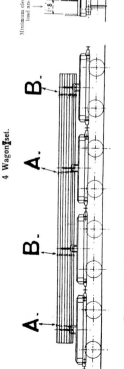

Minimum clearance between load and stanchions.

Total weight of load not to exceed two-thirds of the carrying capacity of the four wagons.

A Load chained to Bolsters, Stanchions in position, and Shackles outside Stanchions.
B Load chained free of wagon.

23. **Four-wagon Set** (Diagram No. 7).—Loads requiring four wagons must be carried on all bolsters and chained to the bolsters of first and third wagons. The load must also be chained, free of wagons, near centre of second and fourth wagons and the outside stanchions left in position on all wagons. The load to be centrally placed and the clearance between the load and the stanchions must not be less than 1 foot 8 inches at each side. The total weight of the load not to exceed two-thirds of the carrying capacity of the four wagons.

METHOD OF CARRYING RIGID LOADS, SUCH AS GIRDERS, LARGE SQUARED TIMBER, &c.

5 Wagon set.

NOTE.—Maximum width and overhang at this end.

4'·0"

24'·0"

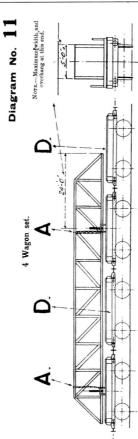

D.   A.   D.   A.   D.

A   Load chained to Bolsters, Stanchions in position, and Shackles outside Stanchions.
D   Bolsters to be removed.

28. **Five-wagon Set** (Diagram No. 12).—Loads requiring five wagons must be chained to the bolsters of second and fourth wagons and stanchions used. Where bolster wagons are used as under-runners, the bolsters to be removed from the first, third and fifth wagons. The load to be centrally placed and the width at the overhang ends not to exceed 4 feet at a maximum overhang of 24 feet. Neither of the carrying wagons to be loaded beyond its registered carrying capacity.

METHODS OF CARRYING RIGID LOADS, SUCH AS GIRDERS, LARGE SQUARED TIMBER, &c.

3 Wagon set.

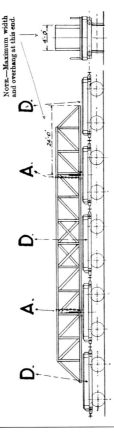

A.   D.   A.

A   Load chained to Bolsters, Stanchions in position, and Shackles outside Stanchions.
D   Bolsters to be removed.

26. **Three-wagon Set** (Diagram No. 10).—Loads requiring three wagons must be chained to the bolsters of first and third wagons and stanchions used. The bolster on centre wagon to be removed. The load to be centrally placed and the weight on either wagon not to exceed its registered carrying capacity.

NOTE.—Maximum width, and overhang at this end.

5'·0"

24'·0"

4 Wagon set.

A.   D.   A.   D.

A   Load chained to Bolsters, Stanchions in position, and Shackles outside Stanchions.
D   Bolsters to be removed.

27. **Four-wagon Set** (Diagram No. 11).—Loads requiring four wagons must be chained to the bolsters of first and third wagons and stanchions used. The bolsters of second and fourth wagons to be removed. The load to be centrally placed, the width at the overhang ends not to exceed 5 feet at a maximum overhang of 24 feet. Neither of the carrying wagons to be loaded beyond its registered carrying capacity.

OVERHANGING LOADS.

Load overhanging one end.

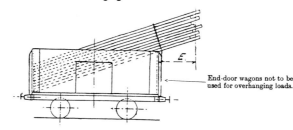

End-door wagons not to be used for overhanging loads.

Table for overhanging Loads.			
Average overhang E in feet.	Max⁹ Load in Tons.		
	8 Ton	10 Ton	12 Ton
2	6	7	8
3	5	6	7
4	4	5	6
5	3	4	5

Ropes must be used to secure the overhanging end of loads to wagon.

Load overhanging both ends.

Diagram No. **14**

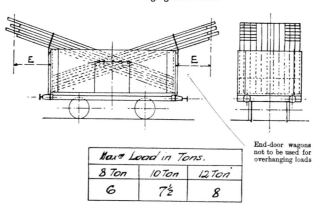

End-door wagons not to be used for overhanging loads

Max⁹ Load in Tons.		
8 Ton	10 Ton	12 Ton
6	7½	8

Ropes must be used to secure the overhanging ends of load to wagon.
Average Overhang E not to exceed 5 feet and load to be equal at each end.

L. W. HORNE, Euston Station, London, N.W.1 (K^L3671).
ASHTON DAVIES, Hunt's Bank, Manchester (G2/18111 H).

APPENDIX 4
EARLESTOWN WORKS AS REVISED 1928

In April 1928 *The Railway Engineer* published an article on the reorganisation of Earlestown Wagon Works by the London Midland and Scottish Railway. Whilst this is strictly outside the main time period of this book, Earlestown Works was so fundamental to LNWR wagons that we opted to print it here in its entirety. Some of the text adds information on the facilities of the Works during the ownership of the LNWR, and will be relevant if you are interested in the LMS. The photographs and diagrams which accompanied this article appear in Chapter 1 on pages 24–32.

A PROGRESSIVE SYSTEM OF RAILWAY WAGON BUILDING.

The Reorganisation in part of the Earlestown Shops of the London Midland & Scottish Railway for the more rapid production of Mineral Wagons has resulted in a very considerable Increase in Output.

The shops originally laid down by the London & North Western Railway at Earlestown and known as the Viaduct Works have been engaged in the building and repairing of goods wagon stock and goods road vehicles for the past 70 years. The establishment is, therefore, probably the oldest of its kind in the country, and is furthermore unique, in that it has always been entirely devoted to wagon production and altogether independent of coach or locomotive building operations. All types of goods wagons and vans were built there for the old L. & N.W. Railway—from 40-ton trolleys to the 2-ton narrow-gauge wagons used on the Blaenau & Festiniog Slate Line, but with the advent of amalgamation, Mr. R. W. Reid, then Carriage and Wagon Superintendent (and now a Vice-President) of the London Midland & Scottish Railway, introduced the principle of division of labour as applied not only to men but also to factories. Under this scheme the plant at Earlestown was set aside for the building of the standard 12-ton mineral wagon, other factories of the Company being allocated other types of vehicles.

The advantages of such a scheme are obvious, all plant and machinery being designed to deal with the components of a particular vehicle or similar vehicles only, so that the most economical development of repetition methods becomes possible. The repair work at Earlestown is, however, as yet not confined to the standard mineral wagon, as such vehicles are still new, but ultimately as the mineral wagons fall due for reconditioning they will be dealt with at Earlestown only, and the whole of the plant will then be engaged on the preparation of parts for that one vehicle, to be used either in assembling into new wagons or in replacement when reconditioning. For the time being, therefore, the repair shops are engaged on the repair of all types of vehicles—principally the L.N.W.R. types which were previously built there. Under this general scheme, the whole of the plant and lay-out was entirely reorganised by Mr. E. J. H. Lemon, the present Carriage and Wagon Superintendent, during the years 1925-26, when he was in charge of the Newton Heath and Earlestown factories as Divisional Superintendent, and a change over to progressive methods in most departments was made.

The greatest difficulty to be faced when reorganising the works was the small and cramped site, only 36 acres in extent, and the impossibility of extension, as the factory is completely surrounded by canal, railway and public streets. The general principles of progressive machining and jig assembly have been applied at Earlestown, and complete new plants have been laid down for timber handling and machining, drilling and wheel assembling. Other schemes are in hand, the modernising of the practice not yet being complete, but a description of the improvements made and in operation to date will doubtless be of interest to our readers.

Reorganisation Problems.

One of the first difficulties experienced in reorganising the works was the fact that the existing wagon-building shops had been built to suit the old method of manufacturing wagons. The tracks were neither long enough for building vehicles on progressive principles, nor was there sufficient room for the storage of the necessary amount of finished components adjacent to the spot where they were to be used. Bearing this in mind, and also the fact that the assembly lay-out must be in such a position that the sawmill can deliver the finished timbers direct to the site, and the ironwork and wheel plants their products to the spot where they are required,

it was decided to take over the then existing timber drying shed for use as an assembly lay-out. The woodworking machinery was placed in an extension to the existing sawmill, which necessitated taking over part of a wagon repair shop, the wheel plant being fixed in the shop where new wagons have previously been built. This had the effect, as will be seen on the block plan, of placing the timber yard in such a position that it could feed the new sawmill with timber and the wheel plant with its raw material by means of conveyors, which will be described hereafter.

The woodworking machinery was laid out in the sawmill extension in such a manner that it delivers the finished components direct to the wagon assembly shop, which is flanked on the other side by the shop containing the wheel plant and the drilling machines. For the purpose of showing how unnecessary carting of material and man-handling of work on and off machines has been reduced to a minimum, it is proposed in what follows to trace the path of each type of component of the mineral wagon manufactured at Earlestown through its series of operations from the raw material stage to that of taking its place upon the wagon.

Timber Yard Methods.

The timber yard is totally covered by two new 10-ton cranes running on parallel gantries, each 479 ft. long and 35 ft. high, the complete equipment having been supplied and erected by S. H. Heywood & Co. Ltd., Reddish, Stockport. One of these cranes handles, stacks, and feeds the mill with the hard-wood scantlings, whilst the other transfers in a similar manner the deals for the wagon sides, also raw materials for the manufacture of wheels. Each wagon-load of timber is lifted out of the wagon bodily and placed on the stack in one parcel instead of being handled piece by piece as formerly, whilst axles are removed from the wagon at the rate of eight per time, and wheel centres and tyres by the half-dozen.

Great economy in man power and expedition in handling has been achieved by the use of these cranes, together with the centralisation of the distribution point for raw material, and the quick return of wagon empties is obtained by means of the fact that the loaded wagons are received under the crane on the in-going road, and after the load has been removed by the methods previously described, the wagon itself is transferred by means of the crane on to the out-going road for return to traffic.

Sawmill Extension and Equipment.

The new sawmill extension contains the woodworking machinery for the 12-ton standard mineral wagon. These machines are divided into two distinct sections, one for dealing with hard and the other for dealing with soft woods. The hard-wood lay-out comprises:—one adjustable chain-feed, double-ended cross-cut saw, capable of dealing with timbers up to 20 ft. in length (made by T. Robinson & Son Ltd., Rochdale); one four-cutter planing machine, with a capacity up to 14 in. by 6 in. (T. Robinson & Son Ltd., Rochdale); one adjustable double-ended chain-feed tenoner, capable of dealing with timbers up to 20 ft. long (T. Robinson & Son Ltd., Rochdale); three horizontal heavy-type mortising machines (T. Robinson & Son Ltd., Rochdale); one 65-spindle multiple boring machine (Wilkins & Mitchell, Darlaston); one multiple deepway boring machine (Wilkins & Mitchell, Darlaston).

The hard timbers are delivered direct from the stack by means of the 10-ton crane in parcels of 40 (this number being found to be a conveniently sized lot to handle economically) and are placed on a skidway adjacent to a live roller conveyor. From this stack the timbers are placed separately on to the live roller conveyor by one man, and are delivered by this conveyor through a hole in the wall of the sawmill direct on to the saddles of the chain-feed, double-ended, cross-cut saw, which cuts the timber to its dead length. This machine delivers the member by means of its chain conveyor down a sloping skidway on to a self-feeding table which feeds the four-cutter planing machine. After passing through the planer the timber is delivered to the chain-feed double-ended tenoner, which tenons both ends of the timber simultaneously where required, but in the case of the wagon headstock, which is not tenoned, the feed motion of this machine is used as a conveyor. From this machine the timbers are carried to a live-roller conveyor by means of a travelling chain, the timbers being supported on a sloping skidway. The live-roller conveyor then delivers the member to the 65-spindle multiple boring machine, which bores all the holes on the flat in a wagon solebar in one operation, the member being held in position by means of pneumatic cramps. The average time for this operation in and out of the machine is one minute, against 40 minutes by the previous methods. This machine delivers the timber direct into the multiple boring machine for boring all the deepway holes. In this machine the member is also held in position by pneumatic cramps, the holes being bored by bits arranged horizontally on each side of the members. Whilst the member remains stationary, one line of bits moves forward and bores through half the depth of the timber and then recedes, whilst the other line of bits comes forward and meets the holes already bored, thus doing away with any danger of the holes running out of truth. This machine also has a time factor of one minute.

Up to this point the whole of the operations have been in one line, the machines being approximately balanced in production times, but from this point the line splits into three, each one of these lines feeding a horizontal mortising machine fitted with stop bars of a circular pattern, which are very easy to handle, and pneumatic cramps. The timbers after leaving the deepway boring machine are delivered to any one of these machines where the necessary mortises are put in, and from here are delivered by means of roller conveyors direct to the assembly site as a finished article ready for use. From this it will be seen that from the time the timber comes into the works direct from the ship, in no case is a piece of hardwood lifted by means of hand power, as after the member has been delivered inside the sawmill the machines are so arranged that the conveyors deliver the timbers at the exact height for the machines to deal with them.

Gravity Conveyance of Timber.

The deals are taken from the stack by means of the 10-ton crane and are delivered on to a platform 20 ft. high in the timber yard. From this platform an overhead gravity roller conveyor, having a fall of 1 in 16, runs the whole length of the sawmill (a distance of 205 ft.), connecting the platform with the self-feeding table of the 15 in. by 6 in. 6-cutter planing and matching machine, both by T. White & Sons Ltd., Paisley. This is the first machine in the softwood lay-out, which comprises also two inverted pendulum cross-cut saws, and one chain-feed double-ended tenoner, all by T. Robinson & Son Ltd., Rochdale. One man stationed on the platform under the crane deposits one plank at a time upon the gravity conveyor which, without further manual aid, delivers the planks to the self-feeding table of the planing machine.

After the planing machine the line is split into two, there being an inverted pendulum cross-cut saw in each of the two lines. The timbers after being conveyed by means of the self-feeding table through the planing machine are delivered by means of a reciprocating arm alternately to one cross-cut saw or the other, and after the deals have been cut to the desired lengths, the lengths being governed by means of an adjustable stop bar, they are delivered and conveyed to a

central spot by means of live-roller conveyors and are bevelled or rounded as desired by means of a chain-feed double-ended tenoner, which delivers them on to a roller conveyor, whence they are carried to the wagon assembly shop, where the capping is screwed on by means of screw-driving machines prior to delivery to the exact spot at which these timbers will be used. Again, it will be seen that no deals from the time of entering the works to becoming the finished articles are lifted by means of man power.

The whole of the timber components of a wagon are manufactured in this shop, and the path of the timber has been traced from the time it enters the works in the wagon to the spot where it will take its place as a component of a standard mineral wagon.

The Wheel Shop.

The plant in this shop comprises :—1 axle ending and centring machine (Sir W. G. Armstrong, Whitworth & Co. Ltd., Manchester) ; 1 axle roughing lathe (Sir W. G. Armstrong, Whitworth & Co. Ltd., Manchester) ; 3 wheel-centre turning and boring machines (Sir W. G. Armstrong, Whitworth & Co. Ltd., Manchester) ; 3 journal grinding machines (2 for roughing and 1 for finishing) (Churchill Machine Tool Co. Ltd., Manchester) ; 3 duplex tyre borers (Craven Brothers (Manchester) Limited, Reddish, Stockport) ; 1 retaining ring bending machine (Lancaster & Tonge Ltd., Manchester) ; 4 gas rings (L.M.S.R., Earlestown)) ; 1 rolling mill for fixing retaining rings (Henry Berry & Co. Ltd., Leeds) ; 1 wheel press for assembling wheels (Henry Berry & Co. Ltd., Leeds) ; 3 electrically-driven travelling jib cranes (Royce Limited, Manchester).

This shop, as previously indicated, was formerly used as a wagon-building shop, and it was found to be just the right width for two rows of machines, and the machines, therefore, were spaced at the full radius of the crane jibs about the centre line of the rails upon which these cranes travel. The machines also were fixed at the same centre height in order to reduce the amount of raising and lowering required, with the object of saving time in getting the tyres, centres, and axles in and out of the machine.

The axles are placed by means of the crane in a gravity conveyor which extends underground from the timber yard to the wheel shop, passing right under the wagon assembly shop. This conveyor when full holds approximately a week's supply of axles, and the day's user is replaced daily, increased storage capacity thus being obtained. The axles are raised from the lower end of this gravity runway by means of a chain conveyor, which deposits them on to a trestle fitted with rollers at the correct height for entering the machine engaged on the first operation, i.e., the ending and centring machine. After leaving this machine the axle is conveyed by means of one of three walking cranes to the axle roughing lathe, which rough turns the journal and wheel seat to within 0·20 in. of its finished size. From this lathe the axle is delivered by means of the same crane to one of the two grinding machines engaged on rough grinding. On this machine the journal is ground to within ·0·003 in. of its finished size, and the wheel seat finished off. All the axles then pass through the third grinding machine, which is engaged in finish-grinding the journal, and takes off 0·003 in. left over from the rough grinders, all conveying being done by electrically-driven travelling cranes.

After leaving this machine, which it will be noted from the upper diagram, page 130, is so placed as to be near to the wheel press, the axle is delivered on the left-hand side of the press, and there awaits its turn for assembly. The centres are dealt with in a similar manner on one of the three duplex centre turning, boring and bossing machines, being conveyed to the machine by means of the second of the three cranes. The centres are finished in one operation, and delivered adjacent to the gas rings. The tyres are completed in one operation on the three duplex tyre borers, being handled by means of the third crane, and delivered by this crane to a space allocated for tyres adjacent to the gas rings.

Wheel and Axle Assembly.

The retaining ring is bent on the rolling machine, which, it will be observed, is placed next to the gas rings, by the operator, who also deals with the tyring of the centres. The tyre, after being machined and delivered to the space allocated for it, is picked up by a pneumatic hoist and dropped into one of the gas rings, and after it has expanded the desired amount, the wheel centre is picked up by the same medium and placed within the tyre. The whole of this is then withdrawn from the gas ring and delivered adjacent to the tyre roller by means of a compressed air-lift. The retaining ring, already bent, is now placed in position, and the whole lifted by means of a pneumatic hoist on to the rolling mill. After the retaining ring has been fixed, this wheel centre and tyre is delivered by the same medium to the opposite side of the wheel press to that on which the axles are stacked. By means of a hydraulic hoist the axle is then removed from its stack and placed on a trestle directly in front of the wheel press. Two tyred wheel centres are then placed in position by the same hoist, the whole being delivered into the wheel press, which, after assembling the wheel, delivers them by means of gravity through a hole in the wall to a storage track, situated in the wagon assembly shop. This storage track, which it will be seen by reference to the diagram, runs parallel to the line on which the wagons are assembled, and during their passage down this track the wheels are blacked.

The storage track extends from the wheel press to a point opposite the spot at which the vehicles on the wagon assembly site are wheeled, the wheel being carried to this point by means of a small bogie running on a narrow-gauge track. During the moving of the pair of wheels from the terminating point of the storage track to the wagon assembly lay-out, it passes the axlebox lay-out, which will be described later, and at this position the axleboxes are fitted on the wheel. Thus, when the wheel is delivered to the site at which it is placed under the wagon it is complete in every way. It will be seen from this that in laying out the shop great care was taken that no needless carrying about of material was incurred, and that the path of the wheel components throughout the whole of their operations should flow directly to the point at which they are required for finally assembling into complete wheels, and after this that the wheels themselves should flow direct to the spot at which they are required for placing under the wagon.

Other Details.

Under the whole of the machines in the wheel plant concerned in the cutting of metals, concrete pits have been formed in the floor and tanks provided so that the chippings and turnings fall into them. These receptacles are then lifted straight out and their contents emptied into wagons by means of the electric cranes in this shop, thus avoiding hand-barrowing. At the bottom of the wheel shop are located six single-spindle high-powered drilling machines (Jones & Shipman, Leicester), two two-spindle gang drills (J. Archdale & Co. Ltd., Birmingham), and one 3-in. screwing machine (Joshua Heap & Co. Ltd., Ashton-under-Lyne).

The bulk of the ironwork, with the exception of body knees and hinges, is here dealt with after reception from the smithy, stamping shop and foundry, and is delivered by electric tractor from the drilling machines direct to the spot on the assembly site at which they are required, where it is painted by dipping and stacked to dry. It was found that to carry out the progressive system of building it was necessary to keep at least a full week's supply of every finished component for the wagon. It will be seen, therefore, that in most cases, though the smaller ironwork is painted by being dipped, a full week transpires before any particular article is required for use, this giving ample time for the paint to dry.

Axlebox Lay-out.

The axlebox lay-out, situated in the wagon assembly shop adjacent to the wheel storage track, comprises a 3-spindle drilling machine (A. Herbert Limited, Coventry), one spindle being used for drilling the pin hole in the lug for the oil hole cover, the second one drilling the oil hole, whilst the third one counterbores this hole to ensure a good fit of the lid. The axleboxes are manufactured on Peacolt moulding pneumatic machines delivered by electric tractors, and the bottoms stacked on a platform at the correct height for handling. Along the front of this platform, and in line with the table of the drilling machine, is a roller conveyor to assist the machinist in handling the bottoms of the axleboxes in and out of the jig. After the machining operations have been performed the axlebox bottom is then placed on a gravity roller conveyor, which delivers it to a fitter a few feet away, who fits the oil hole lid and places the leather liner in the groove, and then passes the casting, by gravity roller runway, to a youth, who finishes the operation of assembling the box. The boxes are then stacked on another platform at the correct height for handling. At this point the complete box is taken by the lifters engaged on the assembly lay-out, as they bring the wheels from the storage track to the point at which they are used.

Soaking of Lubricating Pads.

The plant for soaking pads under pressure is also situated in the wagon assembly shop, directly opposite to the axlebox lay-out, and as the narrow-gauge track, which connects the terminating point of the wheel storage track with the wheeling operation on the assembly lay-out, passes between the axlebox and pad-soaking plants, the finished axlebox is delivered at one side of the wheel and the lubricating pads at the other.

The pad-soaking plant comprises a steam-heated drying oven and two old vacuum cylinders converted into oil soaking tanks. These two cylinders are joined together at the bottom by means of a pipe to allow the oil to be passed from one to the other, an isolating cock being placed between them. Inside the top of each of the cylinders is a suction pipe connected to a vacuum pipe line, the vacuum being made by an injector operated by compressed air. The lubricating pads, after being dried in the oven, are then placed in one of the two soaking tanks. A vacuum is then created above these pads, thus causing the oil to flow from the bottom of the other cylinder and be drawn through the pads under pressure. The pads are then allowed to soak for a definite period, the oil being, of course, under pressure the whole of the time, and at the end of this period the isolating cock between the two tanks is closed, the second cylinder opened and fed with lubricating pads from the ovens. The isolating cock is next opened and the vacuum applied to the top of this cylinder, thus drawing the oil from the cylinder previously dealt with into the cylinder which has just been filled with pads, and when all of the oil has been transferred to the second cylinder the isolating cock is again closed and the pads removed from the first cylinder. This cylinder is again filled with pads and the operation duplicated alternately.

The Bolt Shop.

The bolts for use on the mineral wagons are screwed by means of two thread rolling machines (George H. Alexander Machinery Limited, Birmingham). The smaller of the two machines deals with bolts of $\frac{3}{8}$-in. and $\frac{1}{2}$-in. diameter, and turns out 60 bolts per minute, whilst the larger machine deals with the $\frac{5}{8}$-in. and $\frac{3}{4}$-in. diameter bolts, and has a capacity of 45 bolts per minute.

In the case of the smaller machine the bolts are automatically fed, being placed in bulk in a hopper, the larger machine being hand-fed. Though the speed of production is far quicker on a thread-rolled bolt than a screw-cut bolt, the greater economy is in saving in material, as it is essential that the stock from which the bolt is made should be of less diameter than the finished thread. The $\frac{3}{4}$-in. diameter bolt, for example, is manufactured from a bar having a tolerance diameter of not less than 0·664 in., and not greater than 0·680 in. The bolts are delivered, minus nuts, by means of electric tractors to the wagon assembly site, where they are stored in bins at the points at which they are required for use.

Manufacture of Springs.

All the springs used on the mineral wagons are manufactured in a shop specially equipped for the purpose. The material for the bearing springs is stacked adjacent to a weighbridge, and a definite number of bars is removed from the stack and placed on trestles on the weighbridge, situated immediately in front of a shearing, punching, spear-pointing, slotting and nibbing machine (H. Pels, London), which latter performs the five cutting and punching operations required on a spring plate. After leaving this machine, the plates are heated in an oil furnace and then bent on a hydraulic press to the desired shape, and hardened in water. The spring plates are then tempered in an oil furnace, and assembled into springs. The springs are next tested in accordance with the regulations laid down, and delivered to a 30-ton spring buckling press (J. Shaw & Sons, Salford) where the buckles are pressed on and the springs finished. They are delivered, after being painted, to the wagon assembly lay-out by means of trailers drawn by electric tractors.

Hinge and Body Knee Lay-outs.

The hinges and body knees are dealt with specially on two small lay-outs of their own in the smithy. The body knees are heated in oil furnaces and bent by means of a hydraulic press, and delivered to a spot adjacent to a 12-spindle drilling machine (Wilkins & Mitchell, Darlaston), which completely drills one knee in each operation, drilling the side of one and the foot of another simultaneously. From here the knee is delivered to another drilling machine, on which the holes in the foot of the knee are countersunk, the knee being then trimmed on a cutting machine. The lay-out is schemed so that the whole of the operations, from reception as a taper bar from the merchants to completion, are performed within a radius of less than 30 ft. The hinges are dealt with in precisely the same manner on an almost identical lay-out situated opposite to the one described. These articles are then delivered by means of electric tractors to the point on the wagon assembly lay-out at which they will be used.

We have now traced the path of the timber components, wheels, axleboxes, smaller ironwork details, bolts, springs, knees and hinges, and, in fact, practically the whole of the material required for the construction of a mineral wagon through its various operations from the raw material stage to finish and delivery on site for assembly into the wagon.

Wagon Assembly Lay-out.

The building of the mineral wagon is divided into eight main operations; the components necessary for each operation, as already described, are delivered on the site where they are required, and each man is engaged on a particular part of the wagon, which is moved forward at regular intervals. Compressed air is used for cramping, nut running, and boring the holes in the sheeting. The various operations may be set forth as follows :—

Operation No. 1.—At this point the two middle bearers and centre longitudinals are placed in a jig and pressed together by means of pneumatic cramps. This nucleus of the wagon is then lifted by means of a pneumatic hoist and carried to—

Operation No. 2.—At this point it is placed in position on the main assembly jig; the solebars are then placed in position on the jig, being moved by means of a small trolley which conveys them from the gravity roller conveyor situated on either side of the lay-out on which they have been fitted with all the ironwork they have to carry. The diagonals and end longitudinals are then placed in position, and the headstocks similarly dealt with; the whole is then cramped together by means of pneumatic cramps, the bolts driven and the

nuts fixed on and then tightened by pneumatic nut runners. These nut runners have been provided with an extension bar having a universal joint on the end, to enable nuts to be tightened up, which, under ordinary circumstances, would be inaccessible for tools of this type. The buffing springs and buffers are then placed in position and compressed by pneumatic cramps to enable the cotter pin to be put in. The underframe of the wagon is lifted by means of an overhead travelling electric hoist and conveyed to—

Operation No. 3.—The underframe is here placed on its wheels after the springs have been put in position, the brakework is fixed, and from this point the wagon moves throughout the remainder of its operations on its own wheels. The wagon is next drawn forward through one wagon length to operation (No. 4), the drawgear and the bottom door ironwork being now fixed, and the vehicle then moved to operation No. 5, at which stage the body knees and diagonal braces are fixed and the curb rails placed in position, and the wagon moves forward to the next stage, i.e., operation No. 6.

At this point the floor is laid, and the bottom doors, which have already been put together in a jig on the side of the lay-out, are fixed in position. The fixed end of the wagon, which is also assembled in a jig on the side of the lay-out, is carried across to its position by an air hoist and is bolted to the headstock of the wagon.

Operation No. 7 constitutes the next stage. Here the quarter planking and top through planks are placed in position; the side doors, having been assembled in jigs placed on either side of the lay-out, are bolted into position, all the bolts being driven and the nuts run on by hand, and all the holes for the bolts through the sheeting being bored by means of pneumatic tools, the ironwork itself being used in these cases as boring jigs. The wagon is now ready for the final operation—No. 8. Here the end door is placed in position, after having been previously assembled in a jig on the side of the lay-out, and the whole of the nuts on the body of the wagon are tightened by pneumatic nut runners. The wagon is now finished and moves forward for painting.

From this point to the end of the shop is 220 ft., which gives sufficient room for 11 wagons, and during the time that they are passing along this line the wagons receive their first coat of paint. After a wagon is delivered from this shop it is taken to the paint shop, where it receives its final coats of paint, and is lettered, the lettering being done by paint sprayers through stencils, which are so formed that no filling in by hand is necessary, as will be seen from the diagram. After the spraying operation is completed and the requisite amount of time allowed for drying, the vehicle is passed into traffic.

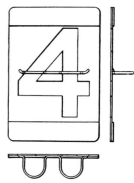

Stencil used for Spray Painting.

Having by the courtesy of Mr. Lemon and with the assistance of Mr. Smalley, Works Superintendent, Earlestown, been enabled to follow all the operations above described in the shops at Earlestown, we are in a position to say from actual observation that the work is carried forward in a smooth and rapid fashion throughout, and it is literally true, though astonishing, to be able to say that one can witness the completion of operations, which by the older hand methods would take at least an hour, in the short space of five minutes. The result is that a new wagon, completely finished and painted with one coat, is turned out of the assembly shop every half-hour, and we

(Continued on page 138.)

APPENDIX 5
LNWR NORTH WALES NARROW-GAUGE SLATE AND COAL WAGONS

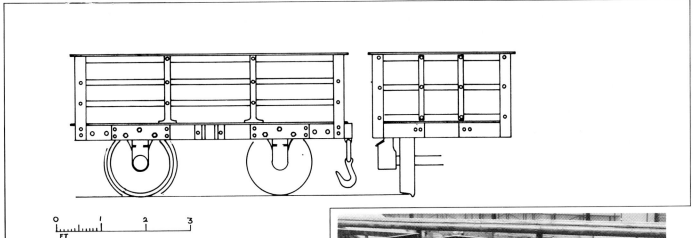

This Appendix gives dimensions and illustrations of the slate and loco coal wagons built by the LNWR at Earlestown and used in the North Wales quarries. It does not attempt to cover Works and other narrow-gauge wagons, only those which would have been transported by the Diagram 7 slate transporter wagons featured in Chapter 3 are included.

SLATE WAGONS

The slate wagons were based on a single design of underframe and running gear and are relatively large in comparison with some other North Wales slate wagon designs. An easy recognition point is the distinctive grease axleboxes clearly indicating 'LNW EARLES-TOWN' and the build year, usually outlined in white. Some slate wagons were fitted with iron brakes on one side only of the curved-lever type but many were completely unbraked. The 1919 table from the Diagram book indicates that none were braked but No.158, now preserved at Llechwedd Slate Caverns, clearly was.

The construction was entirely of metal. The top rim of the sides was made of 2in square angle-iron and was supported on 3in square angle-iron corner posts. There were two lateral straps 1⅛in x ¼in with two vertical straps of the same section on each side. On the ends, only one lateral strap 1⅛in x ¼in was used but with two vertical straps, again of the same section. The base of the sides and ends was 2in square angle, facing outwards. Where one side of a length of angle-iron projects outwards, each end is shaped in a curve back into the side/end, so avoiding any sharp edges which could cause injuries. The vertical straps had a distinctive footing which was presumably hot-welded onto the straps, for it was too large to be produced by upsetting. The footing was welded onto the side away from the slate load and riveted to the floor plate.

The rivets have domed heads on the outside but on the inside of the straps they were flush, presumably to avoid damaging the load. Sizing the wagons to match the slates was never going to be possible; the following is not an exhaustive list but shows the wide variety of slate sizes commonly produced in the North Wales quarries:

This 1ft 11½in gauge LNWR-built slate wagon is one of two now preserved at the Llechwedd Slate Caverns at Blaenau Festiniog. It bears neither number nor brakes but is otherwise identical with the other example, numbered 158. A colourful plate advertising Llechwedd has been affixed by the owners. The livery is plain black and no lettering is highlighted. Note there has been much corrosion and buckling of the floor plate, particularly over the left-hand axlebox. The load is representative of use in service. Note the wheels with their curved spokes. The three-quarter view shows the 2¾in deep bar which was bent to form the central buffer. The hook hangs from a supporting casting on the centre-line of the wagon. CTY. C. NORTHEDGE (NG18)

This second wagon carries the plate 'LNW 158'. The livery is otherwise plain gloss black. This example is fitted with iron brakes on one side only with the distinctive curved brake lever. Note there is no way of locking the lever down, for there is no ratchet or pinning mechanism. The wagons it is coupled to were Great Western Railway slate wagons – note the very different axleboxes. Again, the floor plate is badly corroded and buckled, and the rivets are flush on the load side. These photographs clearly show the distinctive LNWR footing for the mid-side vertical bars, presumably hot-welded on to the bars. This design of footing is also found on the coal wagon.

CTY. C. NORTHEDGE (NG22)

2nd Ladies	– 16in x 8in	Marchioness	– 22in x 11in
Ladies	– 16in x 9in	Duchess	– 24in x 12in
Wide Ladies	– 16in x 10in	Princess	– 24in x 14in
Viscountess	– 18in x 9in	Queens	– 34in x 20in
Countess	– 20in x 10in	Kings	– 36in x 20in

This close-up of the brakes and axleboxes on No. 158 shows it was built at Earlestown in 1887, according to the axlebox lettering highlighted in white. The curved brake lever pulled the central pull lever upwards, so forcing the brake shoes against the wheel, having covered the gap of several inches to make contact. The lever must have been vertical by then! This and the side three-quarter view show the central bracket with two lateral lugs that was used for fixing the narrow-gauge slate wagons onto a parent D7 transporter. The holes in the lug are oval in cross-section with a keyway slot at the bottom. Presumably the bolts on the fixing chains would have been put through the lugs, one from each side of the D7, dropped into the slot and tightened, so preventing any movement as the slate wagon sat across the D7 carrier.
CTY. C. NORTHEDGE (NG29)

These two views show an LNWR-built end-tip coal wagon based on identical running gear to the slate wagons, used for conveying coal to the quarry locomotives and other purposes. It features the same central brackets either side for tying the wagon down when loaded onto a D7. This one is at Llechwedd Slate Caverns, Blaenau Ffestiniog, while another is believed still to be in existence at the nearby Gloddfa Ganol slate mine. There is only one end door but the top is, of course, open. The side straps use the same wide footing as the slate wagons. The axleboxes bear the date 1897 but there is currently no running number. The livery is black for all the ironwork but the planks appear to have been varnished, although the wood is now in very poor condition. There is no sign that they have ever been painted.
CTY. C. NORTHEDGE (NG24)

The wheels were 18in diameter new and 4in wide. Fixed to the centre of each solebar is the double bracket for tying the wagons down onto the Diagram 7 transporter wagons. Each bracket has two lugs and there is a 1in dia. longitudinal hole with a ¼in keyway through at the bottom of each.

A 1in thick bar 2¼in deep was bent to form a central buffer and was riveted to the headstock. A vertical support casting on the centre-line of the vehicle carried a single chain and large hook as the coupling unit. At its inner end it curved up underneath the wagon and was bolted onto an underframe member.

COAL WAGONS

This end-tip wagon design was used to transport coal for the narrow-gauge quarry engines. It has a single end door and is made with wooden planks 6⅛in high by 1⅛in thick. Fifty were built in 1898 (See Chapter 3, Diagram 7) but only two examples still exist in preservation at the time of writing. One is at Llechwedd Slate Caverns, the other at Gloddfa Ganol Slate Mine, both at Blaenau Festiniog. The Llechwedd example has planks which are varnished, not painted. The undergear and running frame is identical to the slate wagons. The side straps incorporate the same distinctive wide footing welded on the side away from the planks as the slate wagons. All the ironwork is painted black.

The non-opening end of the coal wagon, showing the currently poor condition of the planks, and the brake lever pulled sharply up. The slate wagon, mostly out of the picture to the left, is of Great Western design, as evidenced by the axleboxes. CTY. C. NORTHEDGE (NG30)

FUTURE VOLUMES

The remaining volumes are already in preparation and will complete this description of the London & North Western goods stock. The contents are planned to be:

It was very rare for Diagram 9 10-ton open wagons to be photographed in LMS days and rarer still to be seen with a toggle brake fitted one side only — they were normally fitted only to loco coal and coke wagons. Note how thin and prone to bending under Euler load the brake pushrods appear. The tare reads 5 (or 6?) -10-2. The later period LNW livery on No. 29625 was still clear, with the number on the side at lower left and the label holder underneath the 'R'. The location is uncertain — the original is labelled 'Crewe?' but the 'Liverpool Steamers' sign of Robert Gillchrist & Co. casts doubt on that interpretation.
H. J. STRETTON-WARD

Diagram 84 No. 51654 was another wagon still in LNWR livery in LMS days, October 1932. Two-rib buffers indicate a build date of 1910 or after; the tare was 6-4-0 and bulbous No. 18 or 20 axleboxes were fitted.
H. J. STRETTON-WARD